SIXTH EDITION

Copywriting for the Electronic Media

SIXTH EDITION

Copywriting for the Electronic Media

A Practical Guide

Milan D. Meeske

Professor Emeritus, University of Central Florida

THOMSON

WADSWORTH

Australia • Brazil • Canada • Mexico • Singapore • Spain
United Kingdom • United States

Copywriting for the Electronic Media: A Practical Guide, Sixth Edition
Milan D. Meeske

Publisher: Michael Rosenberg
Managing Development Editor: Karen Judd
Development Editor: Laurie K. Runion
Assistant Editor: Christine Halsey
Senior Editorial Assistant: Megan Garvey
Technology Project Manager: Stephanie Gregoire
Marketing Manager: Erin Mitchell
Marketing Assistant: Mary Anne Payumo
Marketing Communications Manager: Heather Baxley

Content Project Manager: Georgia Young
Senior Art Director: Maria Epes
Manufacturing Buyer: Susan Carroll
Permissions Editor: Roberta Broyer
Production Service/Compositor: Rajni Pisharody/
International Typesetting and Composition
Text Designer: Carolyn Deacy
Cover Designer: Marsha Cohen

Printed in the United States of America
1 2 3 4 5 6 7 11 10 09 08

Library of Congress Control Number: 2007930096

ISBN 0-495-41117-5

Thomson Higher Education
25 Thomson Place
Boston, MA 02210-1202
USA

For more information about our products, contact us at:
Thomson Learning Academic Resource Center
1-800-423-0563

For permission to use material from this text or product, submit a request online at
http://www.thomsonrights.com

Any additional questions about permissions can be submitted by e-mail to **thomsonrights@thomson.com**

Contents

PART 3 ADVERTISING BASICS

CHAPTER SIX

Organizing the Broadcast Commercial 85

CHAPTER SEVEN

Broadcast Copy Preparation 93

PART 4 RADIO COPYWRITING

CHAPTER EIGHT

The Radio Commercial: The Mechanics 111

CHAPTER NINE

Types of Radio Copy   125

PART 5 TELEVISION COPYWRITING

CHAPTER TEN

The Television Commercial: The Mechanics   135

CHAPTER ELEVEN

Types of Television Commercials   169

PART 6 THE ELECTRONIC MEDIA: OTHER WRITING NEEDS

Preface

An ongoing goal of this book has been to provide students with plenty of copywriting practice. Writing is like swimming; you have to do it to get better at it. That premise still guides this book, even though it has gone through extensive revisions.

There have been many changes in the electronic media. Offshoots of the radio and television industries have brought changes and new opportunities. Audio and video are important in corporate communications and on the Internet. In addition, media writers may find opportunities writing news or articles for the Web. Of course, writing commercials or station promotional materials still provides opportunities and paychecks.

Given these circumstances, this text emphasizes exercises that can teach and sharpen copywriting skills in a variety of venues. Realistic situations typical of entry-level copywriting positions are included. This approach combines the information of a textbook with the practicality of a workbook. More than 80 exercises are included—more than enough for a normal 15-week semester. The structure of the text is appropriate for an introduction to writing for the electronic media, where many topics are covered, or it can be used for focusing on writing for radio and television alone. Along with the usual copywriting materials, the text includes material not always found in texts, such as a chapter on copywriting style, another on consumer behavior, and another on legal and ethical aspects of copywriting. Examples of storyboards and actual aired copy are used extensively to help students understand the concepts. This variety strengthens the real-world orientation to copywriting in the electronic media.

Changes in This Edition

The sixth edition includes many improvements. The organization has been streamlined to retain the chapters from previous editions and to integrate new information. Specifically, the following changes were made:

- Chapter 18, which is new, discusses "Getting the First Job."
- Chapter 7 has been extensively revised to clarify the targeting of an audience and developing a copy platform.
- The role of the Internet has been expanded in Chapter 8, "The Radio Commercial," and in Chapter 10, "The Television Commercial."
- The grammar review in Chapter 2 has been simplified and expanded.
- Illustrations involving script considerations have been revised to provide added uniformity.

- New illustrations for key concepts have been added.
- The bibliography has been updated to include new editions of reference sources and sources not previously cited.

An Overview of Contents

Part 1 sets the stage for electronic media writing, both commercials and other forms of content. Parts 2 through 5 focus on various aspects of copywriting. Part 2 presents two elements of copywriting: basic style mechanics (Chapter 2) and legal/ethical considerations (Chapter 3). Part 3 emphasizes advertising basics. Chapter 4 examines consumer behavior, and Chapter 5 presents a detailed look at motivation. Chapters 6 and 7 look at techniques for planning a commercial. Chapter 6 presents a time-tested format for structuring a commercial, and Chapter 7 details the targeting of an audience and the copy platform, a helpful structure for adapting a commercial to its desired audience. Parts 4 ("Radio Copywriting") and 5 ("Television Copywriting") focus on the mechanics of these media and the types of commercials written for each. Part 6 deals with specialized forms of electronic media content other than commercials. Chapter 12 covers promotional writing; Chapter 13, public service, political, and issue announcements; Chapter 14, broadcast advertising campaigns; Chapter 15, broadcast news; Chapter 16, writing online material; Chapter 17, corporate media content; and Chapter 18, getting a job.

Exercises follow each chapter so that students can practice the skills taught in that chapter. Because each chapter builds on the previous ones, material learned in doing earlier exercises helps in performing later assignments.

To the Student

This book contains instructions, examples, and exercises designed to help you learn to write electronic media messages. Your instructor might want you to localize the book to your own city by directing you to use the name of your community in the assignments. Be sure to ask.

Your instructor may ask you to vary the assignments to meet certain course objectives. The exercises will usually stand on their own, but they can be combined with other materials or built into larger assignments.

You'll find that the exercise information includes essential facts and, in many cases, data you may not need to use. Your task is to sort out the key facts, as any copywriter would, and place them in a meaningful framework. Listen to and watch the electronic media to see how copywriters have focused their messages. Be alert to any information you feel might be missing from a message.

A number of actual scripts and photo boards are used in the text to illustrate points discussed. Study them carefully; they show how professionals use format and stylistic development. You may notice that style rules vary; they are not absolutes. Be aware of the variation, but follow the style rules in the text—they will help you to present your message well.

The sixth edition of this book includes a number of new exercises. Once you complete them, you may discover problems or omissions. If you do, please let me know.

Acknowledgments

Many people deserve credit for completion of this book. I have many fond memories of R. C. Norris, who provided important content in the first edition but who passed away before the second edition began. Similar memories and gratitude exist for Rebecca Hayden, now retired from Wadsworth, who was an important inspiration in making this book a reality.

Several individuals played an important role in completing the sixth edition. Deborah Ainsworth again served as my local editor and advisor. She was a great help checking facts and making suggestions. Joe Hall of the Nicholson School of Communication provided continued updates on digital/high definition TV. And special thanks to Laurie Runion and Rajni Pisharody who represented Wadsworth in the production of this book.

My thanks also to the following reviewers for their helpful comments and suggestions:

Mike Branstetter, *Eastern Kentucky University*

Mary Ann Carroll, *Herkimer County Community College*

Darrell Dahlman, *Kutztown University*

Brenda K. Jaskulske, *University of North Texas*

Brian Larson, *Aims Community College*

Fred Owens, *Youngstown State University*

Chris Pruszynski, *SUNY Geneseo*

Glenda C. Williams, *University of Alabama*

Finally, students and faculty at the University of Central Florida and elsewhere also deserve credit. Their constructive criticism is much appreciated.

Milan D. Meeske
Email: Mike3836@embarqmail.com

About the Author

Milan D. "Mike" Meeske (Ph.D., University of Denver) is a professor of radio and television in the Nicholson School of Communication at the University of Central Florida in Orlando. He previously taught at the University of Hawaii and worked for broadcast stations in Nebraska and Colorado. He has published numerous articles in journals such as *Journalism Quarterly* and the *Journal of Broadcasting & Electronic Media* and served on the board of directors of the Broadcast Education Association. He is coauthor of *Electronic Media in Government* and has written chapters for several other books. He developed an interest in radio at an early age and began working in radio as a weekend announcer while he was a sophomore at the University of Nebraska. His hobbies include golf, travel, and rock 'n' roll music.

The Broadcast Copywriter

The electronic mass media—radio and television (both broadcast and cable TV)—consume vast quantities of written words. There are commercial messages, news stories, public-service messages, programs (informational, entertaining, and persuasive), and promotional announcements. These messages or versions of them may also be communicated online.

Those responsible for the verbal content of the electronic media are the copywriters, the creative people who write those compelling words about a sponsor's product or the scripts for humorous sitcoms. Such a person might as well be you. Broadcast stations, corporate media departments, and networks cannot operate without copywriters. They may have different titles, such as news writer or script writer, but their function is the same: to write the messages that the electronic media send to their audiences.

Historically, copywriters for the electronic media have focused on specific media and content. For example, a writer might have worked solely on television commercials. However, the media environment has changed, because today you might write for more than one medium. This might mean that a writer creates a television commercial as well as a sales slogan that must be translated to a Web page. Or a writer/producer in a corporate media department might produce messages for a number of media. The result is that the electronic media industry has embraced the integration of media as a way to cut costs. Thus, writing for the technology of today and tomorrow requires a degree of versatility that was uncommon in the past. A copywriter may need to write imaginatively and appropriately for several media, either in the course of a career or certainly when writing interactive media applications.

This book has been expanded to provide you with a wider range of writing opportunities than in previous editions. Certainly excelling at any one medium is difficult enough, but the convergence of technology requires a familiarity with—if not an expertise at—writing for several of the mass media. My goal in this book is to help you gain that familiarity.

◆ A Model of Communication

Writers for the electronic media need to know how communication works. Communication is a process that involves nine factors, as shown in Figure 1.1. The sender and the receiver are the key parties in communication. The major tools are the message and the media. Encoding, decoding, response, and feedback are the communicator's major tasks. The final item is noise in the communication system. We'll define these terms and apply them to a television commercial for Sears:

■ **Sender.** The party sending the message to another party—Sears.

■ **Encoding.** The process of putting thought into symbolic form—Sears' advertising agency puts words and symbols into a commercial that will convey the desired message. Encoding and decoding can result in communication difficulty because, in writing a commercial, the sender must encode a message using words, sentences, sounds, music, and so on, which will translate such that it has the same meaning to the receiver (the target audience). A common frame of reference is needed to communicate effectively.

■ **Media.** The communication channels through which the message moves from sender to receiver—in this situation, television and the specific television programs Sears selects. Advertisers may also use radio, magazines, newspapers, direct mail, and the Internet.

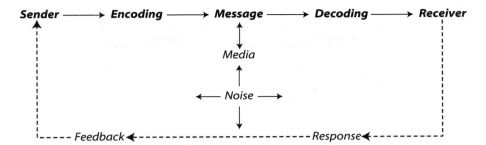

FIGURE 1.1 A Model of Communication

- **Message.** The combination of symbols that the sender transmits—the actual Sears commercial. The message is a symbolic expression of the thoughts encoded by the sender. For our purposes, the message is a commercial.

- **Decoding.** The process by which the receiver assigns meaning to the symbols encoded by the sender—an individual watches the Sears commercial and interprets the words and pictures it contains. As the receiver translates the message that has been sent, the meanings of words, symbols, and actions may differ, depending on the similarity of attitudes and experiences of the encoder and the receiver (target audience).

- **Receiver.** The party receiving the message sent by another party—the person who watches the Sears spot. In broadcast advertising, the receivers are the prospective and present customers of the business's product or service.

- **Response.** The reactions of the receiver after being exposed to the message. Such reactions may include buying a Sears product, liking Sears better, or planning to shop at Sears. The nature of the response determines the effectiveness of the message. If the receivers do not respond as the encoder planned, the communication transaction will fail.

- **Feedback.** The receiver's response communicated back to the sender—consumers contact Sears praising or criticizing the spot or Sears products. Feedback allows the sender a way of monitoring how effectively the intended message is being received. Feedback enables the sender to determine whether the message hit the target as planned or whether it needs to be altered to provide the receiver with a clearer understanding of the message. Advertisers often find that their target audiences do not interpret campaign themes as intended. If that occurs, they can use research-based feedback from the intended audience to correct or replace ineffective advertising messages.

- **Noise.** Unplanned distortion or static during the communication process. Noise leads the receiver to get a different message than the one that was sent—for example, if the consumer once had a bad experience with a Sears product, he or she may tune out of the message. Noise can occur at any stage of the communication process. For example, the sender may encode a message that is poorly focused and cannot be easily deciphered by decoders. Noise also occurs in the media—broadcast schedules might be so cluttered with commercials that the sender's commercial does not gain enough attention to be effective. Decoders cannot translate the message if the message is not clear or is too hard to grasp. An advertiser for an online firm used a parody of a cattle drive by showing drovers herding cats. This juxtaposition walked a fine line, because viewers might not have grasped the point—that online communication can be as difficult as herding cats.

The model in Figure 1.1 illustrates several factors necessary for good communication. Senders must know what audiences they want to reach and what responses they seek.

They must encode their messages properly—in other words, they must create spots that consider how the desired audience will decode them. Senders must use media that reach the target audience, and they must incorporate feedback that will enable them to evaluate the response of the audience to the message. Finally, senders must anticipate and respond to noise in the communication channel. For example, writing commercials for a brand of automobile tires that are known to have been faultily constructed in the past will require care in assuring potential buyers that the fault has been corrected.

The elements in this model apply to writing any message for the electronic media, whether it's a brief commercial or a half-hour teleplay. Remembering the process of communication will enable you to reach your intended audience with the proper construction of a message.

◆ Basic Definitions

Virtually every line of work has its own vocabulary, and the field of broadcast copywriting is no exception. You'll find it easier to follow the discussion in this chapter if you first go over the definitions given here.

- **Commercial.** The sponsor's message—promoting its products or services—as written by the copywriter.
- **Copy.** Term used for written scripts of all types, such as news copy, commercial copy, and so on; same as a *script*.
- **Copywriter.** The person who writes the script for a commercial, public-service announcement, or station promotion announcement. Similar to and often interchangeable with *script writer*, the person who writes the text of a teleplay, commercial, or program. The person who writes Web scripts may be called a *copywriter*, *script writer*, *writer*, or *Web writer*. The writer of scripts for radio or television news stories could be described as a script writer but more often may be identified as a *news writer*. A writer of broadcast news may have other duties, usually reporting or anchoring, which can lead to other terms, such as *writer/reporter*.
- **News reporter.** A person who specializes in gathering information that can be included in newscasts.
- **News writer.** A person who takes information from his or her own research, the station's other reporters, and wire services and then turns this material into news copy to be read on the air.
- **Public-service announcement (PSA).** A noncommercial announcement carried without charge by a station or cable operation for a nonprofit organization or cause such as the Boy Scouts, a drug abuse program, and so on.
- **Salesperson.** The person who calls on the client, makes the sale, and generally collects information about what the client wants stressed in the commercial. The salesperson may sell for a station, cable operation, or agency. Other titles for this function include sales executive, account executive, and time salesperson. The salesperson sometimes writes his or her own copy.
- **Spot.** A commercial, PSA, or station promo.
- **Station promo.** A promotional message about some feature of the station or one of its programs designed to recruit listeners or viewers for the station.
- **Traffic.** The office that handles all programming and scheduling in a broadcast station.

- **Web master.** A person who designs and maintains a Web site.
- **Writer/producer.** A person in broadcasting or corporate media who writes and often produces commercial, promotional, or public-service copy. Cost cutting has led many communications businesses to combine the tasks of writing and producing.

Develop the habit of turning regularly to the glossary at the back of this book to learn additional terms.

◆ Stations, Agencies, Cable TV, and Related Industries

The United States has nearly 5,000 AM radio stations, more than 5,000 FM stations, and over 1,000 television stations, including both VHF and UHF. More than 200 advertising agencies handle major advertising accounts.

Cable operations reach nearly 70 percent of all television homes over 11,000 cable systems. These carry the messages prepared by the many national and local advertising agencies. Although some agencies may specialize in billboards, direct mail, or print media only, many also handle local broadcast advertising accounts.

You should realize at the outset that writing for cable is no different from writing for broadcast television. Both use TV cameras and other electronic picture-making devices to help sell products and services. Corporate TV and video production houses also interrelate with broadcast television. All these means of communication offer jobs for copywriters.

◆ Writing Principles

You might not have thought of yourself as having writing skills. You might feel intimidated at the thought of writing scripts for the electronic media. Here are some thoughts to keep in mind as you learn to be such a wordsmith:

1. Writing is not an inherent talent that you either have or lack. With study and practice, anyone can become a better writer. We will concentrate on the steps you can take to improve your writing ability.
2. Writing requires discipline. It rarely comes easily. Writing is hard work, and persistence is needed to develop an interesting flow of words.
3. Writing is a process that blends the subject and format of the project; your own thoughts, style, and methods; and the techniques and rules presented in this book. These elements must all work together to produce writing that is good.
4. The only way to learn to write is to write. You should critique your own scripts, and your instructors will do so as well. Accept criticism as something you can learn from and try not to repeat the same mistakes.

In this book, we'll focus on the following aspects of copywriting for the electronic media: broadcast commercial, promotional, public service, and news writing. We'll study these topics for both radio and television. We will also examine writing for the Internet, writing for corporate media, and writing entertainment scripts.

◆ Qualifications of the Copywriter

Broadcast writing frequently involves rush jobs. A commercial must be gotten on the air quickly, and a breaking news story must be aired as soon as possible in order to keep the public informed. Here are some qualifications that you will need to survive in this fast-paced environment.

A Sense of Inquiry

A creative and effective commercial copywriter is likely to be someone who is interested in trying novel approaches. He or she has an inquiring mind that asks, "Why not try this . . ." rather than just staying with the tried and true. The key word is *why*. Why this? Why not that? Use the "Why not . . ." approach when you are searching for an idea. It can help you develop new idea combinations, especially if you're willing to give your mind free rein. Begin a sentence with "Why not . . ." and finish it with whatever pops into your mind. Don't be too critical of your initial ideas; generate as many ideas as you can and evaluate them later. Even ideas that may initially seem outlandish can be worthwhile.

Here are some examples of "Why not . . ." thinking. A copywriter who grew tired of writing spokesperson scripts for automobile dealers wondered, "Why not use someone to play the car dealer's wife and do a parody of the spokesperson approach?" The commercial was written, approved, and has been interspersed in the car dealer's broadcast advertising schedule ever since. In another instance, the owners of a furniture store wanted to run a weekend sale even though the exterior of the building was being remodeled. "Why not call it a remodeling sale?" the copywriter asked. This approach provided a framework for the sale. The remodeling work gave the store an unusual reason to have a sale and to attract customers. The framework gave the copywriter a setting for writing the copy and using production elements (sounds of hammering and sawing).

Discipline

Little needs to be said here. You will go through times when the orders pile up and the ideas just aren't there. Broadcasting doesn't allow writers the luxury of waiting for the idea. You must write copy and prepare it for broadcast. As a copywriter, you must produce the best spot that you can and then move on to the next order.

Ability to Keyboard and Use Computers

You must be able to use a word processor, and to do so quickly and accurately. Also, you should learn to think at the keyboard; copywriters don't have time to compose in longhand. The ability to compose on a computer or word processor is important for several reasons, including the overall speed and ease of making revisions on such machines.

In addition, many stations also develop a home page on the Internet, which is used for station promotion and some forms of advertising. To create a home page or make changes to an existing one, more than simple word processing skills are required. We'll look more closely at writing online materials in Chapter 16. Station program logs are now often done with computerized programs, and salespeople often carry laptop computers with them. This enables them to quickly send a sales order to the station by hooking the computer modem to a phone line. News reporters may also carry laptops so that they can write their stories on location while the information is fresh in their minds.

Knowledge of the Language

Simplicity is the key to broadcast writing. Avoid complex sentences and overblown vocabulary. Unfortunately, poor sentence structure and incorrect grammar do appear. Occasionally, they may be part of a deliberate attempt to be creative. More often, the writer simply doesn't know or care about the rules of correct English. Commercials and news stories should be written in acceptable English and in language that is accessible to the average person. Language in a teleplay may use slang or other language unique to the situation.

Knowledge of the Media

As a broadcast copywriter, you must understand the capabilities of the station for which you work. Many commercial ideas are producible only in a sophisticated studio with adequate time and a large budget. They can't be done in a small-market station. Thus, you must understand two things: (1) what radio or television can best accomplish in selling a product and (2) what level of production capability exists at your station.

Dealing with Matters of Taste

As a copywriter, you will face some personal decisions. You will be asked to write for advertisers and public-service organizations that promote ideas you don't like, and you'll be asked to take approaches with which you don't feel comfortable. News reporters may write stories about public officials they don't admire. This will undoubtedly cause some dissonance for you, but you must be prepared to handle this element of copywriting professionally.

Consider some of these possibilities. If you don't drink alcoholic beverages, you might feel uncomfortable writing a commercial for a night spot that encourages listeners to drink and have a good time. If you're proabortion, how would you feel writing a news story or preparing an informational video where the content is antiabortion?

You must first recognize the nature of broadcasting and corporate media. They are businesses, and you will likely plan to follow company expectations. Keep in mind that stations do not choose advertisers, company policies, or news issues in order to please their copywriters—stations ask writers to conform to company policy.

◆ Creativity and Copywriting

The key to the advertising, promotional, or public-service process is this: someone has to come up with ideas that will sell products. This process may, of course, involve more than one person. The advertiser might have an idea he or she wishes to use, and the salesperson might also have a suggestion. In the final analysis, however, it is up to you, the copywriter, to take someone else's idea or generate one of your own and make it sell the product.

We think of the person who comes up with a new idea for an advertiser's product as being creative. But how are new ideas created? Where do they come from? How does a copywriter remain creative despite the need to generate new ideas for a variety of clients? A closer examination of the creative process will provide some of the answers.

The word *creativity* is mysterious and often confusing. As a result, it's important to define the term. In its simplest form, creativity is just another name for finding new combinations of ideas. That is exactly what you'll do when you prepare a commercial. You may occasionally come up with a completely original idea, but more often you'll take some elements of the client's sales data and combine them in a new way. That's what the creative people did for 7-Up when they wanted to stress how it differed from cola drinks. They called 7-Up the UnCola, a new idea combination designed to tell people that the ingredients in the product did not include cola.

The marketing and creative teams for Sears also used a new idea combination. They called a new line of low-maintenance batteries the Incredicell. Though smaller than other batteries, the Incredicell is supposed to generate as much power as larger batteries without requiring maintenance. The battery is an "incredible" cell, so the copywriters used a new word combining these ideas to describe it. Another new idea combination was created for a manufacturer of vitamin supplements. The vitamins, according to a commercial, include everything from "A to zinc."

Finding new idea combinations may be a simple definition for creativity, but the act of creation is not so simple. For one thing, creative thinking doesn't just happen. It requires hard work and discipline, especially when the ideas don't come quickly. Further, there is a common belief that either you are creative or you are not. Actually, all people have some degree of creative ability. Your task as a broadcast copywriter will be to maximize that ability. Developing creative ideas may be especially hard when you encounter new products. You must be willing to learn about new products, both to write a spot and to be creative in doing so.

Here's a four-step process you can use to discipline your mind before you write a commercial, corporate media script, or PSA that will enable you to generate new idea combinations.

- **Step one.** After you've gathered as much information as possible about the product, store, or service, fix it firmly in your mind. Study the information and think about how this client relates to its competitors and to other, noncompeting businesses. Think about the major elements of the client's business.
- **Step two.** Visualize a satisfied consumer reacting favorably to the product, store, or service. Be sure that this is a "postpurchase" impression.
- **Step three.** Evaluate the benefits and rewards that caused the customer's favorable response. Ask yourself, "What factors about this product, store, or service caused the customer's satisfaction?" Consider three possibilities:
  a. Was the customer satisfied because he or she received *tangible benefits* from the advertiser's product? Was the person able to complete a job more easily, quickly, or economically after using it?
  b. Was the customer satisfied because he or she received *personal gratification* from using the advertiser's product? Did the person feel personal pride, satisfaction, or pleasure after using the product?
  c. Was the customer satisfied because he or she received a *desirable response from others* after using the product? Did people display envy or admiration, or did they praise the customer because of the product or service?
- **Step four.** After you've gone through the first three steps, ask yourself a final question: "What strong points of the advertiser's product lead to its benefits?" You should stress these strong points in your commercial.

Let's see how this process might work. Suppose that a discount jeweler wants to advertise on your station. The jeweler has made a special purchase of men's and women's brand-name watches. All styles, including dress and sport watches, are included. All the watches are priced at $48.88 and include a manufacturer's warranty. The watches are to be advertised two weeks before Christmas.

First, you study the information: the brand names being sold, the styles, and the price. Second, you envision a shopper who has completed her Christmas shopping at the sale. She has purchased a sports watch for her son and dress watches for her husband

and daughter as well as herself. Third, you evaluate the reason for this hypothetical shopper's satisfaction. Did this special sale enable her to do a job with more ease? Was she pleased with herself? Or, did others admire her because of her bargains? Although these choices might overlap, the primary reason for the shopper's happiness could be self-satisfaction. She's pleased with herself because she completed her shopping, found gifts her family will really use, and saved money doing so. In the final step, you summarize the main points in your scenario that caused the shopper to be satisfied. They are brand-name watches in a variety of styles, with warranties, all at one low price, all at one convenient location. These are the points you should stress in your commercial.

Use this process to guide your creative thinking before you write a message, whether it's a commercial, a PSA, an online ad, or a promotional announcement. If your time is very limited, use the four steps as a quick guide to planning your message. If you have a day or two to do the work, go through the first three steps and let the information simmer in your subconscious. Even without conscious effort, your mind will react to the input, and you'll find it easier to write a spot when your deadline is near.

➤ POINTS TO REMEMBER

- The writer of a message must analyze the characteristics of the receivers so that they will want to decode the message.
- The sender of a message must encode it properly so that receivers pay attention and can decode it correctly.
- Noise in the communication channel (unwanted interference) must be anticipated by the writer (sender).
- Writing for the electronic media extends beyond commercial writing to news writing, online writing, and writing teleplays.
- You may be expected to do double duty—that is, write and sell time, or write and produce, or perhaps write and announce.
- To copywrite successfully, you must have background skills that include the following: (1) the ability to keyboard, (2) a willingness to strive for accuracy, (3) a knowledge of and feel for language, and (4) a working knowledge of broadcast and cable production procedures
- You must be able to get along with people. Broadcasting and cable are pressure-packed, deadline-filled situations, and a person likely to be at odds with fellow employees does not do well in them.
- Creativity involves disciplining your mind to create new idea combinations.
- An inquiring mind that asks, "Why this? Why not this . . ." can help a copywriter develop new ideas.
- To create new idea combinations, you should envision a satisfied customer enjoying the benefits offered by the client's product or service.

EXERCISES

Exercise 1

Identify an object in your classroom—for example, an eraser, a pencil sharpener, or a chair. Write about the object in free-form style. Describe the object by using a new idea combination. (In other words, don't confine yourself to accepted meanings for the object. Strive for new meanings, new uses.)

Upon completion, read your essay aloud. Compare other essays that merely describe the object and those that place it in a new idea framework.

Exercise 2

This is an exercise in developing "Why not . . ." ideas. For each of the products, services, or businesses listed below, write down both a conventional and an unconventional "Why not . . ." idea. Begin each idea with the words "Why not . . ." Develop your best ideas into partial commercials. Write only an introduction and body for each idea. Expand the list with items you see around your home, city, or school.

1. A Chinese restaurant

2. A high-volume auto dealer

3. A vacuum cleaner

4. An antismoking campaign

Exercise 3

Begin now to listen to radio commercials, to watch television commercials, or to look at Web pages. Choose a message that appeals to you and analyze it as follows:

1. Was music or a sound effect used?

2. How many voices were involved?

3. If more than one voice, was the commercial dramatized—that is, did it employ actors rather than announcers?

4. What was the length of the message?

5. Was the product or service advertised for a local business or a national corporation?

6. Do you think the message was written and presented by the local station, or do you think it probably originated with a larger organization with full production facilities?

7. Which messages do you feel have the best new idea combinations?

Exercise 4

This is an exercise in using the four-step process to develop new idea combinations. You're planning a commercial for Import Motors. The dealership has been in business since 1962. It sells Audi, Porsche, and Mercedes cars. Its address is 4403 Main Street. The service department is noted for high-quality work. New and used cars are available. Stress the nature of these imported cars rather than prices or colors.

1. Identify the major facts about this client.

2. Visualize and describe a satisfied Import Motors customer.

3. What caused the shopper's favorable response? Explain. Pick one of the three:

   a. Tangible benefits

   b. Personal gratification

   c. Favorable responses from others

4. Summarize the strong points of the advertiser's business that provided these benefits.

Exercise 5

This is an exercise in using the four-step process to develop new idea combinations. You're planning a commercial for Valu-Stores, a discount department store with locations throughout Yourtown. The stores carry the following items: clothing, sporting goods, jewelry, automotive supplies, notions, health and cosmetic items, and electronic goods—television sets, radios, and home computers. This spot is aimed at housewives. Its emphasis should be on back-to-school shopping.

1. Identify the major facts about this client.

2. Visualize and describe a satisfied Valu-Stores customer.

3. What caused the shopper's favorable response? Explain. Pick one of the three:

   a. Tangible benefits

   b. Personal gratification

   c. Favorable responses from others

4. Summarize the strong points of the advertiser's business that provided these benefits.

Copywriting Style— Basic Mechanics

Broadcasting is a matter of one-to-one communication. Although radio, television, and cable TV are classified as mass media, they are received by individuals. A noted broadcast performer once remarked that he formed a mental picture of an individual and then talked directly to that person. To communicate effectively, you should write, talk, or perform for an audience of one.

Throughout this book, your writing efforts will be directed toward this more intimate form of broadcast communication through emphasis on a conversational style. This chapter will give you guidelines for this approach and introduce you to the form to use in presenting your copy on paper. But first, the announcer or performer must be able to read your copy; here are guidelines to help you accomplish that.

◆ Copy Appearance

The physical appearance of your copy as typed can make a difference in its effectiveness because the announcer, the TV performer, or the director who may be producing your spot must be able to read and understand what you've written.

To help you understand what scripts should look like, we're going to show you mock scripts for radio and TV. The various types of scripts used on radio will be discussed further in Chapter 8, and the variations in TV scripts will be discussed in Chapter 10. For now, let's examine the sample scripts and then review the rules for putting scripts on paper.

Radio

Radio copywriters use music, sound effects, and voices to capture the listener's attention. The script should set forth these elements clearly so that the spot can be easily read and produced.

SAMPLE SCRIPT   The following illustration shows you the script form used for radio. We'll use a script with two voices, music, and sound effects. This example is not meant to be of any specific length.

MAN	Radio copy must appeal to the mind. Listeners can't see the sponsor's product, so your copy must help them visualize it.
WOMAN	You can use different voices . . .
MAN	You can use music . . .
MUSIC	"YELLOW ROSE OF TEXAS" UP AND UNDER WOMAN.
WOMAN	You can use sound effects . . .
SFX	CLAP OF THUNDER
MAN	(EXCITEDLY) You can ask the announcer to be excited . . . (WHISPER) or you can use a quiet, intimate style.
WOMAN	(CONVERSATIONALLY) Voices, sound effects, and music. They're your main tools for building attention in a radio spot.
MAN	(INTERRUPTING) Don't forget words! Describe the chicken as finger lickin' good . . . the desserts as sinfully delicious.
WOMAN	Sounds good to me. I'm getting hungry already.
MAN	(EXCITEDLY) Me too. Let's finish up (VOICE MOVES OFF MIKE) and go to lunch.
MUSIC	UP AND OUT

This is the basic script form for radio. You might use more voices or effects, but the form remains the same. If you want to specify character voices, provide instructions at the top of the script.

SCRIPT FORMAT CONVENTIONS   The format rules that follow make a spot easy to read and deliver. The goal throughout this text is to prepare copy with both the announcer and the listener/viewer in mind. Copy must be written clearly so that the announcer can deliver it with ease. Follow these rules when keyboarding radio copy:

1. Write on one side of the page only.
2. Double-space all copy.
3. Write instructions for sound effects and music ALL IN CAPS, and underline.
4. Write talent instructions—for example, (WHISPER)—in parentheses, and capitalize.
5. Write all spoken copy in upper- and lowercase.
6. Put only one spot on a page.
7. Write speakers' names ALL IN CAPS.

Television

Television copy differs from radio copy in that it uses a two-column script. The left column is used for video and the right for audio.

SAMPLE SCRIPT   Just as we showed you a mock radio script, we'll now show you a sample TV script. Again, this example is not meant to be of any specific length.

VIDEO	AUDIO
WS OF MAN IN FRONT OF TV CAMERA	The advantage of television is that you can show the advertiser's product.
ZOOM IN TO CU OF TV CAMERA	You can show the product up close . . . MUSIC: "DIXIE" UP AND UNDER
CUT TO WS OF WOMAN OPERATING ANOTHER TV CAMERA	In television scripts we use a form of shorthand to designate the type of shot we want on the air.
SUPER LETTERS "WS"	The shot we're using now is a wide shot and we use the letters "WS" as an abbreviation.
CUT TO MS OF MAN IN FRONT OF CAMERA	The video instructions should be typed in capital letters, but spoken copy should be in upper- and lowercase.

This is the way you should put a TV script on paper. Length, type of spot, or number of scenes may vary, but the format stays the same. The keyboarding rules are important, too, so let's look at those next.

SCRIPT FORMAT CONVENTIONS   The rules for keyboarding television copy are similar to those for radio copy, but each format has certain specific requirements. Follow these rules when keyboarding TV copy:

1. Write on one side of the page only.
2. Keyboard video instructions in capital letters.
3. Keyboard all spoken audio in upper- and lowercase.

4. Keyboard audio instructions for sound effects and music ALL IN CAPS and underline them.
5. Keyboard audio talent instructions in parentheses and underline.
6. Single-space the video column and double-space the audio.
7. Insert a space between speaker and shot changes.
8. Keep the audio and video for a given scene opposite each other as much as possible.

A computer can easily do two-column TV scripts. The word-processing package you use will determine how to set up the screen. Generally, you look in the instruction manual for "columns" or "tables." For example, if you are using Microsoft Word, use the Document menu and select "table insert." Select two columns, each 3 or 3½ inches wide. This gives you two columns—one for audio and one for video.

As you work your way through this text, you may notice that the formatting rules are not followed consistently in all the illustrations of radio and TV copy. These variations reflect the practices of individual writers, stations, or agencies, some of which have no formatting rules. These copywriters or organizations were gracious enough to let us use their scripts, so we didn't retype their spots to make them conform to our preferred format. Be aware of the variations, but remember that consistency is the key. If you follow the format presented here, you'll write copy that's easy to deliver.

Lengthy Copy

If your copy runs more than one page, it's probably too long. However, if your spot is especially complicated and requires more than one page, observe these rules:

1. Never split a sentence between two pages.
2. Type MORE, centered, near the bottom of the first page.
3. Begin the second page with the same copy data used on the first page, following the client's name with PAGE TWO.

Client's Name: __Smith's Dept. Store__   PAGE TWO

Written by: __Ima G. Copywriter__

Length: __60 seconds__

The Importance of Neatness

Numerous corrections are blocks to good delivery. The spot you write must be legible. If you have a small number of errors—generally not more than three—you can correct them without confusing the announcer or performer. If there are several errors, it's always best to retype.

Use a sharp, soft lead pencil to make corrections. A large, blunt lead will produce corrections that are difficult to read. Don't use copyediting marks to correct errors. A sign for transposing words or letters is likely to confuse the announcer. For example, instead of marking a typing error like this: poeple, retype the word correctly. Remember, editors use copyediting symbols to tell printers which changes should be made in print copy. A typesetter is trained to understand these marks and has time to interpret them, but an announcer does not. When you do need to make corrections, observe the following rules:

1. Correct misspelled words by blacking out the entire word and clearly printing in the correct word. The following examples are acceptable.

celebrating

Smith's is ███████████ its sixtieth year.

or

celebrating

Smith's is ███████████ its sixtieth year.

Note that individual letters should be corrected this way:

i

Poor: You are invɇted to the grand opening . . .

invited

Better: You are ████████ to the grand opening . . .

2. Add small amounts of new material by clearly inserting it above the sentence to be altered.

in stock

Every new car has been marked down.

3. Avoid making corrections in longhand. Print your corrections clearly.

Poor: *this week only*

Better: this week only

4. Eliminate small amounts of unnecessary material in your copy.

The doors open at 9 o'clock Tuesday morning.

This could be corrected to read:

The doors open at 9 ██████████ Tuesday morning.

Limit your corrections to the four types illustrated here and retype if corrections are more extensive.

The Hazards of Simplification

In day-to-day writing, we often use some form of abbreviation to save time and space. This form of simplification is not appropriate in spot announcements because it forces the announcer to translate the abbreviation. Likewise, you should adhere to certain rules when using keyboard symbols or stating the time of day.

ABBREVIATIONS Generally, avoid abbreviations in broadcast copy. They force the announcer to translate a symbol into a word and could easily cause confusion.

Poor: The sale runs through Mon., Sept. 3.

Better: The sale runs through Monday, September third.

As with many aspects of copywriting, there are exceptions to the rule. Some words are so commonly abbreviated that announcers are accustomed to seeing them that way. When in doubt, follow these guidelines:

1. You may use the abbreviations Mr., Mrs., Ms., and Dr. These titles will probably be followed by a name, which will help clarify the meaning of the abbreviation.

> Mr. Jones
> Dr. Smith

2. Some city and local addresses are so commonly abbreviated that they may be written that way. City names such as Ft. Worth, St. Louis, and Ft. Smith are commonly abbreviated. Local addresses may also be commonly abbreviated.

> I-80 for Interstate 80
> S-O-B-T for South Orange Blossom Trail

Accepted practices in your area will help you determine the suitability of such abbreviations.

3. The names of certain organizations, businesses, and government agencies may also be abbreviated if they're well known by their initials.

> *Organizations:* Y-W-C-A, Y-M-C-A
> *Businesses:* I-B-M, A-T-&-T
> *Government:* I-R-S, F-S-L-I-C

If you want abbreviations read as initials, type them in capital letters separated by hyphens, as in the previous examples. Don't use periods to separate the initials because a period is generally used to complete a sentence.

If you want the abbreviated content to be read as an acronym, write the initials in a solid combination of capital letters.

> MADD, Mothers Against Drunk Driving

Keep in mind that abbreviations affect two important links in broadcast communication: the announcer and the listener/viewer. If you don't think the announcer can automatically translate the abbreviation into a word correctly, spell it out. Similarly, don't use an abbreviation if you're not certain the listener will immediately recognize what it stands for.

KEYBOARD SYMBOLS Avoid keyboard symbols such as %, @, ¢, &, and 1/2. Rather, spell these terms out to help the announcer. You can, however, use the dollar sign ($), since it is easily understood.

TIME OF DAY Don't use a.m. or p.m. on the air; they sound too similar. Write out the time of day to avoid confusion.

> *Poor:* The sale begins tomorrow at 9 A.M.
> *Better:* The sale begins tomorrow morning at 9.

Web Addresses

Web addresses sometimes require careful treatment, especially in radio copy, where the address cannot be shown. For instance, a web address for a mail-order clothing firm is complicated and requires explanation. The address is *www.landsend.com*. To help listeners, the copy reads, "Landsend . . . one word, no apostrophe."

◆ Keeping it Conversational

Write broadcast commercials, PSAs, and station promos in a conversational style, easy for the announcer to read and easy for the audience to understand. To accomplish this, follow the copywriter's basic rule: Write each spot so that it can be read and understood the first time through.

It's true that commercials and other spots enjoy repeated exposure, but it's equally true that a listener/viewer doesn't stay tuned to the station just to get a second chance to comprehend your spot. Let these repeat airings of your copy reinforce rather than clarify.

Another factor enters in as well. People are bombarded with advertising messages from all the media. As a copywriter, you must be aware that each spot competes with many other messages for the attention of the listener/viewer. If your commercial can't be easily understood, the potential consumer may not pay attention to it. Keeping your copy conversational is one way to make the listener feel, "Hey, he's talking to me."

Avoid stilted language and awkward wording: Make your broadcast copy both conversational and grammatically acceptable. The following guidelines will help you to achieve a conversational style.

Contractions

Contractions are shortened forms of a word or word group. Use them frequently. Contractions are commonly used in your daily conversation, and they're just as appropriate on the air. For example, we seldom say, "It is not warm today." We more naturally say either "It isn't warm today" or "It's not warm today." Contractions help you write copy that follows natural speaking patterns and is comfortable for the announcer.

Here are some contractions used frequently on the air:

aren't for *are not*	*he'll* for *he will*
doesn't for *does not*	*it's* for *it is*
don't for *do not*	*they'll* for *they will*
he's for *he is*	*won't* for *will not*

Some copywriters question the use of the contraction *it'll* for *it will*. It's not easy to say, and it could confuse the announcer.

Avoid contractions if the advertiser wants to place special emphasis on certain words. Hard-sell commercials, for example, use more formal wording to achieve emphasis. You might want to write such a commercial this way:

ANNOUNCER	Smith's is not kidding! Smith's will not refuse an acceptable offer during its clearance sale. Do not miss this fantastic opportunity!

Clichés and Superlatives

Although we commonly encounter both clichés and superlatives in commercial messages, one of your tasks as a copywriter is to find distinctive ways to convey the message.

TABLE 2.1	Thirty-One Clichés to Eliminate from Your Copy

Conveniently located . . .	The friendly folks at . . .
Now that (season) is in the air . . .	Everyday low, low prices . . .
All the names you know and love . . .	How about . . .
Don't forget . . .	For all your needs . . .
Stop in soon . . .	Friendly, qualified personnel . . .
The next time you're in the mood for . . .	Serving you for over __ years . . .
Doesn't it make sense to . . .	Lowest possible prices . . .
Remember . . .	We refuse to be undersold . . .
It's sale time at . . .	We'll meet or beat any reasonable offer . . .
Stretch your budget with these values . . .	Huge selection . . .
Super savings . . .	People who care about you . . .
Savings throughout the store . . .	But wait, there's more . . .
And while you're there . . .	Fantastic
Check out . . .	Unbelievable
A select group of _____ is 25% off . . .	Don't miss out . . .
You'll save big . . .	

Courtesy Chris Lytle, Chris Lytle and Associates.

CLICHÉS To put it bluntly, don't use clichés. Clichés are overworked words and phrases that lack strong sales appeal. For example, a common cliché is: "When you're thinking of (a holiday, a person, a food item, and so on), think of (name of business or product)." This cliché has been used innumerable times; it lacks originality and thus fails to stimulate. When you write your copy, avoid using this cliché and the others listed in Table 2.1.

SUPERLATIVES Overworked superlatives are as ineffective as clichés. If you describe all sales as "outstanding," all bargains as "tremendous," or all dresses as the "cutest you can find," the listener/viewer is apt to discount your claims. Avoid trite, over-worked words and phrases in advertising copy.

Yes, superlatives have a place in your copy if chosen with care. Look for fresh ways to extol the virtues of your product or service. Try words like *active, alive, brimming, captivating, electrifying, hefty, ingenious, lively, merry, prominent, secluded, striking, tingling, understated,* and *vivid*.

Consult your dictionary or thesaurus for variations of tired words. If you can't find the right word, create your own. It takes inspiration to describe a hamburger as an "incred-a-burg-able," but it's fresh, catchy, and stimulating.

Question Lead-Ins

Avoid lead-in questions that invite a yes or no answer. The listener who pauses momentarily to answer the question may miss your sales key. If the listener answers no to the question, he or she will probably tune out the rest of the message.

> *Poor:* Are you looking for an inexpensive way to cool your house?
> *Better:* Here's an inexpensive way to cool your house.

Be just as careful using questions in concluding statements. "Save dollars at Jones Automotive" is better than "Why not save dollars at Jones Automotive?"

Point of View

Don't use pronouns instead of the sponsor's name unless the spot is to be read by the sponsor. It's misleading to have a staff announcer say, "Come by and see our selection." That wording is appropriate only when a spokesperson from the store reads the commercial. If one of the station's announcers is to read the spot, write, "Go by Smith's and see their selection."

Punctuation

You should punctuate broadcast copy more extensively than other types of writing. Your punctuation marks help the announcer deliver the written copy as intended. Punctuation acts as a guide for pauses, emphasis, and oral interpretation in general.

The period, comma, dash, and ellipsis are the most commonly used punctuation marks, followed by the question mark and exclamation point. The colon and semicolon have almost no place in writing broadcast copy.

THE PERIOD The period is used to indicate the end of a declarative sentence or thought.

It calls for a pause or a change of pace. Periods are widely used in broadcast copy because shorter sentences are often more effective. You may even use the period in incomplete sentences, as follows:

ANNOUNCER	Ice. Snow. Bad roads. These are the signs of winter.

In broadcast copy, however, you might also write the message in this manner:

ANNOUNCER	Ice . . . Snow . . . Bad roads. These are the signs of winter.

In either instance, you, as the writer, want the announcer to pause for emphasis after *ice, snow,* and *bad roads.* As you write, try to "hear" your copy the way you want it to sound on the air. When you have finished writing, read it aloud.

THE QUESTION MARK Use the question mark in broadcast copy as it would normally be used. If you omit a question mark at the end of a question, you may set up a stumbling block for the announcer. The omission of the question mark is often the result of carelessness in the haste to meet a deadline.

The following three sentences help illustrate the importance of terminal punctuation in conveying meaning.

Are you ever going.
Are you ever going!
Are you ever going?

The first is an understatement describing someone who is moving quickly. The second is an exclamation of admiration for someone who is moving quickly. The third refers to someone who has worn out his or her welcome. Clearly, the careless omission of a required question mark can change meaning.

THE EXCLAMATION POINT   Exclamation points appeared in a hard-sell commercial earlier in this chapter; a further discussion of hard-sell copy appears in Chapter 9. For now, remember to use the exclamation point when you want the announcer to emphasize a statement.

ANNOUNCER	Williams's opens its doors at 8 tomorrow morning! That's right . . . one hour early! One hour early so you can start early for the big midwinter sale!

If you replace the exclamation points in this copy with periods, the announcer's delivery will probably be much quieter and more sedate.

THE COMMA   When you use a comma, you are usually indicating a pause shorter than called for by a period. Remember "Ice . . . Snow . . . Bad Roads"? Let's repunctuate the copy using commas.

ANNOUNCER	Ice, snow, and bad roads. These are the signs of winter.

Now the announcer is apt to read the series of words in a more connected fashion. The choice of punctuation depends on how you want your copy to sound on the air.

The comma doesn't always signal a pause, but it is a convention of punctuation. Such is the case of the comma in direct address. When one person addresses another directly by either name or title, as in a dialog spot, a comma is necessary before and after the name or title. A period can eliminate the need for the comma after the name or title. Note the punctuation in the following dialog spot:

MARK	Hey, Joe, where'd you get those wheels?
JOE	Same old wheels, Mark. Had 'em for years.
MARK	Yeah, but, Joe, I never saw that shine before.
JOE	Like I said, Mark. Same old wheels, new auto polish.

THE DASH   The dash (—) calls for a complete break in thought. You use it for a pause longer than that called for by the comma. Its pause length is about the same as a period's, but you use it to indicate a thought grouping, not to mark the end of a sentence.

Use the dash to punctuate parenthetical expressions and to guide oral interpretation.

ANNOUNCER	John Jones—Yourtown's largest volume car dealer—has done it again.

THE ELLIPSIS   The ellipsis—three periods (. . ,)—may be used for a more complete break than a dash to indicate a shift in thought within a sentence or to separate phrases.

ANNOUNCER	William Florez (FLOORess) is an electronics technician, but don't look for him at your local repair shop . . . he's working in the Navy.

THE HYPHEN   The hyphen is used to help the announcer read word or letter groups that go together. Hyphens can make combination words easier to read.

> end-of-month party
> once-a-year event

Hyphens may also be inserted to indicate that alphabetical combinations are to be read as groups.

> A-T-&-T

One word of caution: Don't hyphenate words at the end of a line. Doing so causes the announcer to look to the next line to complete the word and increases the chances of error. Complete the word, even if the margins aren't as precise as you might like.

THE UNDERLINE   Though not a punctuation mark, underlining can be used to let the announcer know which words you want given special stress.

ANNOUNCER	These Moonlight Madness prices are in effect only this <u>Friday night</u>.
ANNOUNCER	These Moonlight Madness prices are in effect <u>only</u> this Friday night.

The use of underlining depends on the effect you want. As with all copy marks, underline only when you want special emphasis. Underlining too many words may diminish the effect you're seeking to create.

Numbers

Write numbers carefully because they might be difficult for the announcer to read and for the listener/viewer to comprehend. Use complicated figures sparingly—and simplify them if possible by making them meaningful for the listener/viewer. Here are some specific rules to follow:

1. Write numbers as figures: 50 cents, 12 o'clock, 5 thousand.
2. Spell out all fractions: one-third, three-fourths.
3. Write out decimal points: 8-point-8 percent, not 8.8%.
4. Round off large and detailed numbers unless instructed not to. For example, if a house is priced at $89,975, you could refer to it as "under 90 thousand" or "eighty-nine nine."

TELEPHONE NUMBERS   Generally, avoid using telephone numbers in a spot because they're difficult to read and even more difficult to remember. The following guidelines apply to the inclusion of telephone numbers:

1. Use phone numbers if specifically requested by the client or if you feel that customers might logically call the business.

2. If you do use a phone number, repeat it at least twice.

3. If you use a phone number in a TV spot, superimpose the number on the screen or present it with both audio and video.

STREET ADDRESSES As a general rule, avoid numerical street addresses, such as 6890 Grant Street. Where possible, use nearby landmarks instead. For example, "Smith's on East Main . . . just two blocks south of City Park" helps orient the listener. If there is no good reference point, however, you must use the numerical address.

Pronunciation

If possible, avoid words or names that are difficult to pronounce. If you must use such words, provide a pronunciation guide in one of two ways:

1. Put the guide in capital letters several spaces above the opening lines of the copy. This approach works well when the spot is to be recorded and the announcer will have time to rehearse.

NOTE: PRONOUNCE SPONSOR AS	GAG-ah-no
ANNOUNCER	Collyville Electric introduces the state of the art in kitchen appliances from Gaggenau.

2. Put the guide in parentheses after the word in question:

Milan (MY-lin) Meeske (MESS-key)

Note that in both cases the copywriter simplified the pronunciation guide for easy use.

Never assume that your station's announcer knows the pronunciation of local place names. These voices are often from out of state. Help them: Accuracy begins with you, the writer.

◆ A Brief Grammar Review

Writing in a conversational style doesn't mean playing havoc with the English language. You do have to sell the product or service, but you aren't called on to offend the educated members of your audience. Language is mainly a matter of habit, something we learn by example. The following review notes some bad examples heard on the air so that you can avoid making these errors in your own copy.

Pronouns

Copywriters frequently make mistakes using pronouns, words that substitute for nouns. Let's look at several specific areas where errors are likely to occur.

THE REFLEXIVE PRONOUN The term *reflexive* simply means to refer to a previous noun or pronoun in the sentence. Any pronoun that ends in *self* is reflexive and must have a previous noun or pronoun for reference. Take the sentence "I did it myself." Here you're on safe ground. The pronoun *I* is at the head of the sentence for the reflexive *myself* to refer back to.

Listen to the way those around you tend to misuse reflexive pronouns. How often do we hear a conversation like this:

"How are you?"
"Fine. And yourself?"

This sentence has no noun or pronoun for the *self* in *yourself* to refer to. Grammatically, the exchange should go:

"How are you?"
"Fine. And you?"

If you're writing a dialog spot, use the straightforward, nonreflexive personal pronoun.

PRONOUN CASE   The grammatical term *case* simply refers to the function of the pronoun in the sentence. Pronouns can be the subject of a sentence (subjective case), a direct or indirect object (objective case), or they can show possession (possessive case). Using the wrong pronoun case is a common error that does occur on the air. Here's one from a station promo spot:

ANNOUNCER	Here at _____we're changing to the music you like best . . . country music. *Willie and me* will be with you every night from . . .

Why not "Willie and I"? As with the reflexive pronoun, we seem to go out of our way to avoid the personal pronoun *I* even when usage calls for it.

On the other hand, take this off-the-air example. In this spot, the announcer was a spokesperson for the sponsor, but the station's copy department wrote the spot.

ANNOUNCER	Hi, I'm back to tell you more about Sanders Home Repair. Bill Sanders invited *Jack and I* to visit his shop last week, and . . .

Invited Jack and I? Would you say, "He invited I to visit"? Invited Jack and me.

Finally, consider this exchange from a dialog spot:

MAN 1	Doesn't someone clean your house?
MAN 2	Sure, *my wife and me.*

My wife and me? No, you wouldn't say, "Yes, me do," as in "me cleans the house." You would say, "Yes, I do," as in "I clean the house." It's "My wife and I." Case closed.

UNCLEAR REFERENCE   The pronouns *it* and *they* are especially troublesome in broadcast copy because they are too often substituted for the sponsor's name. To provide clear reference in the copy, avoid using these pronouns. Consider the ambiguous meaning of the pronoun *it* in the following sentence:

Poor: It's so small I take it everywhere. It uses four batteries and it's easy
    to use.
Better: Kwik Fix is so small I take it everywhere. Kwik Fix uses four batteries and it's easy to operate.

In the poor example, the pronoun *it* has no definite antecedent, and the meaning becomes clear only when the listener knows what noun—in this case, the product name—*it* refers to.

Let's look at another sentence with an indefinite pronoun. In this sentence, the writer had the sponsor's name in mind but used the pronoun *they.*

> *Poor:* This sale ends Sunday, and they will never have lower prices.
> *Better:* This sale ends Sunday, and Clark's will never have lower prices.

Clearly, commercials must make sense when they are aired. Replacing indefinite pronouns with the sponsor's name solves the problem of unclear pronoun antecedents.

Adverbs

Most English adverbs end in *ly. Slowly, rapidly, quickly,* and *freshly* are all adverbs—words that modify a verb, an adjective, or another adverb. A television commercial advertising cat food contained the line "made of fresh caught fish." You could have fresh catfish, fresh redfish, but fresh caught fish? The construction requires an adverb; the line should read, "made of freshly caught fish." To repeat: Why offend the many listeners/ viewers who know better when you can so easily use the correct form?

Verbs

Verbs are words or phrases that express action or a state of being. They can be dull and repetitive in spots. Thus, where feasible, omit verbs to tighten up the copy. Consider these examples:

> *Poor:* Clark's *will not be* undersold.
>   Clark's *is located* on Main Street.
> *Better:* Clark's . . . never undersold.
>   Clark's . . . on Main Street.

If you must use verbs, however, keep in mind the following points.

SUBJECT-VERB AGREEMENT   A verb usually fails to agree with the subject because the copywriter hasn't correctly identified the subject. Consider this sentence: "A group of scientists is studying the problem." Here, the singular subject *group* is followed by the singular verb *is.* But it would be easy to pounce on the plural noun *scientists* and throw in the plural verb *are.* Here's an example from a commercial broadcast in the Northeast:

ANNOUNCER	This fine selection of dresses are going on sale tomorrow.

This selection are going on sale? No, "This selection is. . . ." Even better, you could rewrite to say, "All of these fine dresses are going on sale. . . ."

TROUBLESOME VERB SETS   *Lie* and *lay, sit* and *set* tend to be the most troublesome verb sets. A commercial prepared by a large agency began this way:

ANNOUNCER	When you *lay down* for your afternoon nap . . .

You may *lay* a book on the table, but you *lie* down for a nap. You *sit* in a chair, but you *set* the dishes on the table. If you think of *lay* meaning to *place* and *lie* meaning to *recline*, you'll easily remember which verb is correct. Here are some additional correct examples taken from commercial copy:

ANNOUNCER	Don't just *sit* there, phone Hollaway's Garden Service.
ANNOUNCER	After *lying* around on the beach, you'll find nothing is more soothing than Skintex Lotion.

ACTIVE VERSUS PASSIVE VERBS   Broadcast writers usually seek to generate a sense of immediacy in their copy—they want to place the listener in a "now" response mode. Whereas passive verbs tend to put copy in a past or future perspective, active verbs stimulate vibrancy in a spot. Further, it's easier to keep listeners oriented to the present if you use verbs that are in the present tense. Passive verbs are especially troublesome because they provide the opposite of the "now" orientation desired in broadcast copy. Look at the following example:

Passive: Used car prices *will be slashed* at Clark's.
Active: Clark's *slashes* used car prices.

VERBS INDICATING TIME   To make the meaning of time clear to the audience, the copywriter must choose the word that best expresses the time element involved. Consider the example with the words *has, have,* and *had*:

Has expresses an action that still exists or one in which the results still exist: "The store has slashed prices."
Have also expresses an action that still exists or one in which the results still exist: "I have completed the exam."
Had expresses a past or completed action: "The man said he had sent the reply."

Similar time concerns may arise with these verbs:

may, might, must
can, could, would, shall, should
do, does, did.

Awkward Sentences

Construct sentences that are conversational in tone; otherwise, listeners are apt to find the sentences awkward if not ambiguous. Here's an example:

Poor: Located at 1210 Main Street, Clark Motors is the best place for used car bargains.
Better: Clark Motors, 1210 Main Street. The best place for used car bargains.

Spelling Problems

Some words sound alike but are spelled differently. Here are some simple tips to help you use the correct spelling.

ITS AND IT'S   *Its* shows possession or ownership. To remember the correct spelling, associate its with *his* or *her*. "Mario's is clearing out its winter merchandise."

It's is a contraction of *it is* or *it has* and always has an apostrophe.

> "It's about time."

YOUR AND YOU'RE   *Your* indicates possession or ownership.

> "This is *your* book."

You're is a contraction of *you are* and always has an apostrophe.

> "*You're* looking tired."

WHOSE AND WHO'S   *Whose* shows ownership as in "*Whose* car is in the street?" It does not have an apostrophe.

> *Who's* is a contraction of *who is* and has an apostrophe.
> "*Who's* coming with you?"

TOO AND TO   *Too* means in addition or also.

> "The water is hot, *too*."

To is used for expressing motion or direction toward something (as opposed to coming from something).

> "Come *to* Nichols clearance sale now!"

THEIR, THERE, AND THEY'RE   *Their* is the possessive form of *they* and shows ownership.

> "*Their* sale is going on."

There refers to a given place or point.

> "He is *there* now."

They're is a contraction for *they are* and always has an apostrophe.

> "*They're* priced below wholesale."

Additional Writing Rules in Brief

Here are a few final rules to consider as you write your spots:

1. Avoid generalizations.

> *Poor:* Harold's has dozens of suits on sale.
> *Better:* Harold's has double-breasted, single-breasted, and European-cut
> suits on sale.

2. Avoid *if*.

> *Poor:* If you want to save money, go to Harold's.
> *Better:* Save money. Go to Harold's.

3. Avoid clumsy prepositional openings.

> *Poor:* At Harold's they offer free alterations.
> *Better:* Harold's offers free alterations.

4. Avoid negatives.

> *Poor:* Don't suffer from the heat this summer.
> *Better:* Stay cool and comfortable this summer.

5. Use the present tense.

In a commercial:

> *Poor:* You'll be able to choose from your favorite styles at Harold's.
> *Better:* Choose your favorite styles at Harold's.

In a news story:

> *Poor:* Legislators were searching . . .
> *Better:* Legislators are searching . . .

> ➤ **POINTS TO REMEMBER**

- To communicate effectively in broadcast commercials, PSAs, and station promos, write in a conversational style. Write for an audience of one. Don't depend on repeated broadcasts of your copy to get your message across. Write so that your message is understood the first time it is heard or seen.

- Keep in mind that accuracy begins with the writer. This means not only getting the price of the product right or being sure you have the sponsor's name and address correct but also using acceptable grammar, spelling, and punctuation.

- Keep the spot's point of view in mind as you write. Is the announcer inviting the audience to visit the station or go to the store? Remember that a misused point of view can rob you of the opportunity to plug the sponsor's name.

- Keep a good dictionary, thesaurus, grammar text or style book and a sharp pencil with a number 2 lead at your desk.

- Limit the number of corrections in a spot. If there are more than three errors, retype the spot.

- Punctuate your copy correctly, because this helps the announcer to deliver the copy as intended.

- Provide announcers with a pronunciation guide if the copy contains words or names that are difficult to pronounce.

- Use proper language in your spots so that you don't offend the audience.

EXERCISES

COPYWRITING STYLE TEST

Exercise 1

In the blank at the left of each series below, write the letter that designates the style form preferred for ease of reading on the air.

———————— 1. a. Once in a lifetime values

             b. Once-in-a-lifetime values.

———————— 2. a. Here are a few exmaples of the bargains.

               examples

             b. Here are a few ▨▨▨▨▨ of the bargains.

———————— 3. a. Located at 1231 W. Major Blvd., next to Red Bird Mall.

             b. Located at 1231 West Major Boulevard, next to Red Bird Mall.

———————— 4. a. This special sale begins TONIGHT at 6.

             b. This special sale begins tonight at 6.

———————— 5. a. You pay only 5 percent down!

             b. You pay only 5% down!

———————— 6. a. Come and see how luxurious condo minium living can be.

             b. Come and see how luxurious condominium living can be.

———————— 7. a. Smith's is open from 10:00 A.M. to 6:00 P.M. Monday through Saturday.

             b. Smith's is open from 10 to 6 Monday through Saturday.

———————— 8. a. These prices will not last long!

             b. These prices won't last long!

———————— 9. a. These special prices begin this evening at 6.

             b. These special prices begin this evening at 6 P.M.

———————— 10. a. Here's what Kissimmee Hardware offers you.

             b. Here's what Kissimmee (Kih SIM ee) Hardware offers you.

———————— 11. a. If you like pizza that's made the Italian way but is still affordable, the Pizza Place is for you.

             b. If you like pizza that's made the Italian way . . . but is still affordable . . . the Pizza Place is for you.

———————— 12. a. MAN: Grumbling. Another rainy day . . . will the sun ever come out?

             b. MAN: (GRUMBLING) Another rainy day . . . will the sun ever come out?

———————— 13. a. Prices start at just $49,939.

             b. Prices start at under 50 thousand dollars.

———————— 14. a. You pay one-half off the original price!

             b. You pay 1/2 off the original price!

_____ 15.   a. Deposits insured by the F-D-I-C.

                 b. Deposits insured by the FDIC.

_____ 16.   a. Low 9-point-9 percent financing.

                 b. Low 9.9% financing.

_____ 17.   a. Smith's two blocks east of the Mall on Main Street.

                 b. Smith's, at 1240 Main Street.

_____ 18.   a. You need not be emplyed.

                 b. You need not be employed.

_____ 19.   a. Drive the Brand X 4 x 4 pickup.

                 b. Drive the Brand X 4-by-4 pickup.

_____ 20.   a. Get a used car bargain at Clark's.

                 b. If you want a used car bargain, head for Clark's.

_____ 21.   a. At Clark's you get dependable service.

                 b. Clark's promises dependable service.

_____ 22.   a. Clark's is going to have the best prices during its clearance sale.

                 b. Clark's cuts high prices during its clearance sale.

_____ 23.   a. Goodies gas is tops. It features high octane, and it costs less.

                 b. Goodies gas is tops. Goodies features high octane, and Goodies costs less.

_____ 24.   a. We'll wake you up every morning on W-A-A-A. Mary and I are here from six to nine.

                 b. We'll wake you up every morning on W-A-A-A. Mary and me are here from six to nine.

_____ 25.   a. SFX:THUNDER

                 b. SFX:Thunder

Exercise 2

The following script contains errors in grammar, style, and spelling. Edit the copy to remove the errors.

Are you tired of high food costs? If you are Johnnies Pizzeria 5705 University Ave. is designed with you in mind. At Johnnies . . . they want you to come in ant try there delicious Italian food weather it after the game after a movie, or just anytime you are hungry. The friendly folks at Johnnies want you to try our pizza or any of the other delicious Italian dishes. Tuesday night is value night at Johnnies; buy any pizza and you can get a second pizza of the same size for 1.2 price. Just think of it. They will give you a second pizza for 1.2 price when you by a pizza. How can you beat it. So if you want great tasting pizza hurry in. We will be serving you the best tasting, lip smachingist, tongue teasing, delicious pizza you have ever eaten. So come on buy. Do not be trapped by high food costs when they can give you great quality pizza and Italian specialties for less. Call them for take out service at 123–1234.

Exercise 3

Write a single-voice, sixty-second radio spot to be read by a staff announcer for the Hometown Sewing Center, 1984 S.W. Main Street. Do not use music or sound effects. The phone number is 123–9854. The Sew Well sewing machine by the Master Corporation is on sale for $169.99.

The price is $40 below list. The Sew Well has twelve different stitches, including a zigzag stitch. It has a built-in buttonholer and will sew stretch fabrics. The store is two blocks southwest of City Hall. Be certain to observe the radio format rules in preparing this spot.

Exercise 4

Write a single-voice, sixty-second radio spot for Italian Grocery and Deli, 231 Park Ave. Phone number: 123-6681.

Facts: Boiled Ham, $1.89 lb., Genoa Salami, $5.39 lb., Domestic Provolone, $3.69 lb., Polly-O-Mozzarella, $3.19 lb. Stress that the Italian Grocery and Deli is the only true Italian grocery in Yourtown. They prepare special party platters. Store hours: Mon.–Fri. 9 A.M.–6:30 P.M., Sat. 9 A.M.–6 P.M.

Refer to Mr. Victor Venturini, owner of the store, but write the spot to be delivered by a staff announcer. Observe all style rules in preparing the spot.

Exercise 5

Write a thirty-second, single-voice radio commercial for Valu-Mart's 99-cent sale. Include items you think might reasonably sell for 99 cents. In writing the spot, use at least six common commercial clichés. When you've finished, rewrite the spot to eliminate the clichés. Use only hard facts and fresh, specific phrases. Hand in both versions of the commercial.

Exercise 6

Write a single-voice, sixty-second radio commercial for your favorite sports car. Describe its appearance, its accessories, and its fuel economy. Use as many superlatives as you can. When you've finished, exchange papers with a classmate and read the spots aloud. Discuss the impact of the superlatives on the selling power of the commercial.

Once you've discussed the commercials, edit out most or all of the superlatives from the spot you've written. Read the spot aloud again. Which approach has more selling power?

Exercise 7

Juan Jiménez processes frozen Mexican food that is distributed over a four-state area. He has picked your agency to write radio copy for him. He is particularly insistent on correct Spanish pronunciation for the following words, which will appear in the copy: Jiménez, jalapeño, frijoles. Go to an authority for assistance. Be sure you can guide the announcer with the word jalapeño. What word or words do we have in English that contain the "ñ" sound?

Exercise 8

The following radio dialog may or may not need editing for grammar, punctuation, or spelling. You be the judge and make such editorial changes as you see fit.

TOM	Wow, Julie, where'd you and Sue go last night.
JULIE	Its this way Tom. Sue wanted to try that new Chinese restaurant …
TOM	The one out on highway 30.
JULIE	Right. It's only fifteen minutes from downtown, and once you get their, boy is the food tremendous.
TOM	Whats the name of the place.
JULIE	The Panda. They got a big, stuffed Panda out front. And like I say, there food is tremendous.
ANNOUNCER	It's just like Julie said … The Panda … tremendous Chinese food … only five miles out highway 30 north, next to the Raceway.

CHAPTER THREE

The Legal and Ethical Implications of Writing Copy

All the commercial, public service, and promotional copy you write must comply with certain laws and regulations. Both federal and state laws apply to broadcast copy, and stations must also be concerned with copy that, though not illegal, raises questions of taste. However, few legal restrictions apply to copy for cablecasting.

When copy might violate state or federal laws, your foremost concern should be the impact of possible violations on the station's license. Your copy can actually jeopardize the station's license to broadcast, so you must be aware of the laws and regulations that apply and be cautious about copy that might violate them. This chapter examines the various types of government regulation of advertising and its implications for commercial, promotional, and public service copy.

◆ Federal Regulation

At the federal level, broadcast advertising comes under two jurisdictions: the Federal Communications Commission regulates radio and television broadcasting and the Federal Trade Commission regulates advertising content.

The Federal Communications Commission

The Federal Communications Commission (FCC) exercises little involvement in advertising, leaving most issues to the Federal Trade Commission. The following section covers the most important FCC provisions that affect the broadcast copywriter.

SPONSORSHIP IDENTIFICATION   The Telecommunications Act of 1996 requires stations to identify the sponsor or product during commercial announcements or sponsored broadcasts. The goal of this requirement is to avoid deception by letting the public know they are hearing a paid advertisement.

In most cases, this requirement does not pose a problem because advertisers want their names or product names to be mentioned frequently. Sometimes, however, a station might not want to identify a sponsor in a spot. For example, teaser announcements are designed to attract the audience's attention without revealing the sponsor's identity until later in the advertising schedule. Here's an example of an illegal teaser that might start a campaign:

ANNCR 1	Save money on food for your family.
ANNCR 2	Where at?
ANNCR 1	Can't tell you till Friday.
ANNCR 2	Why not?
ANNCR 1	'Cause it's a surprise. One you'll like!
ANNCR 2	But I have to wait till Friday?
ANNCR 1	Yes, but the wait will be worth it. Listen Friday for details about the greatest food-buying plan ever to come to Yourtown.

This announcement looks and sounds like any other commercial, but it's strictly a teaser. No sponsor is mentioned, and the FCC considers that to be a serious offense. A station and its advertisers can attract attention and build interest, but they must mention the advertiser's name at least once in each announcement.

PAYOLA AND PLUGOLA   Another identification problem that violates the Telecommunications Act is a failure to disclose payments that involve programming. This may occur in *payola,* an illegal payment for promoting a record or other product on the air. A record promoter, for instance, might make under-the-table payments to a disc jockey to play a record. Because the payment is not disclosed, payola violates the Telecommunications Act and carries a penalty of a $10,000 fine and a year in jail.

Payola payments began in the 1950s and have been an ongoing problem. In 2007, four major radio broadcast companies reached an agreement with the FCC to pay the government $12.5 million and provide free air time for independent record labels as part of a settlement following a federal payola investigation.[1]

Plugola is a variation of payola in which a commercial product is gratuitously mentioned during an entertainment program. For example, a disc jockey might urge listeners to go to a rock concert that the station is not advertising without mentioning that he or she has been given free tickets to the event. Items promoted through payola or plugola can generally be advertised legally if the promoter is willing to buy advertising on the station and the station identifies the payment on the air.

STATION-CONDUCTED CONTESTS   To protect the public from deceptive contests, the FCC stipulates that a station must disclose the material terms of the contest. Although subject to some variation, the material terms of a contest generally refer to how to enter or participate: eligibility restrictions; entry deadline dates; whether and when prizes can be won; the nature, extent, and value of prizes; the basis for evaluating entries; time and means of selecting winners; and the method of breaking ties. The station is obligated to disclose the terms of the contest when the audience is first told how to enter, as well as periodically during the contest.

POLITICAL SPONSORSHIP IDENTIFICATION   The FCC requires that the sponsor of a political broadcast be clearly identified. The reason for this is to make certain that listeners know they're hearing a political message and understand who paid for the broadcast time. To avoid confusing the public, the FCC requires that political commercials: (1) announce that the message was sponsored (by use of the phrase *sponsored by* or *paid for*) and (2) identify the sponsor in such a way as to reveal to the public the true sponsor's identity. Thus, each political announcement must conclude with a statement such as "Paid for by the Committee to Reelect Joe Jones County Commissioner."

The script that follows is typical of the kind written for candidates for local political races. Because the script is for radio, the identification announcement is included at the conclusion of the copy. In political spots on TV, the identification announcement need not be read aloud on the air but may be presented visually over the final shot.

---

[1] "Broadcasters to Pay $12.5M Over Payola," *USA Today*, March 6, 2007, B1.

This is Dick Batchelor. Over the past eight years, you have elected me to four terms. As your senior representative, I've received the support of Republicans, Democrats, and Independents in past elections. I've never needed your vote more than on this November second. The Fifth Congressional seat in Washington is not going to be won by special-interest groups' excessive campaign spending. Even with almost half a million dollars, my opponent cannot buy the Fifth Congressional District. It's going to be won with your vote for honesty . . . experience . . . and my promise to continue my fight for you in Washington. The choice is clearly yours. Vote Dick Batchelor November second. Paid political announcement, Campaign Committee to Elect Dick Batchelor Fifth Congressional District.

Courtesy Kerns & Associates, Inc.

It is important to note that Section 315 of the Telecommunications Act prohibits a broadcaster from censoring the political advertising of a legally qualified candidate. Thus, even though a station may judge a candidate's message to be vulgar, obscene, or in poor taste or may disagree with the political views expressed, the station can neither censor nor edit the content.

Liquor Advertising

For decades, the liquor industry voluntarily banned the advertising of liquor on broadcast stations. The liquor industry removed that ban in 1996, and Congress proposed legislation banning liquor advertising. The legislation did not pass, which left broadcasters free to advertise liquor. Nevertheless, few stations do so, fearing that the advertisement of liquor could lead to restrictions on the lucrative advertising of beer and wine.

The Federal Trade Commission

The Federal Trade Commission (FTC) is charged with protecting the public from unfair and deceptive business practices, including false and misleading advertising.

A number of other federal agencies including the Consumer Product Safety Commission, the Food and Drug Administration, and the Environmental Protection Agency also play a role in prohibiting harmful trade policies. All fifty states also have laws permitting consumers to sue over deceptive advertising. The following sections summarize some of the FTC policies most relevant for the commercial copywriter.

Deceptive Advertising

Ads are deceptive if they contain deliberately false demonstrations or statements, or if they contain true statements that convey a misleading implication. Such advertising can take several forms, as discussed in the following sections.

RIGGED DEMONSTRATIONS   A major advantage of television advertising is that the product can be shown being "put through its paces." Because it's not always easy to demonstrate a product, the temptation may be to alter the demonstration so as to make the commercial—and thus the product—more appealing. However, manipulating the demonstration can be deceptive. The FTC expects advertisers, their agencies, and their television producers to show a product as it really is, not as it might appear under circumstances that are altered for effect.

The FTC tolerates a certain level of exaggeration in advertising. For instance, the FTC ruled that it was reasonable for the makers of Bayer Aspirin to claim that "Bayer works wonders," and a court ruled that Pennzoil could claim that its motor oil "offered better protection against engine wear." Such exaggerations are known as *puffery*—broad, vague, laudatory language. The FTC accepts puffery because it believes that everyday consumers are intelligent enough to recognize puffery and not take it seriously.

When claims become so exaggerated that consumers can't discern whether they are true, the FTC becomes concerned. Volvo was fined for misrepresenting the strength, crashworthiness, and structural integrity of its automobiles. This occurred when Volvo ran a television commercial that showed an oversized pickup driving over a row of automobiles. All were crushed except the Volvo station wagon. The FTC said the Volvo had been structurally reinforced, whereas structural supports in some of the other cars had been weakened.

The FTC asked six hearing-aid manufacturers to tone down the pitches in their advertising. The problem was not that the hearing aids didn't work, but that the claims exceeded what the devices could do.

The FTC wants the public to see products in television commercials as they really are, not as doctoring will make them appear. Most television producers present legitimate demonstrations in TV commercials. But those who alter the product or setting or who deliberately manipulate the visual presentation through deceptive tape or film editing risk being liable for legal action by the FTC.

TESTIMONIALS AND ENDORSEMENTS The FTC wants to be sure that testimonials and endorsements are genuine. This can pose a major problem in selecting talent for commercials. Actors and celebrities are asked to endorse products because they lend credibility to the message. Endorsements are expected to reflect the honest views of the endorser, and the person must actually use the product at the time of the endorsement. Thus, if a famous athlete endorses a soft drink, he or she must consume the product and give an honest opinion of it. Of course, endorsers are paid for their remarks, so they are likely to react favorably to the product they're pitching.

Testimonials are often delivered by paid actors because ordinary people generally don't come across well on the air. However, if the commercial says we're hearing Mrs. Jones of Omaha describe the efficiency of brand X laundry detergent, we should really see and hear Mrs. Jones. Professional actors deliver similar messages, so there is room for confusion: Is it Mrs. Jones or not? When actors are paid to play the part of actual consumers, they need not even use the product but merely pretend that they have used it.

The problem is an ethical one because the public has no way of knowing if the testimonial is genuine.

COMPARATIVE ADVERTISING Advertisers today frequently identify their competitors by name and make a direct comparison in their commercials. For example, Anacin claims more headache-killing power than other leading brands of pain relievers and names them. Coke claims that it beats Sprite in a taste test.

A comparative ad is most effective when one brand is clearly stronger than others and its strong points can be demonstrated. Pepsi-Cola used taste tests to show that many people preferred the taste of Pepsi to Coke; the taste tests were included in Pepsi commercials. However, comparative ads should not disparage or unfairly attack competitors. Consumers may react negatively to a comparison that belittles a competitor and therefore decide not to use the product.

Finally, consumers should be able to verify the claim made for the product. This might be difficult, because they might not come to the same conclusion as shown in the commercial. Still, if consumers use the product claiming to do the best job, they should see the promised results.

RESEARCH DATA Advertisers commonly run tests on their products to show the public that the product will produce better results than a competitor's. Because consumers like to feel they're spending money wisely, advertisers find research data to be effective in convincing people to buy a product.

Claims based on research data can be used as long as they're not false or misleading. Only when data are presented recklessly does the FTC act to protect the public. Copywriters can present research data in several ways. Comparisons are often used, and they require the care previously mentioned. Dramatizations can also be used, but abuses have led to a set of guidelines. Commercials using actors to play doctors, dentists, or pharmacists are unacceptable. So are commercials with statements such as "Doctors recommend . . ." or "Doctors at a leading hospital have found . . ." or presentations by a third party—for example, an actor who says, "My pharmacist told me. . . ."

Research material can also be presented by couching it in qualified language. One pain reliever, for instance, claims that millions of users suffer no upset stomach as a result of taking the product. The commercial doesn't state, however, what percentage of users *do* experience stomach upsets. Other products claim they "can be effective" or "can help relieve" certain problems. Although legal, such wording does not tell the full truth and may imply results that the product doesn't deliver.

Truth in Lending

Federal Truth in Lending laws apply to broadcasters and cable systems and pose some difficulties. The rules require advertisers to fully disclose all credit terms if any of the terms of a loan are mentioned in an ad. Since the disclosure must be given in some detail, advertisers face the challenge of explaining credit terms that are often detailed and complex. As a result, these terms are often disclosed in small graphic print at the conclusion of television commercials or in hastily read copy in radio ads.

Real estate and auto commercials frequently must disclose loan terms, and they often fail to comply with the rules. For instance, a commercial that cites a down payment or monthly payment must explain additional details of the financing. Similarly, any identification of an interest rate must stipulate the "annual percentage rate," or APR. Certainly, consumers deserve to know the terms of a loan, and although it might not seem desirable to explain these details in the precious seconds of a commercial, the public's right to know is at stake.

◆ State Regulation

Even though federal agencies are primarily responsible for regulating broadcast advertising, most states also have some form of regulation. For example, some states have laws prohibiting or regulating broadcast advertising of lotteries and alcoholic beverages.

Of more specific concern to the copywriter are state consumer protection laws. Practically all states have laws that discourage false and misleading advertising. In addition, each state has its own laws that regulate the advertising of professional services. Physicians, dentists, opticians, chiropractors, attorneys, and health-care facilities may be permitted to advertise on radio and television. State laws vary widely, so you must be familiar with the statutes of your state and those of adjacent states if your station's signal reaches them and if advertising time is sold to businesses in those states.

Professional Services

State laws regulate two aspects of advertising professional services. First, each state determines whether a given service can be advertised. If it can, state statutes typically spell out guidelines.

Although it is impossible to describe the relevant laws of all states, some generalizations will illustrate the concerns with which you should be familiar. State laws typically stipulate that advertising of professional services cannot be false, deceptive, or misleading. This means that advertising copy cannot create false or unjustified expectations of beneficial assistance or successful cures. A law firm, for example, cannot guarantee that it will win a client's case, and a chiropractor cannot promise that treatment will eliminate all aches and pains. Advertising rules for physicians and dentists often state that advertising copy cannot appeal to a layperson's fears, ignorance, or anxieties regarding his or her health or well-being.

Another problem pertains to professional specialties. If a dentist or a physician has the education required to practice a specialty, state laws usually permit the specialty to be advertised. Thus, a dentist with the required training to practice orthodontics may advertise that specialty. In the event that a dental clinic has only one orthodontist as part of its dental team, however, the clinic would not be permitted to advertise itself as an orthodontic clinic.

Some state laws also prohibit celebrity or authority figures from narrating advertisements for professional services on television. Where these laws apply, they stipulate that only the advertising professional may appear and speak on camera. If the professional does not want to use the spokesperson approach, the station can use a staff announcer to deliver the commercial.

Because of such rules, commercials for professional services often appear as straightforward, institutional-style announcements. The result is a low-key, soft-sell approach for advertisers that want to appear serious and responsible.

Commercials for medical clinics have also been written in an institutional style. The spot in Figure 3.1, however, takes a bolder approach, advertising a clinic for alcohol and drug rehabilitation. This is a sensitive topic for both the client and the public. Clinics and hospitals don't want to seem crass in their attempt to fill rooms and beds, and the public may not be receptive to a commercial that is not in good taste. Still, clinics and hospitals compete for patients, and each facility hopes to convince those who need specialized treatment to use its facilities. Good taste and sensitivity are essential in such

BROOKWOOD
RECOVERY CENTERS
Adolescent Services

"Crying Out" :30 TV

Your child may be crying out for your help...

and you may not even know it. Because the warning signs of alcohol and drug dependency

are so very hard to recognize.

A drop in grades, a change of friends

an irrational change of mood. They're your child's cries for help.

If you're listening, call Brookwood Recovery Centers Adolescent Services.

Now at Chocolate Bayou.

We're a unique treatment center in the Houston area dedicated solely to Adolescent chemical dependency problems.

And we can help.

FIGURE 3.1   A Professional Services Ad *(Courtesy Brookwood Recovery Centers. Not to be reprinted without the express written permission of Brookwood Recovery Centers)*

commercials. That point is illustrated again in the following script, which addresses the problem of cocaine abuse.

SFX	ROLL OF GUN BARREL, COCK AND CLICK OF HAMMER
ANNCR	A lot of people are playing a deadly game these days. It's called cocaine.
SFX	ROLL OF GUN BARREL, COCK AND CLICK OF HAMMER
ANNCR	Maybe they think cocaine isn't addictive. That's just not true. Cocaine can make life unmanageable. Unbearable. Unlivable.
SFX	ROLL OF GUN BARREL, COCK AND CLICK OF HAMMER
ANNCR	If someone you love is dependent on cocaine or other drugs, get help. Now. By calling Brookwood Recovery Centers' 24-Hour Crisis Line. Qualified, caring counselors are ready to listen. And ready to help you help someone beat this deadly game. So call now. Brookwood Recovery Centers' 24-Hour Crisis Line is open. Because if they don't win . . .
SFX	ROLL OF GUN BARREL, COCK OF HAMMER, SHOT
ANNCR	Sooner or later, cocaine will.
TAG	Brookwood Recovery Centers. (APPROPRIATE TAG INFORMATION) Someone you love needs you to call.

Courtesy Brookwood Recovery Centers. Not to be reprinted without the express written permission of Brookwood Recovery Centers.

Remember, each state has its own laws regarding the advertising of professional services. If a professional service can be advertised in your state, check the appropriate regulations. They will usually be available at a good library. You can also check with the state attorney general's office, the local Better Business Bureau, and the chamber of commerce. The professional firm that wants to advertise on your station might also have a copy of your state's rules. Ask the salesperson to check for you, or call the client yourself. Legal action can be brought against the station if a commercial for a professional service violates state guidelines. It is your responsibility to become familiar with the rules in your state and to follow them.

Lotteries

For decades, broadcasters were subject to federal restrictions that prevented them from airing commercials or station promotions that constituted a lottery. We're not referring to a state-approved lottery such as the Oregon State Lottery but, rather, to contests and promotions that stations themselves, or their advertisers, wanted to broadcast. Regulators felt that such announcements could mislead the public and thus deserved to be regulated. Before proceeding, let's explain what a lottery is. A broadcast lottery consists of three elements:

Prize. Is a prize, which can be anything of value, offered to participants?

Chance. Is the winner selected by chance, rather than by a test of skill or other factors within his or her control? Is the amount of the prize determined by chance?

Consideration. Must the contestant spend money or substantial time or effort to qualify for the contest?

Suppose that an advertiser wanted you to include the following material in a commercial:

A local sporting goods store wants to promote the start of Little League baseball season. With each purchase, contestants can try to guess the correct number of baseballs in a large container. The winner, who will receive a new baseball glove, will be drawn from the entrants guessing the correct number. Could you safely include this material in a commercial if your state prohibited a lottery? The answer is no; in legal terms, this contest would be a lottery. First, a prize, the baseball glove, will be awarded. Second, consideration is present because participants must make a purchase to enter. And third, an element of chance exists because participants must guess at the correct number, with the winner being drawn at random from the correct entrants. FCC licensees bear the ultimate responsibility to see that contests are not operated as lotteries. As structured, the contest would violate their licenses.

The promotion could, however, easily be made legal by removing the consideration—the requirement that only those making purchases can enter. If anyone going to the store could fill out an entry blank without a purchase, only two elements would exist and the contest would not be a lottery.

Keep in mind, too, that these rules do not apply to lotteries approved and run by the state. The airing of prize drawings and advertising for state-run lotteries has been acceptable since state governments approved these lotteries.

When Congress passed the Charity Games Advertising Clarification Act in 1988, it removed the federal ban on lotteries and allowed the states to restrict or ban lottery advertising. As a result, charitable lotteries and promotions and prize drawings by businesses are generally free of federal restrictions. However, some states may still enforce the lottery provisions discussed previously. If state law makes a lottery unlawful, it remains illegal and cannot be advertised on broadcast media.

State-Run Lotteries

Government-approved lotteries, such as the Georgia State Lottery, are quite different from the lotteries discussed previously. They are state-approved games of chance and do not involve the three elements we have already examined. If a government lottery is lawful under state law, stations licensed to that state may broadcast advertising for the lottery. But what happens if one state has a state-run lottery and broadcasters in an adjacent state want to carry advertising for it? That issue arose when WMYK-FM, a radio station licensed to a North Carolina community, wanted to carry ads for the Virginia state lottery. The town was located near the Virginia border and many of its listeners were from Virginia. The U.S. Supreme Court ruled that because North Carolina had no state lottery, the North Carolina station could not carry ads for the Virginia state lottery. In other words, a station in a nonlottery state cannot carry advertisements for a nearby state's lottery, even if many of its listeners are there.

Casino Gambling

Historically, federal law has restricted advertising for casino gambling even if the gambling activity is lawful, as it has been in Atlanta City and Las Vegas. The public policy on casinos has exhibited inconsistencies. States have legalized gambling activities, yet they have also tried to restrict the detrimental effects of gambling on the safety and welfare of state residents. Until recently, casino gambling has been thought to be especially harmful because of the threat of vice and corruption believed to accompany casinos.

Nevertheless, restrictions on the advertising of casino gambling have been challenged. In 1988, the Federal Indian Gaming Statute permitted broadcasters to advertise most forms of gambling conducted on Indian reservations. In 1997, a federal appeals court (*Valley Broadcasting v. U.S.*, 107 F.3d 1328) held that state statutes and FCC rules forbidding casino advertising violated the First Amendment rights of Nevada broadcasters. In 1999, another appeals court *upheld* the ban on the advertising of casino gambling in New Orleans, but the U.S. Supreme Court overturned the ruling (*Greater New Orleans Broadcasting Association v. U.S.*, 527 U.S. 173). The issue was whether federal law prohibited broadcast stations from advertising private casino gambling when such gambling was legal under state law. The Supreme Court held that the federal laws could not ban gambling advertising if such gambling was legal in the state. As a result of the high court's ruling, broadcasters in New Orleans and in many other states can carry casino gambling ads. The key is whether casino gambling is legal in the state where the station is located.

◆ Self-Regulation

Stations, networks, and cable systems must assume an active role in reviewing commercials. Each network and each station must determine what it will accept or reject. This is a difficult task for smaller stations because they often lack the staff to systematically evaluate commercials with questionable content.

As discussed earlier in this chapter, the more blatant excesses in commercials are covered by existing regulations, but some approaches that are not illegal nevertheless raise ethical questions. Some commercials are too loud, some promote products of questionable value, and some use techniques that raise questions of good taste.

Such ethical questions can be regulated only by advertisers, networks, stations, and advertising agencies. Standards of acceptance constantly change, so it is imperative that those who write and prepare broadcast commercials be alert to words, slogans, and presentational techniques that might offend the audience.

Stereotyping

Stereotyping is a kind of shorthand used in the mass media to facilitate communication. Consider some of the common images that have been presented in movies, commercials, and television programs. A cowboy in a black hat is a bad guy. A befuddled young man with thick glasses is a geek, and a burly, athletic male is a dumb jock. These are generalizations or stereotypes that we have come to accept after repeated exposure in the media. The problem is that these stereotypes might not be accurate generalizations. In other words, athletes might not be dumb and the befuddled young man with thick glasses might not be a technophile. Nevertheless, stereotypes are used because they allow a movie producer or a commercial director to avoid detailed character explanation and move quickly to the story line simply because consumers hold generalizations about stereotyped individuals.

GENDER STEREOTYPES In the 1960s, feminists began challenging the roles assigned to women. American culture was male-dominated, and feminists argued that society led females, from childhood, to think of themselves as wives and mothers. Males were taught to become leaders in business and politics.

Ad makers repeatedly used images of women as brainless housewives and sex objects. A 1964 commercial depicted the Ajax White Knight, who rode into a home wearing shining armor and turned laundry sparkling white with a wave of his wand. An astonished homemaker watched breathlessly. Advertisers believed that idealized stereotypes such as these were the way to reach women. Advertisements showed women with smooth skin, a shining-bright smile, and freshly shampooed hair who were focused primarily on "landing a man."

As women in the 1960s began to move beyond traditional jobs as teachers, nurses, and secretaries, they joined the professional ranks of engineers, lawyers, doctors, and so on. By the 1970s, ad makers had adopted the feminists' concern with gender issues and cast women in business and managerial roles. That trend now continues, with women being depicted as leaders in business, politics, and sports.

ETHNIC STEREOTYPES　Advertisers have generally become culturally sensitive about presenting stereotypes of minority groups, but the change did not come quickly. Very few African Americans appeared in print ads or commercials during the 1950s and 1960s. However, by the 1970s, the number of African Americans shown in mainstream advertising had grown considerably.

The major change was to cast African Americans in more usual occupations and tasks. The Aunt Jemima advertising character "mammy" was presented in a less stereotypical style. Although critics acknowledged the improvement, they were still offended by the stereotype. In other cases, advertising agencies revised campaigns for white-oriented media by substituting nonwhite models and aiming the campaigns at African American audiences. Eventually, well-known African American celebrities like actor Bill Cosby (Jell-O) and singer Lena Horne (Sanka) pitched products to the mass audience and helped to break the color line. The commercial in Figure 3.2 illustrates the increased use of African Americans in advertising. The businessman is an African American, depicting the changed roles in the business world.

Other ethnic audiences, especially Hispanics and Asian Americans, have had less success in the new social consciousness. They rarely appear in advertisements and still suffer stereotypes when they do. Italian Americans and Jewish people have also complained about being stereotyped in advertisements. Italian Americans argue they have been depicted as gangsters, and Jewish people object to being depicted as tight with money.

In the late 1960s, an unflattering character developed for Fritos irritated Mexican Americans. The character, Frito Bandito, was animated to look like the famous Mexican bandit Pancho Villa. The smirking, gun-toting character held up supermarkets, shoppers, and the like in search of his favorite snack. Funny Face fruit drink ran into a similar problem with ethnic characters initially used to pitch the product. "Chinese Cherry" was changed to "Choo-Choo Cherry," and "Injun Orange" became "Jolly Olly Orange."[2]

A more recent campaign for Taco Bell used a stereotype but weathered a swell of complaints to maintain use of the character. The character, a talking Chihuahua, pitched a variety of Taco Bell products and became an icon of sorts. Although his lines varied, his most famous remark was "Yo quiero Taco Bell," which means, "I want Taco Bell." Critics complained that the "spokesdog" presented a negative view of Hispanics, but others said they found the dog amusing. Toy dogs were sold in Taco Bell outlets, and the Chihuahua appeared in television specials and giant inflated images were placed outside Taco Bell stores.

---

[2]For additional information, see Juliann Sivulka, *Soap, Sex, and Cigarettes* (Belmont, CA: Wadsworth, 1998).

FLORIDA DEPARTMENT OF CITRUS
100% PURE FLORIDA ORANGE JUICE
"ROOM SERVICE" :30

WAITER: Here you are, sir.

GUEST: (CONGESTED)
This orange juice
looked a lot bigger
through the peephole.

WAITER: It did.

GUEST: Well look at this puny thing.

I've got a cold. I need vitamins,
minerals, nutrients – *plural*.
You know, fluid*sss*?

Those mini shampoo bottle makers
are behind this, aren't they?

ANNCR VO: 100% pure
Florida orange juice.
Are you drinking enough?

WAITER: I've found you a mug, sir.

GUEST: A mug? Gee,
how'd you get past security?

FIGURE 3.2   A Commercial Depicting a Minority Businessperson *(Courtesy of Florida Department of Citrus)*

Stereotypes are tempting to use because they often evoke instant recognition. However, stereotypes are not always valid, which raises ethical concerns about their use. Commercials influence people, so you must consider the impact your characterizations will have. Avoid blatant and unflattering stereotypes.

◆ Cable Advertising

Although broadcast stations are heavily regulated by the FCC, cable systems are not. Local franchising authorities determine a cable operator's legal, character, financial, and other qualifications. Cable is considered a nonbroadcast facility that is much more in touch with local franchise stipulations than with federal regulation. As a result of their status, cablecasters are not required to observe the FCC rules for sponsorship identification and station-conducted contests. However, cablecasters must adhere to the FCC Political Sponsorship Identification rules. As we noted earlier, the FTC is empowered to review false and misleading advertising of any sort, including that on cable channels. Cable operators also must adhere to state laws against false and misleading advertising, laws that regulate the advertising of professional services, and laws that prohibit lotteries.

➤ POINTS TO REMEMBER

- The Federal Communications Commission is empowered to consider a station's advertising practices at license renewal time.

- Stereotypes are used in commercials for rapid recognition of people or groups, but they might not be flattering.

- Broadcast commercials must include sponsorship identification.

- Broadcast stations can air ads for casino gambling, but only if such gambling is legal in the state where the station is located.

- A contest or promotion with the elements of a lottery (prize, chance, and consideration) may be illegal in some states.

- A station-conducted contest is illegal if the material terms are not broadcast.

- The Federal Trade Commission is charged with protecting the public from false and misleading advertising.

- Products demonstrated in television commercials cannot be altered for effect; they must be shown as they are.

- Testimonials and endorsements in commercials must be genuine.

- Comparative advertising or the use of research data in commercials is acceptable as long as claims aren't misleading and the comparisons aren't rigged.

- Most states have consumer laws that prohibit false and misleading advertising and laws that regulate the advertising of professional services.

- Liquor can be advertised on broadcast stations, but stations rarely do so.

- Each station and each network must review commercials to determine which they will accept and which they will reject.

- Commercials that are loud or otherwise offensive might not violate regulations but could still be in poor taste.

- Cablecasters are primarily accountable to local franchise authorities rather than to the FCC.

- Information about lotteries operated by state governments can be aired by broadcast stations, but only if the station is licensed to a state where the lottery exists.

EXERCISES

Exercise 1

Examine the following list of advertising claims. Why would you accept these claims rather than hold them to be false?

PRODUCT	CLAIM
Curex	Nothing stops the itching better.
Delta Airlines	Just the quiet desire to give you the world's best flight.
Pepsodent	Pepsodent Baking Soda Toothpaste helps get your teeth their whitest.
Bayer Aspirin	Nothing is stronger than Bayer.
Cascade	For virtually spotless dishes.

Exercise 2

Watch television and identify three commercials that use stereotypes to carry the message. Explain the nature of the stereotype and how it is used.

Exercise 3

Study a group of advertisements and look or listen for exaggerated claims that you believe constitute puffery. List five of them. Explain why you, as an average consumer, accept these exaggerations rather than believe them to be false.

Consumer Behavior

The term *consumer* has several definitions. One says that a consumer is a person who *uses* goods or services to satisfy his or her needs. A second definition indicates that consumers are people who *buy* products or services. The buying behavior of consumers is our focus.

Consumers make many buying decisions each day, and the goal of an advertising copywriter is to influence those decisions. Consider a typical buying decision: you need to buy laundry detergent. There are many types and brands, so you must make some decisions. Is liquid or powder detergent better? Is a product with bleach or softener desirable? Does a cheaper brand clean as well as a more expensive and possibly better-known brand does? Ultimately, the consumer makes a buying decision based on his or her needs.

Consumer researchers examine buying behavior to learn what consumers buy, where they buy, when they buy, and why they buy. Such data helps advertisers understand how consumers respond to advertising approaches a company might use. The company with a strong understanding of how consumers respond to a product has a decided advantage over its competitors. Discovering what makes buyers tick is not easy because much of the information is locked in the consumer's head. However, a good starting place is to look at the characteristics that affect consumer behavior.

◆ Personal Characteristics

Consumers' buying decisions are influenced by cultural, social, personal, and psychological characteristics that affect buying behavior. By and large, marketers cannot control the influence of the characteristics that affect a buying decision, but these factors must be considered.

Cultural Factors

Culture is the most basic determinant of an individual's wants and behavior. Human behavior is primarily learned from the society around us. A child learns perceptions, behaviors, basic values, and wants from key institutions and from the family. These values include material comfort, freedom, achievement, individualism, fitness, and humanitarianism.

Marketers track cultural changes so they can develop new products people might want. Marketers have responded to several recent cultural trends in America. For instance, Americans spend much of their time in their cars and desire safety, room, and comfort. Auto makers have responded with sport utility vehicles. These vehicles suit the "soccer mom" who transports her children to various activities as well as outdoors-oriented individuals who need room for camping gear.

Office cultures have changed too. Entire business segments such as Internet and computer companies have developed casual dress codes. Many traditional businesses have dropped the conservative dress style, at least on "casual Fridays," and in some cases throughout the week. As a result, people are choosing more casual clothing and informality in their lifestyles.

SUBCULTURES   America is known as a vast melting pot because it is made up of numerous subcultures, or groups of people with shared value systems based on similar life experiences. Racial groups such as Hispanics, blacks, and Asians have unique cultural styles and values. Religious groups such as Baptists, Catholics, Mormons, and

Lutherans have their own preferences and beliefs. Age groups include baby boomers, teens, and seniors. Groups such as Italians, Japanese, Irish, and Cubans are found within many cities and have specialized interests and ethnic tastes. Geographical areas such as the Southwest, New England, the South, and the Pacific Northwest include subcultures with distinct lifestyles.

SOCIAL CLASS   Virtually all societies include social classes, which are uniform and relatively permanent partitions within society whose members share values, behaviors, interests, and even buying behavior. In some societies, members of social classes are born into certain positions and cannot change them. In the United States, however, people are not fixed in rigid social classes. They can move to higher or lower social classes as conditions change. No single factor determines social class. Rather, a combination of variables such as income, education, and occupation interact to determine social class.

Sociologists have examined social structure over many years, and a model constructed in 1983 is still considered to be a sound representation of class structure in America.[1] This model, by Richard P. Coleman and Lee P. Rainwater, identifies six levels of class structure, as shown in Table 4.1. Even though the model represents an abstraction of reality, it is useful in helping an advertising manager understand the characteristics of these basic classes.

TABLE 4.1   ## Levels of American Class Structure

Upper-Class Americans

Upper-Upper (0.3%)—The world of inherited wealth and aristocratic names.

Lower-Upper (1.2%)—The new social elite, drawn from contemporary professional and corporate leadership.

Upper-Middle (12.5%)—The remaining college graduate professionals and managers; lifestyle centers on the arts, causes, and private clubs.

Middle-Class Americans

Middle Class (32%)—White- and blue-collar workers who make average pay, do "the proper things," and live on the "better side of town."

Working Class (38%)—Blue-collar workers who make average pay and lead "working-class lifestyles" regardless of school, job, income, and background.

Lower-Class Americans

Upper-Lower Class (9%)—Working, not on welfare but having a living standard just above poverty.

Lower-Lower Class (7%)—On welfare, usually out of work, visibly poverty-stricken. Hold the most menial jobs.

---

[1]Richard P. Coleman, "The Continuing Significance of Social Class to Marketing," *Journal of Consumer Research* (December 1983), 267

◆ Social Factors

Social factors such as the consumer's status, family, and reference groups influence a consumer's behavior.

Status

We all belong to groups such as clubs, organizations, and families. Two elements, role and status, define an individual's position in each group. A *role* is defined as the activities a person is expected to fulfill according to the people around him or her. Each role carries a *status* that reflects the position given to it by society. People often choose products that show their status in society. For instance, the sales manager of a television station might buy a pricey foreign import automobile to show his or her job status to coworkers and peers. Likewise, an upper-class family might not want just a sedan to haul the family but rather a Lexus or Infiniti that would also reflect status. The houses people buy, the neighborhoods they choose, and the furnishings they select express their roles in society and the status with which they identify.

Family

Family members can strongly affect buyer behavior. From parents, individuals receive an orientation toward economics, religion, and politics. Thus, some consumers will exhibit little independence in making major purchases if their fathers tended to such decisions. Parents also instill a sense of love, self-worth, and personal ambition. As a result, parents can significantly influence a buyer's subconscious behavior even if the buyer has not lived with his or her parents for a long time.

The buyer's immediate family—the buyer's spouse (or significant other) and children—directly influence regular buying behavior. Marketers must consider the roles played by the husband, wife, and children in the purchase of a variety of products and services. Husbands and wives participate in joint decision making when expensive products and services are involved. Marketers need to determine which family member normally has the greater influence on the purchase of a given product or service. For instance, does the father or mother exert the greatest influence when buying a large-screen TV or a kitchen appliance?

Although some buying patterns were fairly standard in the past, cultural changes have modified them. The wife was formerly the primary purchaser of products for the family, including food, clothing, and household items. However, the increasing number of later first marriages, working wives, and changes in cultural norms have brought major changes. Today, husbands and wives often divide the shopping activities or make joint buying decisions.

Children also enter the process. Even though they may not make most of the purchases, they influence their parents' choices of food, clothing, and entertainment. Thus marketers must understand the dynamics of family decision making to aim their advertising strategies toward the right family members. The commercial in Figure 4.1 capitalizes on the interaction of a mother and her baby.

Reference Groups

Another source of influence on behavior is membership in reference groups—groups that have direct or indirect influence on a person's behavior or attitude. Reference groups influence people by exposing them to new behaviors and lifestyles, influencing the

FLORIDA DEPARTMENT OF CITRUS
100% PURE FLORIDA ORANGE JUICE
"WHAT A NICE MOM" :30

ANNCR VO: Gina didn't wait 'til she was pregnant to start thinking about her baby's health.

That's why she made Florida orange juice

part of her daily lifestyle two years ago.

So she'd be sure to have the folic acid she needs

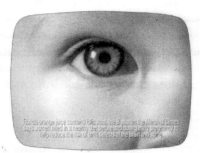

to help reduce the risk

of certain birth defects.

So before you start thinking pink, or blue,

start thinking orange.
100% pure Florida orange juice.

Are you drinking enough?

FIGURE 4.1   Commercial Emphasizing Mother's Love for a Child (*Courtesy Florida Department of Citrus*)

person's attitudes and self-concept because he or she wants to "fit in." Reference groups create pressures to conform that may influence the person's product and brand choices.

When a person belongs to a reference group that has such a direct influence, the group is called a *membership* group. Some—such as family, friends, neighbors, and coworkers—are primary groups with whom there is informal interaction. Others—such as religious groups, professional associations, or political parties—are secondary groups where interaction is less regular but group structure is more formal.

Groups to which people do not belong also influence them. An *aspiration* group is one to which the individual wants to belong. For instance, a teenage female soccer player may hope someday to play for the U.S. Women's National Soccer Team. She has no direct contact with the group but nevertheless identifies with it. A *dissociative* group is one whose behavior and values a person rejects. The same teenager might want to avoid interaction with a gang.

Advertisers seek to identify the reference groups of the target market they are trying to reach. The influence of reference groups varies across products and brands, but it is strongest for conspicuous purchases. Conspicuous products are those that are noticeable because the buyer is one of the few people to own it; they include luxury items of all kinds, or products consumed in public where others can see them. For instance, a college student who joins a fraternity or sorority may be more conscious of norms of dress than a student who doesn't join such a group. Figure 4.2 is a commercial for a conspicuous product—a water recreational vehicle.

Friends may influence purchases of conspicuous products in hopes that they will also enjoy the product. However, reference groups have a weak influence on the purchase of private luxury items such as cappuccino makers, remote-controlled window blinds, bathroom spas, or high-speed cable modems. People choose such private luxuries simply because they want them; the influence of friends is not a major factor.

◆ Personal Elements

Personal characteristics such as age and life cycle, occupation, and lifestyle can also influence a buyer's decisions.

Age and Life Cycle

Preferences for specific items of furniture, clothing, food, and recreational equipment often relate to age. These preferences don't remain static; they change as families pass through certain phases. These phases, identified in Table 4.2, represent a family life cycle.[2] Marketers often define their target audience in terms of the family life cycle and develop products and advertising themes that correspond to these phases. Marketing targeted to specific phases of family life once concentrated on young singles and married couples. Because of societal changes, however, advertisers have reacted to nontraditional, alternative life cycles such as single parents, unmarried couples, and so on.

Occupation

Our jobs affect the goods and services we buy. People working in construction jobs wear boots and jeans. Individuals employed in law firms are usually expected to wear dark, conservative suits. Businesses attempt to identify the occupational groups that

---

[2]Leon G. Schiffman and Leslie Lazar Kanuk, *Consumer Behavior* (Upper Saddle River, NJ: Prentice-Hall, 2000), pp. 285–292.]

TABLE 4.2	Family Life Cycle Phases	
Young	**Middle-Aged**	**Older**
Single	Single	Older married
Married without children	Married without children	Older unmarried
Married with children	Married with children	
Divorced with children	Married without dependent children	
	Divorced without children	
	Divorced with children	
	Divorced without dependent children	

have an interest in their products or services. For example, businesses targeting affluent purchasers include CNN, CNBC, Lexus, and BMW.

Lifestyle

Lifestyle analysis examines a person's day-to-day living pattern and is expressed as an individual's psychographics. Psychographics is the method of measuring lifestyles and developing lifestyle classifications. It measures consumers' *activities* (sports, hobbies, work, shopping, social events), *interests* (recreation, food, fashion, family), and *opinions* (about business, products, social issues, and themselves). These characteristics concentrate on the following:

1. How people spend their time
2. Their interests—in other words, what is important to them in their immediate environments
3. Their view of themselves and the world around them
4. Basic demographic data such as income, education, and location of residence

The thinking behind lifestyle analysis is that advertisers can plan better strategies to reach target audiences if they know more about them. For instance, it could help an advertiser to know that the average member of a target audience for an SUV is 32.5 years old, married, has 1.3 children, and owns a house. These demographic factors are useful, but they don't paint a human picture of the target market. Lifestyle analysis might show that the target audience just described is community-oriented, has a traditional lifestyle, and enjoys outdoor sports and family activities. A commercial for this target market might show a happy family piling into the SUV to attend a soccer match. As a result, the target audience could readily identify with the commercial.

Values

The values a person holds impacts the products they buy and use. The VALS system, a proprietary procedure for understanding consumers' values and lifestyles, categorizes U.S. adults into consumer groups that think and act differently based on a combination of primary motivation and resources. Primary motivations signify distinct psychological characteristics, attitudes, and decision-making styles. The eight primary VALS classifications, illustrated in Figure 4.3, classify consumer behavior in terms of three primary motivations: *ideals* (consumers whose decisions are led by their beliefs rather than by

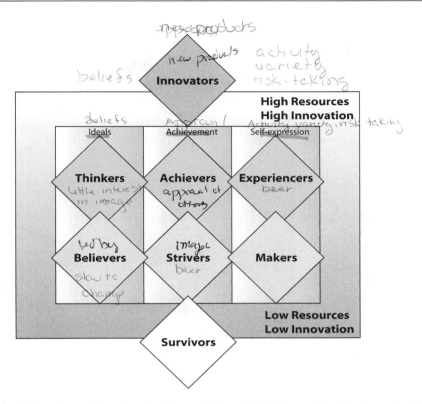

FIGURE 4.3 VALS Typology (*Reprinted with permission of SRI Consulting Business Intelligence, Menlo Park, CA. VALS is a registered trademark of SRI Consulting Business Intelligence*)

desires for acceptance), *achievement* (consumers whose buying choices are regulated by the approval and opinions of others), and *self-expression* (consumers whose purchases are motivated by an inclination for risk taking, variety, and physical or social activity).

Resources, varying from most to least, indicate the material, psychological, demographic, and physical capabilities of consumer lifestyles.

The eight VALS classifications reveal some important distinctions. Innovators are attracted to new and innovative products, whereas Believers are slow to change. Strivers are image-conscious, but Thinkers have little interest in image. A close study of the classifications shows distinct consumer categories that reflect differences in buying behavior. You can determine your own VALS classification by completing the survey at *www.sric-bi.com*.

Study the Celebrity Cruises commercial in Figure 4.4. Which VALS classification might this message appeal to? When used with care, the VALS approach can help advertisers understand changing consumer values and how to affect buying behavior. For instance, Iron City beer, a popular brand in Pittsburgh, used VALS to review its image and target audience (blue-collar steelworkers enjoying Iron City at a local bar). The target audience was drinking less Iron City, and the company was losing sales. VALS research showed that Experiencers and Strivers drink the most beer. A study of this group showed that they no longer identified with the heavy-industry image but saw themselves as modern, hard working, and fun loving. An advertising campaign mixed images of the former target audience with the young Experiencers and Strivers having fun. Sales of Iron City shot up.

Understanding the consumer's needs and the factors that affect buying decisions is the basis of successful advertising. Consumers vary considerably in their cultural

✕ *Celebrity Cruises*®

Exceeding expectations.℠

:30 Television – "Stingray/Caribbean"

VO:
Don't just satisfy my needs,

fulfill my dreams.

There is a cruise line that
can do that.

Celebrity.

MUSIC:
"You're simply the best,

better than all the rest,

better than anyone ..."

VO:
Celebrity Cruises.

FIGURE 4.4 Celebrity Cruises Commercial (*Courtesy Philip E. Cohen, Harris-Drury-Cohen*)

backgrounds, the groups they are in, and the life cycles through which they pass. The roles people play and the way these roles develop will express lifestyle and influence buying behavior. Advertisers must understand how consumers transform advertising messages and other influences into buying decisions.

➤ **POINTS TO REMEMBER**

- A consumer's wants and behavior are primarily determined by culture.
- Advertisers must be aware of cultural shifts that might provide new ways to serve consumers.
- Consumers choose brands and products that reinforce their reference group roles and status.
- Lifestyles—the system of acting and interacting with those around us—significantly influence buyers' decisions.

- Factors in buyer behavior cannot be controlled, but they can be useful to advertisers in efforts to understand the consumers they want to influence.
- Psychographic methods are used to classify consumer behavior by psychological and demographic variables. Psychological researchers evaluate items such as media usage, leisure-time activities, and attitudes toward social issues.

EXERCISES

Exercise 1

What do each of the following indicate about a person's social class?

1. Shops at Kmart rather than Macy's   *Working*

✓ 2. Earns an income of $30,000 versus $80,000   *Working*

3. Drives a Ford pickup truck rather than a Lexus sedan   *Working*

4. Works with a personal trainer at a health spa versus exercising at the YMCA   *upper mid ↑*

5. Plays tennis rather than goes fishing   *middle ↑*

Exercise 2

Compile a set of recent commercials or print ads for the following:

1. beers

2. breakfast cereals

3. pickup trucks

4. cell phone users   *achievement*

5. vacation cruises   *Exp + ach*

What lifestyles do the advertisements depict? How do they depict the lifestyle?

Exercise 3

Examine the VALS classifications in Figure 4.3. What lifestyle segments might respond to advertising for the following?

1. Handheld organizer

2. High-definition TV

3. A nationwide family department store chain

4. Shirt or blouse with designer emblem

5. Rolex wrist watch

6. Four-door Chevrolet family sedan

Exercise 4

Identify four products or services for each of the following by the relative influence of reference groups on product and brand choices.

1. Public luxuries

2. Private necessities

Write a commercial for one of the public luxuries and for one of the private necessities you have listed. Include an explanation of reference group influence on the product or service and the brand selection.

Motivation

As we saw in the previous chapter, consumers make buying decisions and advertisers try to understand consumers so that they can influence their buying decisions. We now come to the heart of the buying decision: the reasons people actually buy the products they do. At any point in time, consumers are affected by different motives, some of which are contradictory. For example, you may say that you took up jogging, spending considerable money to buy shoes, shorts, and so on, to keep in shape. The real reason, however, might be that you think jogging will be a good opportunity to meet the attractive man or woman next door who jogs by your house. Both reasons are real, but one is stated and one is subconscious.

As a copywriter, you must be aware of the reasons that motivate people to buy. Then, you appeal to consumers to buy a product or service because of needs and motives they might have. What motivates people to make purchases? How have researchers categorized human motivations?

◆ The Structure of Motivation

A *motive* is the reason a person behaves in a given way. It is an internal force that stimulates you to behave in a specific manner. *Motivation* is the justification for the behavior. Needs and wants motivate us. *Needs* are the basic forces that motivate us to do something. We also have needs related to our views of ourselves and our relationships with others. Needs are more basic than wants. *Wants* are "needs" that we learn during our lives. For instance, we have a basic need for water—but some people have learned to want a bottle of Perrier. When a need isn't satisfied, it becomes a drive. A *drive* is a strong stimulus to reduce a need—a stimulus that encourages action. Drives are the reasons behind certain patterns of behaviors. The purchase of a product is the result of a drive to satisfy a need. Consider consumer motives in the purchase of bread. At the basic level, bread is necessary for physiological needs; we need it to survive. Why buy whole-wheat rather than white bread? We might feel that whole-wheat bread will give us more vitamins and minerals than white bread will. We might also want others to see that we choose a more healthful bread for our loved ones.

Motives can be strong; in other words, we might buy Evian even though the municipal water supply passes all safety tests. However, motives are highly situational. For example, we may drink an inexpensive beer at home where other people aren't aware of our choice. In public, we might drink Michelob so that other people see that we have picked a good brand. Thus, the situation makes a major difference in ordering our behavior, and the motives driving our behavior may vary from one situation to another.

Some critics argue that advertisers can make consumers buy products against their will. We can't create drives in consumers, but we can study the nature of consumer needs and drives. With this knowledge, we can better understand consumer needs, drives, and wants—and how they can be better satisfied.

◆ Maslow's Hierarchy of Needs

If motivation is to be used to advantage in developing advertising, we must understand it. Maslow's hierarchy of needs is a good guide to human behavior because it categorizes needs. Maslow places needs in ascending order of importance: physiological, safety, social, esteem, and self-actualization. As a person fulfills one need, a higher-level need becomes important. In other words, the most basic level of needs must be satisfied

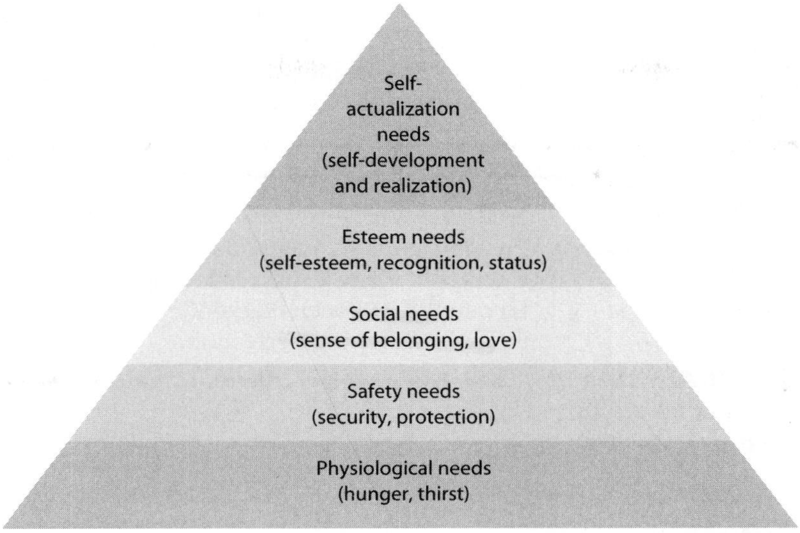

FIGURE 5.1   Maslow's Hierarchy of Needs

at least minimally before other motives are engaged. Figure 5.1 illustrates Maslow's hierarchy with a brief description of each level.[1] Now, we can examine the model with illustrations of advertising slogans for each level.

I. **Physiological:** Needs for water, food, and shelter are physiological motives. This is the most basic level of human needs. Because physiological needs are essential to survival, these needs must be satisfied first.

Products:	Medicines, low-cholesterol foods, health foods, and special drinks.
Sample Slogans:	Wonder white bread—"Wonder helps build strong bodies." I Can't Believe It's Not Butter—"The taste you love without cholesterol." Dairy Farmers—"M.V.B. (Most Valuable Beverage) Got milk?"

II. **Safety:** Needs pertaining to stability, physical safety, comfortable environment, and so on.

Products:	Insurance, retirement investments, smoke detectors, preventive medicines, automotive tires.
Sample Slogans:	BlueCross/BlueShield—"To take care of their mind . . . their body . . . their spirit, their health." Prilosec Acid Control—"24 hours of complete heartburn relief is possible." LIFE—"Life insurance isn't for the people who die. It's for the people who live." Culligan Drinking Water System—"It's a security system for your water."

III. **Social Needs:** Motives that illustrate a desire for friendship, group acceptance, affiliation, or love.

Products:	Clothing, entertainment, foods, personal grooming, and others.

[1]Adapted from Abraham H. Maslow, *Motivation and Personality,* 2nd ed. (New York: Harper & Row, 1970)

Sample Slogans:	ColorSpa for Men—"The new fitness in haircolor." DeBeers—"The diamond engagement ring. How often will you give her something she'll cherish for the rest of her life?" Kay Jewelers—"Every kiss begins with Kay."

IV. **Esteem:** Self-respect, superiority, prestige, and status. Esteem motives relate to a person's desire for accomplishment and usefulness.

Products:	Cars, furniture, clothing, hobbies, liquors, and many others.
Sample Slogans:	Punch Cigars—"A legendary smoke. A knowing choice. For those who value a full-bodied cigar." Lincoln LS—"Reach Higher." Lexus—"Pursuing perfection."

V. **Self-Actualization:** The need for self-fulfillment, of becoming all that one is capable of becoming.

Products:	Hobbies, sports, education, gourmet foods, and some vacations. (Maslow felt that few people reached this level, but advertisers nevertheless focus on it.)
Sample Slogans:	U.S. Army—"Army Strong." National Geographic—"Enjoy the thrill of a National Geographic expedition." Job Corps—"Success lasts a lifetime."

Maslow's explanation of motives provides a good framework for overall behavior, but his hierarchy is not ironclad. A given consumer behavior can satisfy more than one need, as well as different needs at different times. For example, the purchase of a Volvo automobile may satisfy desires for safety, esteem, and self-fulfillment. The vacations advertised in Figure 5.2 appeal to both self-esteem and social needs. Remember that consumer motives may be strong, but they depend on the situation. Nevertheless, evaluating motives can be important in targeting an advertising message.

◆ McGuire's Psychological Motives

McGuire has devised a classification that is more specific in defining motives than Maslow's version is. The following of McGuire's motivational needs are mostly applied to advertising.[2]

Self-Expression

This motive relates to a need to express oneself to others. We want to let others know by our actions, including the purchase and display of products, what we are and who we are. This brings the notion of *self-concept* into play.

Your self-concept is the attitudes you hold toward yourself. Self-concept can be divided into actual and ideal: *who I am now (actual)* and *who I would like to be (ideal)*. The self-concept is developed through relationships with teachers, parents, peers, and important others. One's self-concept is important, and we strive to enhance it.

Certain products serve as social symbols and communicate social meaning about those who own or use them. These products communicate meaning to oneself and to

---

[2]W. J. McGuire, "Psychological Motives and Communication Gratification," in *The Uses of Mass Communications*, ed. J. G. Blumler and C. Katz (Beverly Hills, CA: Sage, 1974), pp. 167–196.

others; they enhance our need for self-expression. The outcome is that we often purchase and use services, products, and media to maintain a desired self-concept. Thus, an individual might want to wear a shirt embossed with the name Tommy Hilfiger because others might recognize it as a brand of quality—a factor that could also reinforce the wearer's self-image. Similarly, a person motivated toward humanitarianism might buy a "Save the Children" necktie rather than a Pierre Cardin tie even though the price and quality might be similar.

Before self-expression can be relevant to the targeting of audiences, there must be a relationship between self-concept and product image. Further, the product purchase must help deliver expression of the self-concept. For example, ordering a well-known brand of wine with dinner may enhance your self-concept if others recognize your knowledge of wines.

Novelty

The need for novelty stems from a desire for variety and difference. In consumer purchasing, this need could relate to impulse buying and brand switching. For example, an individual buying an automobile might believe the top consumer choices to be Toyota and Honda. However, that person might react to the need for novelty by purchasing another brand that is attracting attention. For example, Mazda added a novel approach to its advertising for the Tribute SUV, which it claimed had the soul of a sports car.

The need for novelty is highly situational. Individuals in stable situations become restless and may want change, but people experiencing rapid change prefer stability. A man who has always worn a dark suit, a solid color tie, and a white shirt to work might switch to a sports jacket and a polo shirt to add some flavor to his life.

Reinforcement

Products designed to be used in public (automobiles, clothing, furniture) are often advertised to emphasize the amount and nature of reinforcement that will be received. This reinforcement relates to individuals' need to enhance their self-images. For instance, you might feel that a sporty red automobile reflects you and your image. If people comment favorably on the car, you'll feel good about yourself and the choice you made.

Affiliation

This need emphasizes the development of satisfying and helping relations with others. The focus is on the need to share and be accepted by others, including family members, group members, or significant others. Some products are aimed at mothers who look after the health of their families. Some beers are advertised to suggest a sense of enjoyment and togetherness brought by consuming the product.

Modeling

Modeling is the need to base one's behavior on that of others. Individuals seek satisfying relationships with others and reflect on the desire to maintain conformity with reference groups. Advertisers apply this motive by depicting desirable individuals using their brands. For instance, Buick runs a series of ads that show people trying to learn the techniques used by Tiger Woods. Then Woods is shown driving a Buick.

FIGURE 5.2 Commercial Aimed at Self-Esteem or Social Needs *(Courtesy Philip E. Cohen, Harris-Drury-Cohen)*

WYNDHAM

Television

Where personal experiences . . .

A genuine smile experience etched in your soul.

. . . turn into memories. It's The Wyndham Way.

Singer: The way you hold your knife. The way we danced 'til three.

Singer: The way your smile just beams . . . No, No, they can't take that away from me.

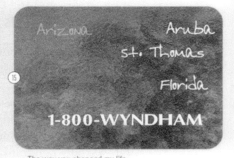

The way you changed my life.
Announcer: Wyndham Resorts . . .

Announcer: The Wyndham Way. A Personal Vacation Planner.

Your memories are waiting.
Singer: No they can't take that away from me.

Ego Defense

One of our important motives is the need to defend our egos or identities. We use defensive behaviors and attitudes to protect our self-concepts when our identities are threatened. Many products are advertised to provide ego defense. Consumers who are hesitant about their purchases of socially visible products may rely on well-known brands to avoid the possibility of making a socially incorrect purchase. For example, the Jeep Wrangler is advertised as the correct purchase for an individual wanting a rugged go-anywhere vehicle. The copy says: "Take a ride in a rugged Jeep Wrangler and you'll see the world like never before. And the world will see you like never before. That's because Wrangler says a lot about you, on the road and off. Your passion for discovery. Your quest for fun." The final line summarizes the message: "Jeep. There's only one."

Other products, such as mouthwash or breath mints, are advertised to protect us from the embarrassment of bad breath. We may be concerned that if people notice our bad breath, they will reject us. A breath mint can solve bad breath and, in the process, make us feel good about ourselves.

Some people may even want to make the right purchase for the bathroom! After all, who would want bathroom appliances that aren't beautiful and elegant? The commercial in Figure 5.3 uses a tongue-in-cheek approach to that situation.

◆ Categories of Appeals

Maslow and McGuire devised categories to explain consumer needs and actions. Beyond them are the basic motivations underlying the purchase of a product or service. These motivations can be classified as rational, emotional, or moral. In writing a commercial, you must determine which motivation will work best. Let's examine the three appeals.

Emotional Appeals

Emotion can be defined as powerful, relatively uncontrolled feelings that affect our behavior. We experience a wide range of emotions, such as joy, anger, grief, and sadness. Even though we sometimes don't recognize it, emotions are usually accompanied by thinking. Our ability to think "rationally" varies with the degree and type of emotion. During a period of great unhappiness, for instance, we may feel that we cannot think at all. We do think, but our feelings may be taking greater control. That is the difference between thinking rationally and reacting emotionally. Emotion is based on subjective feelings rather than logical, fact-based thinking.

Emotional appeals are used to generate either positive (joy, love, pride) or negative (shame, guilt, fear) emotions that can motivate purchase. These appeals are used to get people to stop doing things they shouldn't (eating fatty foods, drinking too much, smoking), or to do things they should (lose weight, brush their teeth). For instance, Quaker Oatmeal stresses that eating the product will lower the user's cholesterol level.

Advertisers may appeal to our emotions in any of several ways.

EMOTION AROUSAL   Emotions are characterized by positive or negative reactions; in other words, a given event can cause us to feel happy or sad. As consumers, we consciously seek products whose primary or secondary benefit is the arousal of emotion. Advertisers capitalize on this behavior by making emotion arousal the primary benefit of many advertisements. For example, makeup products are positioned as attracting favorable attention, and keeping our pets healthy appeals to a desire for pleasure or

American Standard

"No Place Like Home"
:30

The American Standard bathroom.

A study in simple elegance.

Timelessly beautiful.

But its beauty is a function

of its flawless engineering.

Which, after all,

is any bathroom's most important attribute.

American Standard.

American Standard

Living up to a higher standard.

A higher standard.

FIGURE 5.3 An Appeal to Appearance (*Courtesy Margeotes Fertitta & Weiss, Inc.*)

affection. Rational, fact-based thinking doesn't appeal to our needs as well as emotional appeals do; thus advertisers seek to arouse our emotions in their commercials.

EMOTION REDUCTION Many emotional states are unpleasant. We don't like to feel unhappy, jealous, or frustrated. Advertisers respond to this by positioning products to reduce or prevent the arousal of unpleasant emotions.

A number of products are advertised to appeal to emotion reduction. Weight-loss and other self-improvement products are often positioned to reduce shame, guilt, or helplessness. The Hollywood 48-Hour Miracle Diet promises to "help you lose weight while you clean, detoxify and rejuvenate your body." Over-the-counter medications are advertised to cope with depression and anxiety. Flowers are advertised at holiday time as a cure for loneliness.

ELICITING PARTICULAR EMOTIONS Advertisements use emotional arousal to elicit particular emotions such as joy and warmth. Some emotional advertisements are designed to get the consumer to like the ad. Consumers may relate better to commercials they like and thus be more receptive to the message. For instance, ads that convey "warmth" are often used where the goal is to directly or indirectly depict a family, friendship, or romantic relationship. The "Islands Honeymoon" spot in Figure 5.4 shows a couple reinforcing love for each other by using a credit card to pay for a romantic vacation. McDonald's uses commercials that depict a father-son or father-daughter relationship, and Wal-Mart depicts happy families doing their shopping. Advertisements involving pets, babies, family gatherings, and special moments seek to arouse particular emotions.

Rational Appeals

These appeals relate to the audience's self-interest by demonstrating that a product will deliver the desired results. Examples are messages showing the performance, economy, quality, safety, design, or price of a product. We can see how rational appeals work if we look more closely at their use when they feature price and quality.

PRICE Price appeals provide a good example of the blending of motivating factors. Rarely does price alone motivate. Rather, an effective ad combines price with quality. A 12-inch pizza with two toppings may be advertised for an attractive price, thus relating quality and price.

QUALITY Quality permeates and is common to nearly all other appeals. Hallmark combines a message of love with an emphasis on quality in its greeting cards; our heroes endorse a product because of its quality. We are strongly motivated by quality.

The television commercial for Curtis Mathes (see page 82) appeals to our desire for a product that is both dependable and long-lasting. This spot makes a direct appeal to our desire for quality with the slogan "Curtis Mathes costs a little more, but it's worth it." Many customers are willing to spend more money to own a car, a home appliance, or even a home that doesn't require constant repair. The desire to get our money's worth is strong and should be used for appeal whenever possible.

OGILVY & MATHER

2 EAST 48 STREET, NEW YORK 10017
907-3400

Client: AMERICAN EXPRESS
Product: CARD
Title: "ISLANDS HONEYMOON"
Commercial No.: APOW 9056 :60

1. MAN: That's our flight.

2. WOMAN: It was too short, wasn't it?

3. We were almost there.

4. MAN: What do you want to do? (MUSIC UP AND UNDER) WOMAN: Can we get the bags off?

5. (MUSIC)

6. MAN: What do you need?

7. MAN SINGS: I got sunshine on

8. a cloudy day.

9. (MUSIC)

10. I guess you say

11. what can make me feel this way.

12. My girl, my girl, my girl.

13. Talkin' about my girl.

14. My girl...
WOMAN: I wonder what the next ten years will bring.
MAN: I wonder where our luggage is?

15. ANNCR: (VO) Everything you need when you need some time together.

16. Membership has its privileges.

FIGURE 5.4 An Appeal to Love (*Courtesy Gorden S. Bowen, Ogilvy & Mather*)

VIDEO	AUDIO
OPEN TO CU OF FC. SLOW ZOOM TO MED SHOT. FC HOLDS BAMBOO FLYROD.	Quality. Let me tell you something about quality. You want to buy the best car. You're going to pay a little more. Same thing goes for a good suit or . . . a fine fishing rod. It's just a fact of life. Quality costs more. But you're willing to pay the extra because you want a product you can depend on. One that will last. It's called getting your money's worth.
CUT TO CU 5-SECOND PRODUCT ACTION ENDING WITH SUPER OF LOGO LINE	This little bit of wisdom is brought to you by . . . Curtis Mathes. The most expensive television sets in America . . . and darn well worth it.

Courtesy Ron McQuien, McQuien-Matz.

Moral Appeals

These appeals are aimed at our sense of what is "right" or "wrong." They are frequently used to urge consumers to support social causes such as stopping smoking, aiding the needy, keeping the environment clean, and helping starving children.

Other Appeals

The list of appeals that advertisers use is almost endless. Many intermingle with other categories. In addition to those already identified, advertisers use the following:

HUMOR One way to involve the listener or viewer is through humor. We feel good about things that are amusing or funny. Humor can be especially effective if the goal of the commercial is to establish product identification. If the sales goals are more complex, however, humor is not the best appeal. The rules for writing humorous spots are covered in Chapter 9. The following script illustrates the use of humor. Act out this script in class, or better yet, record it. A humorous spot is a miniature playlet, and acting it out or recording it forces you to adopt the characterizations called for in the script. This will help you appreciate the writing and production of humor commercials.

	ESTABLISH PIRATE MUSIC, BOAT SFX, ETC.
PIRATE	Ahoy, mateys. Welcome aboard "Deep Sea on a Discount" Cruise Lines . . . har, har, har.
ARNOLD	This isn't like their brochure.
WIFE	This is the luxury cruise you promised me?
PIRATE	Why sure it be a luxury cruise. Here's yer "welcome cocktail," madam.
	CORK POPPING OUT OF JUG SFX Jest wipe off the neck when yer through . . . har, har.
WIFE	Oh, really . . .
ARNOLD	May I see your brochure?

PIRATE	Not now, trim the mainsail. Then I'd like to trim yer mainsail, lady . . . har, har.
WIFE	Oh, I can't believe it. <u>FADE UNDER ANNCR</u>
ANNCR	If you traveled through American International Traveler, you'd always have smooth sailing. With nothing but firsthand facts from our large, experienced staff. Whatever the budget, destination, or time of year, we've been there. We know. So don't get lost in a sea of blind offers. Call A-I-T at 459–5401.
WIFE	When is dinner served?
PIRATE	Oh, whenever ya catches it . . . har, har, har.
WIFE	Ohhhhh.
HUBBY	Oh fishy, here fishy, here fishy.
JINGLE	The choice is so rational, American International. The most priceless free service in town.

Courtesy of Neal Spelce Communications, Austin, Texas.

CELEBRITY   When a former football star or a well-known actor asks us to buy a product, we are motivated favorably toward the product largely because we trust these spokespersons. They are our heroes, and if one of them trusts a product, so should we. Testimonials—endorsements by those we admire—can have a strong appeal. After all, a football hero or a screen star wouldn't mislead you.

The Hanes Underwear spot in Figure 5.5 uses a famous professional athlete as a spokesperson. The unwritten message for American males is "If this basketball star wears Hanes, shouldn't you?"

You shouldn't assume from the preceding that star appeal is for men only. Many famous women have been effective in selling a variety of products.

FIVE SENSES   Sometimes we buy a product simply because it appeals to one or more of our five senses. We buy candy because it tastes good, a recording because we like the sound, a picture because it pleases the eye, popcorn because it smells so good in the theater lobby, a piece of cloth because of the way it feels. You can show a picture on television, you can sample the recording on radio, but how do you communicate taste, feel, and smell in a broadcast spot? By the use of descriptive terms and demonstration. In a TV commercial for a fabric softener, show a woman holding a towel treated with the softener against her cheek. Let the look on her face convey her pleasure at the towel's softness. Come up with your own fresh phrases to replace the old and worn ones such as "the sweet smell of spring," "the delicious aroma of freshly brewed coffee," "the skin you love to touch."

◆ Features and Benefits

When we buy, we want to benefit from the product. One of the first things a good copywriter learns to do is to translate a product's features into its benefits.

A feature is a characteristic built into the product by the manufacturer, and the consumer might not understand it. Your job as a copywriter is to translate these features into benefits that will make the buyer want the product. Visit any automobile showroom, appliance dealer, or camera shop and look at the brochures. You will find the

Hanes® Fashion Underwear
"Michael Jordan"
Long, Haymes & Carr
Length: 30 seconds

(MUSIC UP AND UNDER)

MICHAEL V.O.: When I'm on the court, I don't just make shots . . . I take 'em.

Michael Jordan
After the game

So when I'm done slammin' (SFX OF SLAM DUNK)

I'm jammin' in Hanes Fashion Underwear.

It has the style I'm used to

with the comfort I can't find

flying through a seven-foot wall of arms and elbows.

BOY O.C.: Got the tickets Michael?

MICHAEL O.C.: Guys, we don't need tickets.

SING: NOW YOU'RE WEARING WHAT YOU LIKE . . .

HANES. NOTHING ELSE FEELS SO RIGHT.™

©1989 Hanes Underwear

FIGURE 5.5 Celebrity Appeal *(Courtesy Long, Haymes, & Carr, Winston-Salem, NC)*

product's features in this literature; your job is to translate them into customer benefits. Here are some examples taken from brochures:

What the Brochure Says (Feature)	What the Copywriter Says (Benefit)
Remarkable McPherson struts (Subaru automobile)	A more comfortable ride
Active infrared autofocus system (Olympus AFL camera)	Gives you pictures that are always in sharp focus
Comes complete with Hi-Vac (Snapper Lawnmower)	Vacuums grass into an upright position for ease in cutting even damp grass

A particularly good place to study benefits is in television commercials. You'll notice that most TV spots show the benefit of the product near the conclusion of the sales message. For example, if the commercial is for a laundry detergent, you'll see the person admiring the clean clothing. If the spot is for mouthwash, you might see the person being kissed after using the product. These are benefits that derive from using the product. Remember, benefits satisfy needs. Thus, when you write a commercial, think of a consumer who wants a given product or service. Analyze the benefits your product or service might supply and motivate the consumer to buy to achieve the benefits.

➤ POINTS TO REMEMBER

- Understanding motives and behaviors enables advertisers to focus on the forces that lead consumers to make buying decisions.
- Maslow's hierarchy of needs states that basic motives must be minimally satisfied before more advanced motives can be activated.
- The self-concept is one's beliefs and feelings about oneself.
- The self-concept is important to advertisers because consumers purchase products to enhance, express, and maintain their self-concepts.

- Consumers seek products whose primary or secondary benefit is to arouse emotion.
- Advertisers may seek to arouse, reduce, or elicit certain emotions.
- Rational appeals demonstrate that products will deliver the desired results.
- Moral appeals aim at the consumer's sense of right and wrong.
- As a copywriter, you must convert the features of a product into benefits that will arouse the consumer's desire to purchase it.

EXERCISES

Exercise 1

How could Maslow's motive hierarchy be used to develop an advertising strategy for each of the following:

1. A sports car *Appeals to the need for esteem (superiority + prestige) The car that will get you noticed - by friends and foe alike*

2. Orange juice *Appeals to basic physiological needs Vitamin C - One of the ABC's for health*

3. A large-screen TV *Appeals to social need for friendship + group acceptance + esteem the way to make your Rec room the center of the universe the place where friends gather*

4. A gourmet wine *Appeals to need for esteem, prestige + stature Share a bottle with the savy upper crust*

5. Men's cologne *Appeals to social need for love + acceptance She'll be intoxicated by your presence*

6. Supplemental Medicare insurance *Appeals to need for Safety Don't get caught on the wrong side of retirement without a safety net.*

7. Habitat for Humanity *Appeals to need for esteem through usefulness When all your needs are met, isn't it time to start thinking about the needs of others.*

8. A casual shirt or blouse advertising a famous brand *Appeal to social need for acceptance. Everyone who is anyone scores with American Eagle*

9. A candidate for political office *Appeal to need for esteem (usefulness) or self actualization (being all one is capable of) Be the person you were meant to be - the person who not only knows how to represent his own needs, but who knows how to represent the needs of others*

Exercise 2

How would you use self-concept to advertise the following?

1. Viagra

2. Scandinavian furniture

3. A fitness center

4. An Internet stock-trading firm

5. Antibacterial hand soap

6. Life insurance

7. Instant breakfast

Exercise 3

Which of McGuire's motives would be valuable in developing an advertising campaign for each of the following? Explain.

1. An expensive restaurant

2. A luxury sedan

3. Underarm deodorant

4. The Red Cross

5. An ocean cruise

Exercise 4

Outdoor Lighting Experts is a firm selling outdoor lighting systems for houses and yards. Points they stress: improving your home and landscaping investment, lengthening the hours of outdoor enjoyment, safety, and security. Write a 30-second television spot that appeals to the need for esteem.

Exercise 5

Write a 30-second television spot for Body Enhancers, a medical firm devoted to skin care and appearance improvement. The firm's doctors perform facelifts, breast surgery, rhinoplasty, and plastic surgery. It has a licensed staff. Appeal to the need for affiliation.

CHAPTER SIX

Organizing the Broadcast Commercial

The effectiveness of a broadcast commercial, whether for radio or television, stems from good structure and good organization. Your commercial needs a functional floor plan: an inviting front door through which you entice the listener/viewer, an interest-holding interior in which you inform and create the desire to purchase, and a ready exit through which members of your audience may hurry to the store to take advantage of the benefits you offer.

◆ Organizing the Message

You've undoubtedly written essays and term papers, but now comes the task of writing a 30- or 60-second spot announcement. That's what will be sent to the audience or receivers. Most of you have probably never written a spot before, so how do you get started?

To assist you, we'll keep things simple. For now, we'll concentrate on straightforward single-voice announcements. Later, after you've grasped the feel of writing a short spot announcement, we'll add sound effects, music, additional voices, and video.

◆ The AIDA Formula

A widely used formula for organizing a broadcast commercial message is known by the initials AIDA: *A* for *attention*, *I* for *interest*, *D* for *desire*, and *A* for *action*. The AIDA formula shows you how to create interest and desire in listeners. Let's examine the four steps in the AIDA formula more closely.

Attention

A spot must gain attention and do so quickly. You have no more than three or four seconds to gain attention in a spot before you risk losing the interest of the listener/viewer. Your attention-getter should be as unique as possible, though it's not always feasible to begin each spot with an earth-shattering opening. Use your imagination to say something startling, humorous, or important so that people are compelled to listen to the message.

Some broadcasters say that you should use the attention step to *hook* the listener/viewer just as you would hook a fish. In radio, you hook attention with three elements: words, sound effects, or music or a combination of these elements. In television, you can use words, sound effects, and music, but, more important, you can use video to *show* the viewer something interesting. Remember, if your commercial doesn't attract attention, receivers probably won't focus on it and the message will not achieve its goal.

Interest

The crossover from attention to interest is a subtle one and not always clear-cut, nor does it have to be. What gains attention may also hold interest. Not every commercial is going to hold the interest of every listener/viewer. You aim for the interest of your target audience. For example, teenagers rarely show interest in life insurance, and elderly individuals show little interest in sports cars.

Here are several ways you can arouse interest in a product or service:

1. Expand on your attention-getting lead. Interest can often grow out of the lead. You've already gained attention, so stick to the main idea and relate it to the target audience.
2. Tell about the benefits of using the product or service. Show how using the product or service will make life more enjoyable, easier, or safer.
3. Explain selling points that will produce the benefits you describe. Identify and explain the points to substantiate the main thrust of the spot.
4. Use a "you" posture in your copy. Direct the copy to *one* listener/viewer, hooking his or her attention and interest.
5. Introduce the sales goal and the name and address of the sponsor or the name of the product. This lets the audience know what the spot is about. Identify the sponsor atleast three times in a spot.

Desire

Building interest in the product or service also means creating a desire in the receiver. These two elements of your message should work together. *Desire* means "I want one of those." It means "I want the Tommy Hilfiger shirt, not the no-name shirt from the shopping mart." Desire grows out of benefits, and to create desire, you have to make your audience want what you're selling. This means you must understand how the target customers think, behave, and make decisions, and then give them a reason to buy. Consumers decide to buy products or services because they want an item and, finally, because having it will meet their needs.

Thus, arousing desire is a process of matching consumer wants and needs with product benefits. For example, if my current auto is in constant need of repairs, I could use a new one. I may want an appealing sports car but might have to settle for a car with the most benefits—room for four, good mileage, and a nice enough appearance to say "this is me."

Action

This is the conclusion of the message and should constitute no more than 20 percent of the spot. Your goal is to convince listeners/viewers to become customers, so tell the audience what you expect them to do: hurry to the sponsor's business, buy the product, call for information, and so on. Be specific and be direct. Stress that now is the time to respond. Be sure the sponsor's name and address, if appropriate, or the product name and slogan, are clear and distinct. This is the final aspect of your message, so it must do its job if receivers are to respond appropriately.

AIDA Summary

In analyzing radio and television commercials for the AIDA formula, the opening and closing *A*'s stand out most clearly; interest and desire frequently merge and attention might blend into interest. As a writer, your concern is to hold interest and create desire for the product. Don't be overly mechanical, taking the approach that after you have written an interest-holding sentence or phrase you must focus solely on creating desire. Instead, feel free to intermix interest with desire if the copy seems to flow better that way.

The AIDA Formula in Action

To get a feel for the AIDA formula, let's examine the following radio script in paragraph form.

Attention	Cooking can be a chore, but having the right kitchen appliances can make the job a breeze.
Interest	Anderson Electronic, Yourtown's oldest kitchen appliance specialists, carry the state-of-the-art in kitchen appliances from Kitchen Queen.
Desire	Kitchen Queen appliances are practical and functional, yet they're striking to look at and a dream to use. The complete line of ultramodern Kitchen Queen cooktops from Anderson Electronic allows you to choose the features for your lifestyle. Choose a classic four-burner arrangement in either gas or electric, or get the latest Kitchen Queen cooktop with *both* gas and electric burners. Add special features like a barbecue grill or a deep fryer. Let Anderson Electronic help you design the kitchen of your dreams, with a colorful sink and drainboards, futuristic ovens and cooktops . . . in fact, just about anything you want for your dream kitchen is made by Kitchen Queen and sold by Anderson Electronic.
Action	Visit Anderson Electronic today. You'll see the kitchen of tomorrow on display today. And make your time in the kitchen productive and enjoyable with contemporary Kitchen Queen appliances. See Kitchen Queen at Anderson Electronic, 1401 Main Street, two blocks south of City Hall.

The AIDA formula works well with this script. Attention is gained by identifying a labor-saving device. Interest is generated by expanding on the attention-getting lead and identifying the name of the product and the merchant. Desire is created by appealing to the concern for convenience and functionality. Action is found in the statement "Visit Anderson Electronic today" and in the phrase "See Kitchen Queen."

At the risk of getting ahead of ourselves, let's also apply AIDA to a spot for TV. This spot gains attention by inserting an unusual twist into an everyday activity—seeing a psychiatrist for advice on relaxing. Interest is developed with a solution to the problem, adding an aquarium to the home from the Tropical Fish Store. Desire to relax is blended with the notion of watching fish in the home tank. Action is urged by stating, "Visit the Tropical Fish Store today," and by showing the store name and address.

VIDEO	AUDIO
LONG SHOT OF MAN ON PSYCHIATRIST'S COUCH. DR. IS TAKING NOTES.	You don't need a psychiatrist to help you relax.
CLOSEUP OF TROPICAL FISH IN TANK.	You need the Tropical Fish Store.
PULL BACK TO SHOW MAN WHO WAS ON COUCH NOW GAZING CONTENTEDLY INTO TROPICAL FISH TANK.	The Tropical Fish Store can get you started on this fascinating and relaxing hobby with over 100 varieties of tropical fish for your selection.

LONG SHOT OF DEN AT HOME. MAN IN EASY CHAIR, FEET ON OTTOMAN, FISH TANK NEARBY. HE IS COMPLETELY RELAXED.	You can relax with your feet up and enjoy the sight of either fresh- or saltwater tropical fish. The Tropical Fish Store has all you need . . . tanks, aerators, and, of course, fish.
SAME AS BEFORE. PHONE RINGS. MAN ANSWERS:	Joe? Sam next door. Got a big business deal cooking. Can I come over and relax with your fish?
TROPICAL FISH STORE LOGO WITH ADDRESS.	You may want to keep it quiet from your neighbors, but visit the Tropical Fish Store today . . . 101 Center Street. You owe it to your peace of mind. The Tropical Fish Store—101 Center Street, across from the courthouse.

◆ National versus Local Commercials

As you watch commercials on television or listen to them on the radio, you should quickly note a difference in the structure of national compared with local spots. Commercials written for local businesses tend to stress the action step of the AIDA formula, especially the closing move to action. Local commercials urge the listener/viewer to go to a specific location for the product advertised—say, Townley Toyota at 1209 South Drive. This is not practical in national advertising, of course. You just can't give the name and address of every Westinghouse or Cadillac dealer in the nation. In many instances, the thrust of a national spot is to put the name of the product before the audience and make the product or service seem desirable. It can be argued that making the listener/viewer want the product is in itself a form of moving to action.

➤ POINTS TO REMEMBER

- The AIDA formula focuses on the need to create interest and desire on the part of the listener/viewer.
- You gain attention in a spot by hooking the listener/viewer so that he or she wants to hear or see the rest of the spot.
- Identifying the sponsor/product name also provides an opportunity to state the sales goal. You should identify the sponsor/product name at least three times in a spot.
- In the action step of a spot, you should tell the audience what you want them to do.
- Aim to hold and expand the interest of your target audience.
- To build desire, convince the target audience that they want the product or service you are selling in the spot.

EXERCISES

Exercise 1

Write a 30-second commercial for SunBlox sunglasses. Concentrate on using the AIDA formula by using paragraphs to identify each step.

Exercise 2

Find a magazine or newspaper advertisement that includes a large amount of copy. From the ad, write a 60-second commercial using the AIDA formula.

Exercise 3

Write a single-voice spot for the House of Music in Yourtown Mall. Use the AIDA formula. The spot should be 60 seconds long. Focus on structure. Base your spot on these facts:

1. Wide selection of records, tapes, and compact discs

2. Music for all tastes—popular, jazz, country-western, classical, and so on

Exercise 4

Observe commercials for products and services. Identify instances of "noise" about the product or service that might interfere with sending a successful message. (Refer to the explanation of noise in the Model of Communication in Chapter 1.)

CHAPTER SEVEN

Broadcast Copy Preparation

The amount of time you spend planning a spot will vary, and your time will be limited at stations that carry a large volume of retail advertising. Ideally, you will have sufficient time to think about the structure of the commercial and the manner in which you will organize it. But even if you don't, you should *always* plan every spot. Even a few minutes, if well spent, can determine whether your spot will motivate people to respond.

Another comment about planning: all too often, copywriters think first about technique—how the spot will look or sound when produced. Planning the sales message becomes a secondary concern. The resulting commercial may look or sound clever, but it may not sell the product. Your job as a copywriter is to motivate listeners or viewers to buy the product. Therefore, it is essential that you plan to sell the product first and concern yourself with technique second.

◆ Planning A Commercial

Before you can effectively plan a commercial, you must consider several important factors. The first of these is the audience to reach. Writing a spot without considering the audience is a waste of time and money. It makes more sense to identify the segment of the population an advertisement should reach and then plan the commercial with that goal in mind. Second, you must determine the objective of the commercial. What does the advertiser want to achieve with this advertising message? Without answering this question, there is no strategy for the commercial campaign. To determine the intended audience and the commercial's goal, you must address several strategic considerations. We will first look at the task of determining the desired audience segment, then the objectives of the advertising, and finally the framework—a copy platform that can be developed to expand the planning of the advertising strategy.

Targeting the Audience

One of the first steps in media planning is to decide whether to pursue all users of a product or service or to focus on a narrower category of users—a *target audience*. In other words, rather than seek a small share of a large market, should the effort be to capture a sizable share of a particular segment? By targeting an audience the advertiser can focus on those who are most likely to buy—the largest potential audience for the product. Some consumers outside the target audience might use the product, but their numbers would be smaller than those in the target audience. Targeting enables advertisers to save money and increase the chances that potential users will see the commercials and respond to them. Broadcast advertising is usually targeted.

In planning for advertising, the creative staff (1) selects a broad overall market worthy of approaching and (2) often subdivides this broad total market into segments (targets) that may call for focus. For example, automobile tires may be sold to a broad market as "the best" for durability. The broad market may be segmented to target families who want safe tires, high-mileage drivers who want economy, and consumers in wet-weather states who want traction. The question is then whether to run specialized advertising to each segment of the broad market or to target one of the subdivisions.

Businesses usually advertise to expand sales, and in some instances the advertiser may wish to focus on those consumers who are the most intensive users of a product. In other cases, the advertiser may seek to persuade occasional users to increase the size or frequency of their purchases. In yet other cases, the advertiser may direct efforts to nonusers of the product. Generating additional business with new users may be easier than stimulating present users. Finally, the advertiser may wish to consider the competitive nature of the marketplace. If some target markets are already subject to strong competition from other brands, the advertiser must determine whether a smaller portion of the market not now sought by the competition may still yield a favorable return.

DEMOGRAPHIC SEGMENTS The most common method of segmenting markets is by specifying demographic factors. Considerable audience and media data is regularly gathered in demographic categories. The primary means of segmenting markets is to divide the population into age groups and evaluate the needs and wants of each group.

AGE AND LIFE CYCLE Consumer needs vary with age and life cycle. Companies often market different products or use different marketing approaches for groups such as teens, baby boomers, "GenXers " ("20-somethings"), and the more mature. For example, the Lexus LS 400 was targeted to reach a new category of affluent/luxury purchasers identified by researchers, a group of 28- to 38-year-olds overwhelmingly populated by millionaire entrepreneurs. Sony targets its PlayStation video game console to children under age twelve, potential female purchasers, and "unconverted" adults. However, its PlayStation 2 is targeted at a predominately male audience of 18- to 34-year-old techies and gamers who exercise considerable influence on household technology purchases. In an attempt to look youthful, sporty and fun, Mercedes-Benz targeted its C-Class sedan to buyers in their 30s rather than people in their late 40s. Kodak targeted its Advantix Access one-time-use camera at GenXers who could use it as a lifestyle accessory. The advertising industry broadly target the 18-to-49 age group, those most likely to have money and spend it. Of course, much narrower demographics are selected for certain programs and brands. Beyond age groupings, population groupings can also be viewed in terms of life cycle.

Life cycles include three age groups: *GenXers, baby boomers, and seniors.*[1] GenXers—also known as Xers, busters, or slackers—are the 20-somethings, the desirable 18-to-29-year-olds that businesses love to reach. GenXers do not like labels and do not want to be singled out. Job satisfaction is more important to them than salary. They prefer to enjoy life and have a lifestyle based on flexibility and freedom. GenXers are more interested in camping, outdoor activities, and jogging shoes than fancy cars or homes.

Baby boomers are the largest distinctive age group alive today, ranging in age from the mid-30s to the mid-50s. They represent 40 percent of the adult population and constitute about 50 percent of those in managerial or professional occupations. Of individuals with college degrees, about half are baby boomers. Each year more baby boomers turn fifty and join the category of senior consumers. Boomers don't like aging; they join health clubs or take vitamin supplements to feel young. Baby boomers are consumption-oriented; they enjoy buying for themselves and others. Businesses react to the aging of boomers with "relaxed fit" jeans, walking shoes, and retirement plans.

Yuppies are a subgroup of baby boomers who are well educated, well off financially, and hold responsible managerial or professional positions. Yuppies are often associated with status brand products such as Lexus cars, designer clothing, and Rolex watches. As yuppies age, they also turn to physical fitness, travel, and thoughts of retirement.

The 50-plus age group comprises *seniors*. People in this age group constitute one-third of adults in the United States. The 50-plus bracket makes up the single longest life stage of any consumer group. Seniors actually constitute a diverse age segment made up of four chronological categories: the mature market (ages 50 to 65), the young old (ages 65 to 74), the old (ages 75 to 84); and the old old (age 85 and above).

---

[1]Advertisers are also targeting "Tweeners," girls who are between puberty and adolescence.

It might be easy to dismiss seniors as a target audience with the view that they are usually in poor health—that they have few resources and few interests. Statistics tell a different story. Among seniors aged 65 to 72, one in four is still employed full time and many more work part time. Many others do volunteer work. Seniors spend money not only on housing and food but also on vacations and recreation, which are important to many seniors.

Overall, seniors are an important advertising target. They are growing twice as fast in numbers as the overall U.S. population and represent diverse interests, actions, and opinions. The mature market segment (ages 50 to 65) in particular is an attractive market for advertisers. Most in this age and life-cycle group still work, are at the height of their earning power, and dominate top positions in business and government. Many medical and health products as well as lifestyle products are advertised to this group.

GENDER Dividing a group of buyers into segments based on sex has long been popular in advertising cosmetics, clothing, magazines, and deodorants. Increasingly, more women work outside the home, giving them considerable influence on how paychecks are spent. Certain industries make extensive use of gender as a consumer variable. Auto makers have recognized that women buy almost half of all new cars sold in the United States and influence 80 percent of new automobile purchases. Cars are marketed to address the concerns of women car buyers—safety plus added space for luggage and for passengers.

The blurring of sex roles has led to changes in the marketing of some products. Women were long the major target for hair coloring products and cosmetics while men were targeted for tools and shaving products. Now, razors are marketed to women and hair coloring products such as "Just For Men" seek the male audience. Yet some products play to the uniqueness women feel. L'Oreal pitches its cosmetics to women by urging them to justify use of the product with the thought, "Because I'm worth it."

Marketers suggest that special techniques can help reach the female consumer. The idea is that women and men differ in the way they receive and process information.[2] Women take in information quickly on many levels and weave together the threads for an inner meaning. Men tend to look at the big picture. Starbucks has responded to this premise. It has created an attractive context for female customers, 60 percent of their total: a relaxing ambience with books to browse through and, of course, coffee to enjoy and comfortable places to sit and chat.

Men can be special targets too. After conducting extensive research, TBS redefined its target audience as regular "midwestern" guys, median age 42. They targeted these average guys because they watch a lot of TV and their families watch with them.[3]

Commercials target diseases that affect men only; for example, for advisements for prostrate medications.

INCOME Businesses commonly target markets on the basis of income because they believe that it is a strong factor in the ability or inability of consumers to pay for a product or a specific model of the product. Items such as automobiles, boats, clothing, travel, and cosmetics are frequently targeted at buyers based on income.

Education, income, and occupation correlate closely and are often targeted jointly. High incomes result from high-level occupations that generally require advanced education. Consumers with little education rarely achieve high-level jobs and high pay.

---

[2]Faith Popcorn and Lys Marigold, *Eveolution: The Eight Truths of Marketing to Women.* (New York, NY: Hyperion, 2000).

[3]Deborah D. McAdams, "Where The Average Joe is King," *Broadcasting and Cable*, April 10, 2000, p. 114.

EDUCATION   In general, the higher the education, the more likely the person is to have a high income. Further, better-educated consumers spend more, on average, on housing and recreation than do those with less education. Trends indicate that Americans are completing higher levels of education. This translates to better income and increased spending power. In two-income families, women often have more education than in the past and generally earn more.

OCCUPATION   Occupation is related to income in that some occupations are traditionally better paid than others. Nevertheless, the pay differential between blue-collar and white-collar incomes has decreased. But even though levels of pay may be similar, spending patterns can be quite different. It's not so much that one occupational group outspends the other but that they spend their money differently.

RACE   Purchasing decisions cannot be distinctly traced to race; to do so raises questions of ethnic stereotyping, as discussed in Chapter 3. Still, demographic groupings create major target-market opportunities. Blacks and Hispanics each constitute about 12.5 percent of the U.S. population respectively.[4] Advertisers seldom focus on racial characteristics in their advertising, but they do show members of specific ethnic groups using their products. Major advertisers recognize that this is a part of the audience that cannot be overlooked.

GEOGRAPHIC FACTORS   Buyers can be classified into different geographic units such as states, regions, or cities. A company may decide to operate in one or two geographical areas, or it might advertise in all areas but focus on geographic differences in needs and wants. When Nestle advertised a line of frozen meals and dips by its Ortega Mexican foods line, it practiced geographic targeting by launching the campaign in markets west of the Mississippi. Chili's targeted an even narrower audience with a Spanish-language campaign aired in Miami. The goal was to reach Cuban and Caribbean consumers.

Climate can also be related to geography. People in southern states have less need for heating products than those in the North, but they use more air conditioning. Southerners have a greater need for pest-control products, but they don't need snow blowers.

PSYCHOGRAPHICS   Psychographic targeting divides consumers into different groups based on lifestyle characteristics. People with the same demographic characteristics can have very different lifestyles. How audience members view the world—how they feel, think, and act—is more important than demographics. Psychographics tells us how people see themselves and how they live. Psychographic data may be combined with demographic data or used alone.

Narrowing the scope of advertising to the consumers who have a desire for the product is good business, whether the audience is subdivided on the basis of demographics or lifestyle factors. A retailer specializing in women's clothing is an example of one who would consider lifestyle factors. One such retailer, MNG by Mango, doesn't target an age group; it aims for independent women who are interested in fashion but who also create their own trends.[5]

Here is a further example. People who buy pickup trucks are often thought to be blue-collar workers who toil outdoors and engage in physical labor. But what of the suburban white-collar worker who spends weekends improving the lawn and house?

---

[4]U.S. Department of Commerce, Bureau of the Census, *Population by Race and Hispanic or Latino Origin, for All Ages 18 Years and Over for the United States.* Washington, DC: U.S. Government Printing Office, 2000.

[5]"MNG by Mango Brings European Flavor to Florida." *Orlando Sentinel,* February 6, 2007, p. C1.

| TABLE 7.1 | Target Audiences for Consumer Markets |

Variable	Typical Breakdowns
Geographic	
City size	Major metropolitan, small cities, towns
Density	Urban, suburban, rural
Climate	Hot, cold, dry, rainy
Region	South, Pacific, Mountain, Southwest, Midwest
Demographic	
Gender	Male, Female
Marital status	Single, married, divorced, living together, widowed
Age	Under 6, 6– 11, 12– 17, 18– 34, 35– 49, 50– 64, 65+
Income	Under $25,000, $25,000– $35,000, $35,000– $50,000, $50,000– $75,000, $75,000– $100,000, $100,000 and over
Education	Some high school, high school graduate, some college, college graduate, postgraduate
Religion	Protestant, Catholic, Jewish, other
Race	White, Black, Asian, Hispanic, Native American
Family size	1–2, 3–4, 5+
Occupation	Professional, white-collar, blue-collar, agricultural
Life cycle	Baby boomers, GenX, seniors
Psychographic	
Lifestyle	Achievers, strivers, believers

Commercials for pickup trucks could theoretically reach both groups, since both watch TV on nights and weekends. What if an advertiser, attempting to spend money wisely, wanted to reach only culturally upscale consumers? Focusing on the passions and prejudices of the upscale viewer "psychographically" makes that possible. Showing a weekend warrior hauling building supplies in the same rough, tough pickup the blue-collar worker drives may target the lifestyle of this audience.

Whether targeting is accomplished with demographics or psychographics, the audience should always be subdivided. Targeting the desired audience is good business and can enable the advertiser's schedule of commercials to be all the more effective. Table 7.1 summarizes the major characteristics that might be examined in targeting an audience.

◆ The Copy Platform

An important aid in planning a commercial is a *copy platform,* a checklist that helps you prepare a successful sales strategy. A copy platform helps focus planning by drawing your attention to the key elements of the sales data. It helps you work more efficiently to prepare a sales message that really works.

The copy platform we'll present here can be used for a radio, television, or cable TV spot. This platform is designed primarily for the copywriter working at a station or cable system; however, it can be adapted to higher-budget accounts at advertising agencies.

Many variations of the copy platform are used, but the following example has been devised for its logic and ease of use. It consists of seven items: client (and product, store, or service), target audience, advertising objective, sales slogan, bonus items, approach, and positioning.

Client and Product, Store, or Service

This item is a simple recognition of the client and specific commodity being advertised. For example, the client might be:
Federated Department Stores—Spring Sale

Target Audience

As we have seen, companies seldom try to reach everyone; instead, they seek targeted audiences, which helps them to focus on the consumers who have the greatest desire to purchase. Audiences are commonly targeted with demographics including age/life cycle, income, education, occupation, and race. Geographic and psychographic data may also be used to target an audience.

For example, a typical target audience might be men ages 25 to 45 living in a metro area, with incomes greater than $50,000. This targets gender, age, and income. Demographics are often combined to gain more strength from the data.

In a campaign for Volvo, the company decided to target a group of non-Volvo consumers. Volvo's goal was to get 24- to 35-year-old non-Volvo drivers to consider the Volvo C30.[6] Mars Candies took a different approach in introducing a new line of nutrient-fortified kids' snacks called Kid-Didits. Mars targeted 6- to 11-year-old children, the consumers most likely to eat the snacks.[7] The television industry most covets the 18- to 34-age demographic but seeks many segmented target audiences as well.

Advertising Objectives

An advertising objective is a specific communication function to be accomplished with a specific target audience during a specific period of time. It is the goal of the advertising to be planned. An advertising objectives can be classified by its purpose: to inform, to persuade, or to remind. Table 7.2 includes examples of each objective.

Informative advertising is used extensively when a new product category is introduced. In such circumstances, the objective is to develop initial demand. Thus, producers of digital camcorders presented the product as one producing high-quality video that could easily be connected to the computer. Toyota introduced its Tundra pickup truck to compete with American-manufactured trucks. Its commercials show the power of its new pickup.

Persuasive advertising is important as competition increases, forcing the company to urge consumers to select its brand. For instance, when Canon decided to compete with Sony and JVC in marketing digital camcorders, it set out to persuade consumers that its camera was capable of producing a Hollywood-quality home movie. Persuasive advertising may take the form of *comparative advertising*—advertising in which a company compares its brand, directly or indirectly, with one or more competing brands. For example, Clorox pitted its Clean Up Cleaner with Bleach against Lysol to back its claim that Clorox destroys 99 percent of allergens.

---

[6] Jean Halliday, "Volvo Lets People Recognize the C30—In It's Own Ads." *Advertising Age,* January 1, 2007, p. 6.

[7] Stephanie Thompson, "Critics Can't Stomach Mars' Healthful Play." *Advertising Age,* January 15, 1007, pp. 4,36.

TABLE 7.2	Advertising Objectives

To Inform

Explaining how a product works

Telling the market of a price change

Advising new uses of a product

Telling about a new product

Lowering buyers' fears

Strengthening a company image

Changing false impressions

Explaining company services

To Persuade

Building brand preference

Urging switching to your product

Altering buyer views of product features

Encouraging buyers to purchase immediately

Urging buyers to accept a sales call

To Remind

Reinforcing brand awareness

Reminding buyers that the product may soon be needed

Reminding buyers where to buy the product

Keeping buyers aware of the product during the off season

Reminder advertising is designed to establish products in the minds of consumers. Advertising campaigns for Geico auto insurance seek primarily to remind people about Geico, not to persuade or inform them. Geico campaigns have used a talking gecko, cavemen, and show business personalities to remind consumers of the brand name.

Sales Slogan

Now that you've decided whom you want to reach and what you want to accomplish, it's time to move to the heart of the copy platform and develop the major selling point you hope the spot will convey.

The sales slogan or central selling point is the focal point of your commercial. It consists of (1) a major sales point tied to (2) a strong consumer benefit. The benefit should be a relevant, believable effect of the sales idea.

To see how the sales slogan works, let's look at a nationally advertised product with which you may be familiar. Figure 7.1 shows a commercial built on the slogan "Orange you smart." The sales point is that Florida orange juice is good to drink anywhere. The benefit is that it's refreshing and healthful. That point leads back to the slogan "Orange you smart for drinking orange juice."

FLORIDA DEPARTMENT OF CITRUS
PROCESSED ORANGE JUICE
"ORANGE YOU SMART – FISHING"

COMM'L NO.: FCOJ 2336   LENGTH: 30 SECONDS

(MUSIC UNDER THROUGHOUT)

ANNCR: (VO) Isn't that Florida Orange Juice?

SINGERS: (VO) Orange You Smart . . .

(SFX: MUSIC TO ACCENT FINGER TAPPING) for drinking orange juice.

for that clean sunny taste.

Hey, Orange You Smart --

(SFX: MUSIC TO ACCENT FINGER TAPPING) for drinking orange juice.

pure refreshment any place.

Hey, Orange You Smart for drinking

to your body's content -- the taste only

nature could invent. ANNCR: (VO) 100% pure from Florida.

SINGERS: (VO) Hey Skipper,

Orange You Smart!

(SFX: MUSIC TO ACCENT FINGER TAPPING)

FIGURE 7.1   TV Commercial Using a Sales Theme *(Courtesy Florida Department of Citrus)*

Remember that the sales theme should be the strongest single thing you can say about the client's product, store, or service. Note, too, that the benefits must be meaningful to the audience. Build benefits for your clients that are so exciting, so believable, so provocative that people can't wait to respond.

A sales slogan must be planned and nurtured: Its success will depend on the time and effort you devote to it. What is a sales slogan? It's a forceful, imaginative, persuasive idea presented in a striking phrase. A cheese snack is advertised, for example, with the following sales theme: "Combos cheeses your hunger away." You're told the product name and that it *cheeses*, a play on the word *chases*, your hunger away. The slogan is clever and brief, but memorable.

Here's another. An automobile dealer's sales theme states: "Seminole Ford . . . where a great deal is happening." This slogan identifies the advertiser and tells you that many people shop for cars at this dealer because they get great deals. That's the thrust of a sales slogan. It should be brief, clever, and memorable and should include the advertiser's or product's name. Even negatives can be turned to advantage. Retailers located in outlying locations urge customers to "drive a little and save a lot." Major advertisers take a similar approach. For example, the sales slogan for Clorets tells you that "Clorets cost more, but they're worth it."

Remember, the sales slogan is the key to a persuasive message. It helps viewers recall the advertiser's or product's name and the product's selling benefits. On television, the sales theme can be presented aurally, visually, or both. A carefully developed sales slogan can be your best aid in developing audience recall.

Bonus Items

Too many selling points confuse, so it's best to emphasize *one main* sales idea. You may add an extra copy idea or two, but be certain they relate to the main idea of your sales theme.

To help identify your major and optional selling points, make a list of sales items. List anything that comes to your mind. This exercise helps you get to know the product, store, or service better. You may even stumble across a major selling point or benefit that you hadn't thought of.

Once you've completed the list, examine it and arrange the items in order of importance. Delete any items that seem too farfetched. Determine the single idea that should be used in your sales theme. Use optional ideas only if they relate to the main idea. Bonus ideas are not always needed. If bonus items will dilute a strong, clear sales theme, it's best not to include them.

Approach

A suitable approach (tone, mood, or style) must be established for each commercial to match the objective and the target audience. A soft, understated, dreamy approach, for instance, would suit an elegant ladies' boutique. On the other hand, a spirited, upbeat approach would be better for a car dealer's model clearance sale. Mood must always match the audience and the message, so the copywriter must plan for it.

Remember that this copy platform is designed to help you organize the data in a sales order so you can write a commercial that hits its mark. You may not need to follow each step in every commercial, but even a brief copy platform will help you to organize your data and identify your audience.

Note that this copy platform is for an individual commercial, not a group of spots or a full campaign. (See the examples that follow.) A set of spots for a given order may have nothing more in common than a sales slogan. Each spot may have a different target audience and a different objective. As a result, additional spots for the same client require preparation of a separate copy platform. We'll discuss the copy platform again in Chapter 14, which covers broadcast campaigns. You may wish to read Chapter 14 in conjunction with this chapter to gain an appreciation of the use of the copy platform in a full campaign.

Positioning

When the client's product, store, or service has a number of competitors, it becomes difficult to make a unique claim for your client. When this happens, you may want to "position" your client against the competition.

Positioning involves the creation of a separate identity for the product, store, or service—an identity that helps consumers distinguish the client from its competitors. Although this separate identity must have substance, it is actually a matter of using a commercial to reorient the consumer's perception of the client's product, store, or service. Burger King, for example, created an identity for itself in the competitive world of fast-food hamburger chains by claiming that its hamburgers were flame-broiled and not fried like those of its competitors. Wendy's carved out a niche, too. It offered baked potatoes as well as hamburgers, and consumers loved them. These efforts involved attempts to distinguish the advertiser as an entity, separate from the crowd.

Insurance companies also use positioning. One company might stress low rates while another advertises service. The Ætna spot shown in Figure 7.2 positions the company as one whose agents are involved in helping to solve problems.

Positioning a product or service is most likely to be accomplished by an advertising agency as part of long-term management of a business's advertising. A product or service is positioned for advertising in all media and is part of the total marketing presentation. Thus, positioning becomes a major task that requires careful analysis of the positions established by competitors and the unique factors of the product or service being positioned. This is not a task that can be accomplished quickly and typically is a team effort. A writer in a small- or medium-sized market agency or station might establish a position for a client that does a great volume of business with the agency/station. In such a case, an individual writer can fulfill the functions of a creative team in a large advertising agency. Further, there may be no one else to establish a marketing position for a product or service. Nevertheless, positioning a product or service is more commonly done by an advertising agency that has full command of a company's advertising program.

Eventually, the position established by a firm may no longer be correct. Consumer habits may change, business practices may be altered and competing products may come into the market. When that happens a business may need to "reposition" itself to reorient the consumer's perception of the product, store, or service.

Midas Mufflers, the auto repair shops, repositioned themselves as offering a wider range of services, not just muffler and brake repairs. The goal was to generate more frequent customer visits instead of just the infrequent visits for new mufflers or brake repairs. As part of a marketing effort, Midas shops were remodeled, the company logo was updated, and the word "muffler" was taken out of the company name. An advertising campaign was designed to make consumers aware of the change.[8]

Now that we have examined the criteria used in a copy platform, let's look at two examples of copy platforms. The second platform also includes a spot that was written for this specific campaign.

---

[8]Jean Halliday, "Midas Repositioning Shows It's More Than Just a Muffler Shop." *Advertising Age,* May 15, 2000, 87

"HURRICANE" :60

ANNOUNCER: When a hurricane this strong hit Houston...

Houston found out you need...

an insurance company...

this strong behind you. Within hours...
AIRLINE CAPTAIN'S VOICE: Houston's got one runway working. So we're gonna take you on in.

ANNOUNCER: An Ætna task force was coming, over a hundred men and women strong...from 'round the country...

ÆTNA CLAIMS ADJUSTOR: Bob Nichols, Atlanta.
CLAIMS MGR.: Bob, keep your coat on, we've got some messy ones down here.

ANNOUNCER: each assigned to the hardest-hit...
SCHOOL SUPT.: Builders are talking months. This school's gotta open in two weeks!

ANNOUNCER: and they plowed ahead, chasing down contractors...

paying a thousand claims a day...
BOY: Is the school gonna stay closed?
BOB NICHOLS: Not if I can help it!

ANNOUNCER: working five A.M. until ten P.M., until Houston was back in business!

THE STANDARD FIRE INSURANCE COMPANY

ANNOUNCER: When there are deadlines to meet, payrolls to meet, challenges to meet...

that's when you're glad you met Ætna!
SCHOOL SUPT: You're not Texas, are you?
BOB NICHOLS: Atlanta.
SCHOOL SUPT.: Atlanta Ætna, we're glad we met ya!

FIGURE 7.2   TV Spot That Positions a Client *(Courtesy Ætna Life and Casualty)*

The first platform was developed for Fiber Lite, a new product being considered by the W. K. Kellogg Company.[9]

Copy Platform for Fiber Lite

1. **Client and Product:** Fiber Lite, a high-fiber, light cereal.
2. **Target Audience:** Health-conscious women, ages 25 to 54. These women are achievement-oriented and are involved in keeping themselves healthy and fit.
3. **Objective:** To build awareness among the target audience of Fiber Lite's offering of high fiber in a light cereal that is packaged to promote a healthy eating program.
4. **Sales Theme:** Fiber Lite provides high fiber in a lower-calorie, fat-free, and cholesterol-free cereal. Fiber Lite helps you feel good about yourself.
5. **Bonus Item:** Packs are stay-fresh and provide product portability. Fiber Lite is low in sugar.
6. **Positioning:** Fiber Lite is a high-fiber, light cereal for adults who know that good health is essential to feeling good about yourself.
7. **Approach:** Light, sincere.

A second award-winning campaign was conducted for the Adolph Coors Company for Coors Beer. It was devised at a time when so-called college crazes—such as jamming as many people as possible into a car, eating as much exotic food as possible, and so on, were popular. This is the copy platform and a commercial that were developed for the campaign.[10]

Copy Platform for Coors Beer

1. **Client and Product:** Coors Beer
2. **Target Audience:** Joe College type males, legal drinking age to age 24. These are heavy users of the product who (1) socialize with friends, (2) are involved with fraternities and clubs, and (3) enjoy having fun.
3. **Objective:** To (1) establish a personality for Coors Premium Beer as *the* college beer, (2) to appeal directly to the college market by creating interest and involvement, and (3) to develop an image for Coors as the fun, popular beer.
4. **Sales Theme:** The campaign uses the college craze approach and associates Coors with everyday college life. Coors is depicted as a fun, popular beer with the slogan "Coors, the taste of college life."
5. **Bonus Item:** A number of events will accompany the campaign to develop involvement by the target audience.
6. **Positioning:** Coors is to be advertised as the ideal beer for the college market rather than as a light beer.
7. **Approach:** Fun and upbeat.

---

[9] Donald E. Schultz, *Strategic Advertising Campaigns,* 3rd ed. (Lincolnwood, IL: NTC Business Books, 1991), pp. 584-616. A campaign and copy platform was developed by a student group. It was judged as the best regional entry in the 1989 National Student Advertising Competition by the American Advertising Federation.

[10] Don E. Shultz, Dennis Martin, and William P. Brown, *Strategic Advertising Campaigns,* 2nd ed. (Lincolnwood, IL: NTC Business Books, 1984), pp. 483-509.

The following script was written for the Coors campaign:

SFX	NEWSROOM SOUNDS, UP, 4 SEC., TYPEWRITER FOLLOWED BY RIP OF PAPER, DOWN, FADE INTO BACKGROUND.
ANNCR	GRAVEL-VOICED, FAST-TALKING
	And hot off the press is today's Coors College update. Jalapeño pepper–eating contests have become one of the hottest crazes at college campuses. Crowds watch as contestants gulp down the fiery pickled peppers. One heroic participant at the U of X swallowed 17 peppers in less than 10 minutes. Coors put out the fire. PAUSE Universities across the country report that more students are cramming and actually enjoying it. Twenty-three crazy students from X College decided cramming into phone booths was more fun than cramming for exams. A cold Coors got them out of this very tight spot.
SFX	RATTLING OF PAPER AS ANNOUNCER TURNS PAGE IN NOTES
ANNCR	Several western universities are kicking around a new idea. Hacky-sack has become a favorite pastime among the college crowd. Students at U of X managed to keep the leather footbag off the ground for 21 minutes. Afterward, they got their kicks with Coors.
SFX	SHUFFLING PAPERS
ANNCR	This concludes today's Coors College Update. If your craze can top these, we'll feature your school on Coors College Update. Get instructions for the college craze competition when you're buying Coors at your favorite store.
VO	MALE, NORMAL VOICE
	Coors . . . the taste of college life.

◆ Sources of Copy Information

As we noted previously, you must have sufficient information about the product, service, or place of business you want to promote before you can write a commercial that will sell. Let's look at where the copy information should come from and what you should do to supplement the normal information sources.

The Salesperson

The person making the sale is the primary source of information. The salesperson is in direct contact with the advertiser and probably maintains regular contact with the account. The salesperson should present copy instructions in a clear, comprehensive form that provides enough information to enable you to write an acceptable sales message.

Newspaper and Magazine Ads

Local newspaper advertisements for retailers are another source of copy information. Advertisements from print sources should not be relied upon, but they can be helpful. They often provide sufficient data for a spot—but sometimes too much. More important, print ads are written for the eye, not the ear. The copywriter cannot just copy the wording but must rewrite the ad so that it will be appropriate for presentation on the air.

Brochures and Pamphlets

Brochures and pamphlets for products can also be a useful source of copy information. A brochure about a given model of car or a given brand of lawnmower may provide the information you need to write the spot as well as a fuller understanding of the product. With this background, you can then apply the data to the spot for the local retailer. Note, however, that brochures and pamphlets are written in print style and must therefore be rewritten for use on the air.

Prepared Announcements

In some instances, the station may have access to broadcast commercials that are already written but do not include the sponsor's name and address. Such commercials may be supplied by the national advertising representative for use in cooperation with a local distributor. This use of nationally written co-op advertising is fairly common. When such copy is available, it is a great help to the copywriter. In other cases, small stations may subscribe to a commercial writing service that provides generic commercials for banks, hardware stores, and the like. In addition, the Radio Advertising Bureau provides generic spots and sample scripts from other stations that can be adapted for local use.

The Client

If possible, you should maintain personal contact with the station's clients, but visit them only if you have the salesperson's permission. If the salesperson wants you to visit the advertiser to inspect a new store, have lunch in a new restaurant, or observe a complicated product firsthand, try to make the visit.

◆ Copy Preparation and Traffic

In addition to the facts you need to prepare the content of a commercial, you also need to know certain items about the scheduling of the commercial. You obviously need to know how long the spot is to be, the number of spots needed for each order, the date on which the spots are to begin, and when the spots will be aired during the broadcast day. A carefully prepared copy information sheet should supply most of this information. If you don't get the information from the salesperson's copy information sheet, you should consult with the traffic department—the department that receives the sales orders and schedules them on the station log as requested. If you don't coordinate your work with the traffic department, you can't properly date the copy.

➤ POINTS TO REMEMBER

- A spot must be planned if it is to motivate people to respond.
- A copy platform helps the copywriter prepare a successful sales strategy by identifying—in addition to the client and the product, service, or store—the (1) target audience, (2) objective, (3) sales theme, (4) bonus items if any, (5) positioning, and (6) approach.
- The salesperson is the copywriter's primary source of information.
- Newspaper ads, magazine ads, and brochures help the copywriter gather

background information but are written for print, not for broadcasting.
- Prepared announcements, with space for the local sponsor's name and address, are sometimes available.
- A copywriter should maintain personal contact with clients but visit them only with the salesperson's approval.
- The copywriter must consult with the station's traffic director to identify the date on which the spots are to begin as well as when the spots will be aired during the broadcast day.

EXERCISES

Exercise 1

Prepare a copy platform for Smith's Department Store.

COPY INFORMATION

Smith's, a well-known department store in your community, is having its seventy-fifth anniversary sale. The store has specially reduced prices on housewares, appliances, and clothing for men, women, and children. The sale runs Wednesday through Sunday. Commercials begin running Monday. Items and prices are too numerous to mention. The audience should see the ad in Tuesday's paper for details. Stress that these are the best prices in Smith's history. Special store hours for the sale: Wed.–Sat., 9 A.M.–9 P.M.; Sun., 12 P.M.–6 P.M. Shoppers can also register to win a free $500 shopping spree at Smith's.

Exercise 2

Write a 60-second radio script for Smith's Anniversary Sale. The spot is to be broadcast only on Monday and Tuesday. Be sure that the spot reflects the information in the copy platform. Use the AIDA formula.

Exercise 3

Prepare a copy platform from the following information. Write a 60-second radio spot based on the copy platform.

Down South Airlines has a new frequent-flyer program called "Fast Flight." Features include the following:

- Passengers need fly only 20,000 miles to earn a free one-way flight in the United States on Down South (most airlines require 25,000 miles).
- Passengers need fly only 30,000 miles to earn a free round-trip overseas flight on Down South (most airlines require 40,000 miles).
- The card is honored by a number of car rental and hotel outlets.

CHAPTER EIGHT

The Radio Commercial: The Mechanics

A recent media campaign put it well: Wherever you go, there's radio. Radio is with you at the shore, in a hunting lodge in the mountains, in the bathroom, the kitchen, the bedroom, the den. It's in your car, your plane, your boat; it's on your bike. Radio is by far our most portable means of mass communication, and it remains one of the world's chief media for entertaining, informing, and selling goods and services.

Radio is a theater of the mind. The listener builds the scenery, does the costuming, and decides what the face behind the voice looks like. But you, the writer, provide the materials to build the scenery, the fabric with which to fashion the costume, and the features from which to form the face. You do all this with four elements: sound effects, words, music, and voice. Above all, the spoken word creates most of the selling impact of radio. The words that you write for the station announcer to read and those that you write for the sponsor himself to deliver on mike are the words that move products and sell services. Music and sound effects are adjuncts. We do not want to underplay the effectiveness of well-selected music or well-executed sound effects in a radio commercial; rather, we want to put these elements in perspective. Words come first.

◆ Radio Today

In addition to being a highly portable medium, today's radio tends heavily to specialization in programming. Actually, we don't refer so much to programming in radio as we do to a station's "sound." A given station may be all country and western, or all rock, or all news and talk. National networks, along with wire services, do provide national news, and special networks let the local listener hear play-by-play broadcasts of out-of-town sporting events. National spot sales by major agencies expose listeners across the country to the same commercials with the same jingles. All stations have access to the same list of top tunes, so that the music on a given local station often sounds the same as that of any other station with a similar "sound."

How Radio Is Delivered

Radio stations are of two types: AM and FM. AM stands for *amplitude modulation*, a method of sending the audio signal by varying the amplitude, or size, of a radio wave. The AM radio band extends from 535 to 1705 kilohertz (KHz). AM stations have several disadvantages. AM signals are vulnerable to electrical interference from thunderstorms or high-power transmission lines. They do not have the bandwidth of FM stations and are thus unable to provide the quality of music reproduction available on FM. Finally, most AM stations must control the transmission of their signals to prevent interference with stations on the same or adjacent frequencies. To do this, their signals may be directional—that is, boosting the signal in one direction while reducing it in other directions—or they may have to cease operating at night when AM signals are prone to travel varying distances from the transmitter.[1] As a result of these factors, AM radio is more widely used for news, talk, sports, and other specialty formats rather than for music formats.

FM stands for *frequency modulation*, a method of sending an audio signal by varying the frequency of the wave. FM transmissions have little static and use a larger bandwidth than AM stations. This makes FM an excellent means for broadcasting high-fidelity music.

---

[1]AM signals use a sky wave, a nighttime signal that bounces off the ionosphere and, under favorable conditions, returns to earth great distances from the transmission site.

FM signals are line-of-sight and depend heavily on antenna height. The FM band extends from 88 to 108 megahertz (88 MHz through 92 MHz is reserved for noncommercial educational stations).

Networks link stations and provide news, sports, stock information, and so on. Satellites permit networks to provide stations with excellent signal quality, and satellite program providers supply affiliated stations with complete 24-hour hour formats in a variety of styles.

Radio is sold on a time basis, from an hour or more to as little as 10 seconds. Advertisers may also purchase sponsorship of entire programs. The most common lengths of time-based commercials are 60 and 30 seconds, with 60-second spots being the most common. Spots are usually sold on a rotating basis; in other words, they rotate throughout a part of the day, such as 6 to 10 A.M. Monday through Friday.

Strengths of Radio

RADIO CAN TARGET SPECIFIC AUDIENCES   In this era of market segmentation, radio has the ability to focus on desirable demographic groups—teenagers, baby boomers who like oldies, yuppie "New Age" listeners, news buffs—who represent narrowly defined target audiences. Advertisers can select a radio station whose programming format will attract those listeners who are most likely to be prospective customers.

RADIO IS MOBILE   People can take it anywhere. We listen at home, in the car, at the ball game, and at the beach. Advertisers can reach listeners and sell products at all these locations.

RADIO IS INTRUSIVE   It's very difficult to avoid hearing a commercial. Radio is everywhere, and radio commercials can create consumer interest where none existed before. People may listen to a creative and compelling commercial while they are involved with other people or activities.

Some radio formats are more intrusive than others, a factor that can assist in selling a product. If listeners are paying close attention to the program, there is a good possibility that they will also pay attention to the commercial. Spots on talk and news stations are intrusive because listeners pay close attention. Stations with established personalities capitalize on their popularity by having the personality present commercial messages. Commercials presented by established personalities are the most memorable of all types of commercials.

RADIO IS FLEXIBLE   If an advertiser wants to get on the air quickly, even on the same day, radio can do it. It would take several days for a similar message to appear in a newspaper or on television. This flexibility also allows advertisers to make changes in their commercial copy. Advertisers can get up-to-the minute information included in radio spots, but television stations would have to reproduce the commercial.

Weaknesses of Radio

RADIO IS AURAL ONLY   Radio is a sound medium; it does not have pictures. Advertisers cannot demonstrate their products or show them. They cannot show addresses and phone numbers. In radio, advertisers must write messages with care and build emotion into a spot. That is hard to do in all cases, but if radio advertising is to be effective, the announcers, sound effects, and so on must stir the listeners' emotions.

RADIO MESSAGES ARE SHORT-LIVED Commercials are intangible. Once the spot has been played, there is no way to retrieve the message. This makes it difficult for listeners to jot down phone numbers, addresses, and names. To counter this fleeting quality, advertisers schedule a number of commercials so that the message gets repeated.

RADIO LISTENING IS PRONE TO DISTRACTION Radio engages only one sense—hearing. Thus, people can do other things while listening and can be distracted. How many times have you caught a fragment of a commercial and wanted to hear the rest of the message? This is where repetition is important; if you didn't hear the entire message the first time, you may catch it when the spot is repeated.

◆ Radio Basics

Like any other medium, radio has its own terminology, conventions, and requirements. To be an effective radio copywriter, you must know not only the language but also some tricks of the trade.

Timing Radio Copy

Radio (and television) spots are sold by time. Your most frequent assignment in radio will be to write a 60-second spot.

How do you write to time? Although experience certainly helps, the only sure way is to read the copy aloud while timing it with a stopwatch. Thus, you'll need to learn to time your copy while reading silently at an out-loud rate.

Gaining Attention

People don't buy radios just to tune in to your commercials. They own their sets for entertainment and information. For many, the commercial is an intrusion, and if your spot doesn't hook the listeners, they may change stations. Unless your spot opens with an attention-grabber that carries the listener into the sales message, you've failed.

In radio, you gain attention in three basic ways: (1) with words, (2) with a sound effect, or (3) with music. A possible variation is to use an attention-getting voice for the words you've written: a Brooklyn cab driver, a Vermont farmer, a Deep South secretary, or a Texas rancher. Using words alone, a radio spot for a hamburger stand might open with "Love at first bite. That's what you'll find when you bite into a juicy hamburger from Tom's Hamburgers." Radio reaches for the ear with combinations of sound. It reaches for the mind with the mental images provided by carefully chosen words, voices, music, and sound effects. These are the tools of the theater of the mind.

There is no absolute formula for gaining attention. Your creativity and insight into human nature are your best guides. As one station manager put it, "Keep it simple, keep it honest."

Terminology

As a copywriter, you need to become familiar with the following terms because of their relevance to radio writing and production.

- **Bed.** Music that is played behind a commercial.
- **Board fade.** A decrease or increase in volume made at the audio control board. Could be either *board fade out* or *board fade in* (see *mike fade*).

- **Cross fade.** To fade from one sound or music to another. Same as *segue*. This is to audio what a *lap dissolve* is to video.
- **Echo chamber.** A device used in broadcasting and recording to produce echo effects.
- **Establish.** To bring sound effects or music to full volume, permitting the listener to hear enough to understand the sound or music.
- **Hold under.** After establishing the sound effect or music, fading it to background and holding it (as in *bed*) behind the spoken message.
- **Mike fade.** Performers move away from mike (*mike fade off*), or move to on-mike position (*mike fade on*), from off-mike position. Mike fade is a decidedly different effect from *board fade*. In the mike fade, acoustical relationships change because of the performer's movements. In a board fade, only volume changes.
- **Mike filter.** An electronic means for eliminating high and low frequencies. Often used to give the effect of speaking over a telephone line.
- **Reverb.** Short for *reverberation*. An electronic device sometimes used in lieu of *echo*, but the effects are not the same.
- **Segue.** Pronounced SEG-way. To make a transition from one musical number or sound effect directly to another without interruption.
- **Sneak in (or out).** To bring music or sound effects into the background of a spot or program at a low level by increasing the volume until the desired level is reached. The process can be reversed to *sneak out* music or sound effects.
- **SFX.** An abbreviation for *sound effects*.

◆ Radio Copy and Commercial Formats

The term *format* as used here simply refers to the physical form of your copy on paper. The format governs such points as when to use single, double, or triple spacing, when to type in all caps, and when to use caps and lowercase. Using a consistent format leads to a uniform presentation that all concerned will understand. Unfortunately, no universal format for typing exists for either radio or television spots, so stations tend to evolve their own formatting peculiarities. For example, some announcers insist that what they read be typed in all caps, whereas others prefer the more common practice of using caps and lowercase. The format given here is a common and effective one. You should follow it unless your employer tells you otherwise.

Here is a summary of the keyboard format rules introduced in Chapter 2. Observe these rules to ensure that radio copy will be easy to read.

1. Double-space all copy.
2. Write all spoken copy in upper- and lowercase.
3. Write instructions for sound effects and music ALL IN CAPS and underline.
4. Write talent instructions, for example, (WHISPER)—in parentheses and capitalize.

In addition to the basic rules outlined here, format also involves both the number and the kinds of voices used as well as the way sound effects and music entries are typed. These matters are discussed next.

Single-Voice Copy

The basic format for single-voice copy was introduced in Chapter 2; we'll expand on it here largely as a matter of review. Note the format used in the following copy:

ANNCR.	Only two days are left to take advantage of the outstanding values at
(URGENTLY)	Fingers Department Store. That's right, only two days. Everything in the
	store has been reduced 25 percent at Fingers!

This format tells you that only one voice is required for the spot. The all-caps instructions tell both the producer/director and the announcer what style of delivery to use. The copy itself is typed apart from the production instructions in caps and lowercase.

The practice of using all caps for instructions to the announcer also helps separate what is to be read aloud from instructions that must appear in the body of the copy.

ANNOUNCER	How often do you check the oil in your car? Every fill-up? Every six
	months? Stop and think about it. (SLIGHT PAUSE) Now that we go to self-
	service stations, we often forget to make that important check on our
	motor oil.

Within the body of this copy, you'll note the all-caps instruction SLIGHT PAUSE. The writer wants the announcer to pause briefly to let the message sink in. If the entire body of the copy had been written in all caps, this instruction would not stand out for the announcer, and his or her delivery might not convey the message fully.

Two-Voice Copy

It's sometimes desirable to have two voices alternate in reading the copy. Two-voice (or alternate-voice) copy should be distinguished from dramatic or dialog copy. In two-voice copy, the two voices merely alternate phrases or statements:

VOICE ONE	How often do you check the oil in your car?
VOICE TWO	Every fill-up? Every six months?
VOICE ONE	Stop and think about it. Your car's engine can't think about it, but you can.
VOICE TWO	Preston's wants your car to give you the best performance possible, but you've got to help.

In the preceding two-voice spot, the nature of the content, auto upkeep, tends to call for two male voices. If the writer wants to indicate the gender of the voices, the format makes it easy to do so:

MAN I	How often do you check the oil in your car?
MAN II	Every fill-up? Every six months?
MAN I	Stop and think about it.

It follows that in other commercials, the writer could alternate two female voices, alternate male and female, or even indicate the age of the voices, such as ELDERLY MAN or YOUNG CHILD. It also follows that as a writer you may have no control over who is cast to read your copy. These decisions may be left entirely to a production director.

Finally, no rule other than practicality dictates that you are limited to two voices. However, using more than two voices may tend to confuse the listener—and casting more than two good voices could be a problem, especially in smaller stations. Keep these problems in mind when you are tempted to write a spot with a "cast of thousands."

Dialog Copy

A variation on the two-voice spot just illustrated is the dialog spot, which is usually a minidrama. The format is the same; it is the content that changes. Here is a dialog spot illustrating the consistency in format:

JOHN	What's for dinner tonight, honey?
MARY	Same old question. Same old answer. Leftovers from last night's dinner.
JOHN	I thought that would be the answer.
MARY	So?
JOHN	So I took a tip from the boss.
MARY	The last time you took a tip from him you lost 30 bucks at the track.
JOHN	Yeah, but this is different. Now he's got a working wife like I do who really doesn't have time to slave away in the kitchen.
MARY	You've got that "slave away" part right. Now what's the tip?
JOHN	See this package I picked up at the supermarket on the way home? It's Quick-As-A-Wink chicken and dumplings. Just pour in a pan, add water, heat, and you've got homemade chicken and dumplings.
MARY	Hey, why didn't I think of that? Sue had Quick-As-A-Wink chicken and dumplings when she had me over while you were out of town. Just hand me that saucepan . . . we're gonna have Quick-As-A-Wink chicken and dumplings tonight.
ANNOUNCER	And you can too. Just a quick trip to the supermarket and a quick meal of delicious Quick-As-A-Wink chicken and dumplings.

Although dialog spots may seem to be a desirable approach, producing them can entail certain problems. The dialog spot calls for a dramatic talent that the average radio announcer may not have. Large agencies with sizable budgets can cast a dramatic dialog spot with little or no trouble, but small-market stations may encounter difficulties. Before you write such a spot, you must know if it can be produced. Is the talent available? If so, how much will it cost? Is the necessary money available? If you can answer yes to these questions, then proceed—with one more caution. Don't become so clever in your writing that the listener remembers the witty dialog but not the product. That has happened with national spots produced by large agencies. Don't let it happen to you. Finally, remember to keep your dialog copy conversational and pattern it after the way people actually talk.

Sound Effects and Music

Sound effects, music, or both—when carefully and well integrated into a spot—can do a great deal to make the commercial special and attract listener attention. Sound effects and music are instructions rather than copy to be read aloud, so they are typed in all caps and underlined. The underlining is used for clarity; it helps the eye see immediately that this element of the production differs from instructions to the performers.

Here is an abbreviated example:

SOUND	FIRE TRUCK WITH SIREN APPROACHING. ESTABLISH AND FADE UNDER FOR:
ANNOUNCER	This can be a terrifying sound, especially when the fire truck stops at your house.

SOUND EFFECTS   Sound effects in spot announcements can serve a variety of purposes:

- Establish a setting, such as a baseball game, a wedding, or voices in a cave
- Set a mood, as might be done with conversation and music to suggest a nightspot or with the sound of strong wind to suggest winter weather
- Establish time, as with an alarm clock ringing or a metronome ticking
- Represent action, such as hitting a golf ball or closing a door

In some cases, you might produce your own sound effects: a metronome to indicate the passage of time, or you might use the technical capability of a radio or audio studio to create an echo effect for a voice in a cave. You might also record one or both parts of a phone conversation to add realism. Generally, however, copywriters use prepared sound-effects libraries for most sounds needed in production. Many of the recorded sound effects are not that distinct, so it's wise to tell the audience precisely what they're hearing, as was done in our example.

MUSIC   Music can be most effective in gaining and holding listener attention. Even the smallest radio stations have a music library, and many stations have mood music libraries. Mood music libraries include instrumental recordings of varied tempos. When stations purchase such libraries, they are entitled to use the music in commercials without paying additional fees. Music in a spot announcement, like sound effects, can serve several functions:

- Create a mood, as with a sharp musical interjection (called a *sting* or *stab*) to create a feeling of fright, or light, breezy music to create an expression of fantasy
- Establish a location, as with a Hawaiian melody or music from a five-string banjo
- Create a sound effect, such as playing "Auld Lang Syne" to indicate New Year's Eve
- Establish a theme, perhaps by using a pleasing melody in each spot to establish advertiser identification (but don't pick a song that's too familiar; it may draw away attention)
- Establish direction, that is, to introduce a spot, to gain attention, to suggest transitions, and to add a conclusion

Music can be used in spots in several ways. It can be played under all of the spot, it can be played under part of the spot, or it can be used as a *bridge*, or transition, as in the following spot:

ANNCR:	The drink has a bright and pleasingly palatable taste. This refreshing beverage was actually developed by a pharmacist and sold to promote temperance among the rowdy coal miners of Philadelphia. What was this drink that was introduced at the eighteen seventy-six Philadelphia Centennial?
	MUSIC BRIDGE
	To make your Business Travel more pleasingly palatable, there's United Airlines and the American Express Card. United serves more of the U.S. than any other airline. And the American Express Card is the card rated best by frequent business flyers for their travel and entertainment.
	MUSIC BRIDGE
	Charles Elmer Hires wanted to call his new drink "root tea," but a friend suggested the coal mining crowd might take to it a bit more if he called it "root beer." And so a national favorite was born.
	MUSIC BRIDGE
	United Airlines and the American Express Card. Two other national favorites that make great travel partners.

Courtesy United Airlines.

A word of caution: stations and cablecasters have to pay copyright fees for the music they use in their programming, including music used in commercials. Music licensing firms such as BMI, ASCAP, and SESAC represent the musicians and collect copyright fees from stations and cablecasters. But their concern with copyright does not extend to the use of recorded music in spots. For example, to use a given popular record in a spot because the lyrics are recognizable is a specialized use of the record, a use for profit. The music licensing firms do not handle copyright matters in such instances. Other firms, such as the Harry Fox Agency in New York, should be contacted to obtain permission to use a popular recording in a spot. When stations or cablecasters use recorded music in commercials without permission, they run the risk of being charged with violations of copyright law. If convicted, they might have to pay penalties greater than the charges to use the music legally.

As noted previously, stations and cable systems often purchase music libraries to avoid the copyright problem. When a music library is purchased, the rights to use the music are usually included in the purchase price.

Now, back to format. You might want to use both sound effects and music in the same spot. Again, the basic rule of all caps and underlining pertains. At least two interchangeable terms should be in your writing vocabulary: *cross fade* and *segue*. Simply stated, these terms mean that as one sound (whether music, voice, or sound effect) fades out, the second fades in over it and comes up to full volume. Here's an example:

MUSIC	CUT I: MOOD MUSIC LIBRARY CD. ESTABLISH FOR 3 SECONDS AND CROSS FADE INTO:
SOUND	RAGING FIRE. FIRE TRUCK SIREN IN BACKGROUND. HOLD UNDER FOR:
ANNCR	Up-to-date fire insurance is important. Don't wait for a fire to check your home insurance.

In this example, the writer has selected specific music from the station's mood music library and has given instructions for the location and use of the music. Instructions for the sound effect show that the siren remains in the background, or bed, while the announcer reads the copy.

It follows that you could write for one piece of music to segue into another or for one sound effect to segue or cross fade into another. The glossary at the end of the book includes production terms often used in writing commercials for radio.

◆ Donut Copy

A variation on the local tag is *donut copy*. It works like this: The agency produces a sound effect/music open and close for a commercial. The music may be a nationally recognized signature for a product that opens and closes the spot, while the local announcer reads copy prepared by the agency between the opening and closing music/sound. If you are writing for a local station receiving a donut commercial, you may have to prepare a local tag. Timing is critical in this type of spot. Once the tape starts rolling, the announcer has a precise number of seconds in which to read the live message. If the announcer is not finished reading in time, the closing music will quite possibly drown out his or her voice.

◆ Live Ad-Lib Copy

When an announcer has developed a wide listener following and become a strong air personality, a sponsor may want him or her to ad-lib the sales message. Does this situation require anything of the writer? Often it does. As a writer, you may be asked to prepare a fact sheet for the announcer or DJ. Such a fact sheet is a list of things the sponsor wants to get across in descending order of importance. These lists are often referred to as *announcer's fact sheets*.

Many radio stations have their top DJs ad-lib live copy and charge advertisers a premium for that service.

◆ Production Copy

Any copy that goes through the studio process of being recorded is production copy. Most of these spots come through agencies. Large radio stations offer production services to their sponsors, and some stations serve as production centers for agencies.

Production copy offers the advantages of rehearsing until you get it right, so the result sounds more professional. The chief disadvantage is cost, a factor that could be outweighed by the greater effectiveness of the spot. The disadvantage to small stations is that a spot that reads great on paper may overtax the station's ability to produce it.

Many stations follow the practice of prerecording all radio spots, including straight announcements. This is done largely because of the complexity of production scripts. For example, the following script uses voices, music, and sound effects:

MUSIC	SOFT, BUT ELEGANT. ESTAB., THEN UNDER
ANNCR	Once upon a time in an office not too far away, you were having trouble deciding what to have for lunch.
MAN	What will it be? A hot dog? No, I had that yesterday. A pizza? No, the day before.
VOICE	(ON FILTER) Not again. Are you going to treat me to indigestion because of a greasy, hurried lunch again?
MAN	Who's that?
VOICE	(ON FILTER) I'm your stomach, and I've had it with that stuff you feed me. I need a change. SFX: EXPLOSION I don't need another blast of indigestion.
MAN	What do I do?
MUSIC	HARP TRILL
WOMAN	(WITH SLIGHT ECHO) Go to the Salad Buffet. You build your own salad from dozens of delightful choices, crisp lettuce, sliced carrots, sliced celery …
MAN	(INTERRUPTS) Now, who are you?
WOMAN	(SLIGHT ECHO) I'm your conscience. I agree with your stomach. Those greasy hot dogs have got to go, and you know it. A delightful salad from the Salad Buffet keeps you fit and helps you eat right.
MUSIC	ORCHESTRAL. REACH CRESCENDO THEN SNEAK UNDER
ANNCR	And so you went to the Salad Buffet at 1201 Douglas. You created a delightful salad that pleased your stomach, your conscience … and your pocketbook.
MAN	You should try the Salad Buffet too! Downtown at 1201 Douglas. You'll like it!
MUSIC	STING. UP AND OUT

The complexity of this spot makes it poorly suited to be produced live.

◆ Radio and the Internet

Radio stations are finding that the Internet is a significant way to expand service and reach consumers. Their Web sites include a variety of information such as real estate, employment, traffic and airline listings, plus information on local news and weather. Most sites emphasize information about station personalities, no matter the format of the station. A photo gallery of personalities is usually included, along with a schedule of shows for each individual. Many sites include a link to an on-air broadcast, and station bloggers are common.

Stations with music formats include items that enable listeners to provide feedback. These techniques may allow listeners to rate songs played on the air and a listing of the top songs played. Audio of the station may be streamed so that listeners can tune in anywhere they have Internet access. Concert listings are common on sites for stations with music formats.

Many Web sites include advertising with links to sponsors. As listeners seek information on the site, they also see the ads, just as they would hear them on the radio.

➤ POINTS TO REMEMBER

- Radio is everywhere; it helps people get through drive-time traffic and is a constant companion for many. Still, radio has limitations, the chief of which is the lack of a picture. The radio copywriter must therefore make the product or service come alive in the listener's mind by helping create a mental picture.

- The radio commercial comprises four elements: sound effects, words, music, and voice. You must use these tools to capture the listener's attention and create the desire for your client's product or service.

- Timing radio copy by reading it at the rate at which it will be read on the air is an important part of the copywriter's job because there is no precise way to time copy by counting the number of words or lines written.

- The term *format* refers to the physical form of your copy on paper. Stations tend to evolve their own formats for writing copy. However, unless your employer directs differently, you should type instructions in all caps and spoken copy in caps and lowercase.

- Copywriting for radio involves a variety of formats: single-voice announcements, two-voice spots, dialog spots, and fact sheets.

- Copy can be presented in a variety of ways: live, live ad-lib, donut, and prerecorded.

EXERCISES

Exercise 1

Write a 60-second straight spot for Yourtown Transit. Stress the convenience of taking the bus and the savings involved (lower gas bill, no parking fees, and less mileage on the car). Ask listeners to look for coupons in the paper that entitle an individual to one free trip anywhere in Yourtown.

Write this spot so that the talent seems to be talking to him- or herself or thinking out loud. Be sure to follow the format recommended for radio. Give at least four specific instructions to guide the announcer in reading this spot—for example, URGENTLY or CALMLY. Exchange your scripts and read them aloud.

Exercise 2

Write a 60-second dialog spot for Howard's Housekeepers. Howard's Housekeepers provides temporary help for the house and yard. The phone number is 292-4357 (292 H-E-L-P). The service is reasonably priced. Howard's will do house, yard, or both. Aim this spot at young couples.

Exercise 3

Write a 60-second production spot for SavMor Supermarkets (four locations). Use both sound effects and music (assume that you have clearance for the music). SavMor has been in Yourtown for 26 years, longer than any other supermarket chain. Stress that they provide the lowest prices, top quality, and a wide variety. The stores are open 24 hours, 7 days a week. This client takes pride in its reputation, so a hard sell would not be an appropriate approach.

Exercise 4

Write a 60-second spot for Valu Stores, a discount chain with locations in Yourtown. Use two voices (not dialog) and a sound effect. The spot should emphasize Value Days, next Wednesday through next Sunday. Hours are 9 A.M. to 9 P.M. through Saturday, 12 P.M. to 6 P.M. Sunday. There will be specially reduced prices in every department. Many items are reduced 30 to 40 percent. Slogan for the client: "Your Value Leader."

Types of Radio Copy

In the previous chapter, you learned the mechanics for putting a radio commercial on paper. Before that, you considered what motivates people to buy, and you examined the AIDA formula. You also studied the writing style used in broadcast commercials. Now it's time to bring all of these elements together by examining the various types of radio commercials. You could think of this as the approach you're going to take for a given radio spot. Will you take a humorous approach, write a hard-sell commercial, or use a testimonial or endorsement spot?

The choice might not be entirely yours, of course. The sponsor may dictate the type of commercial desired. In some instances, the nature of the product will influence your decision. Funeral homes, for example, don't lend themselves to humorous announcements. Used-car dealers often prefer hard-sell copy, whereas banks sometimes use institutional spots.

◆ Straight Copy

Many of the spots you write will be *straight copy* commercials, which are perhaps the backbone of local radio advertising. Straight copy (or straight announcement copy) is virtually always written for one-voice delivery. It lacks the urgency of hard sell but doesn't use the understatement of institutional copy. Rather, it's written to be delivered in a conversational, informative voice. Straight copy certainly follows as nearly as possible the AIDA formula, making every effort to motivate the listener.

The following examples should help you learn to recognize straight copy when you hear it. Consider first this spot from a medium-market radio station in Nebraska:

ANNOUNCER	The all-American Cavalier meets the foreign challenge head-on. Drive a Cavalier at DuTeau Chevrolet. Steer it through a curve and understand precision handling. Drive it over a rough road and feel solid construction all around you. Discover the advantages of front-wheel-drive traction in rain, mud, snow, and ice. Cavalier is quality and performance . . . advanced technology and engineering. Cavalier is an exceptional all-American car that meets the foreign challenge head-on. See it today at DuTeau Chevrolet, 18th and "O."

Courtesy KFOR, Lincoln, Nebraska.

Straight-copy spots are not screamers, but they do convey information to the listener, and they are persuasive. Such spots are often recorded to ensure consistent on-air delivery.

◆ Hard-Sell Copy

Hard-sell commercials go by a variety of names: bargain basements, screamers, hard hitters, urgents, quick-sale spots. The following elements appear in most hard-sell radio copy:

■ **Price reduction.** These examples are typical: "Reduced 30 percent!" "Everything in the store is 30 percent off!" "At Jackson's, we will not be undersold!"

■ **Urgency.** This is communicated by using two techniques: (1) crowding so many words into the commercial that the announcer has to read it at a breakneck pace to finish the spot in the time allowed and (2) using urgent phrases such as "This bargain ends tomorrow," "These cars must be sold by midnight," "Madman Mike has done it again," and "You can't beat this!"

- **Sound effects**. Explosions, dramatic music, and echo effects are common elements.
- **Punchy sentences**. Short, punchy sentences are easy to read, especially when the pace is fast.
- **Slogans**. Hard-sell spots often use the hammering of slogans or the repetition of phrases such as "See it at Goss, the tradin' hoss, located on Ross," "Drive in today and drive out a bargain," or "You always save when you shop at Sampson's."

Hard-sell copy lends itself to a variety of formats: one-voice and multiple-voice formats are common. Frequently, the sponsor will elect to deliver his or her own spot. In this latter category, the personal pronoun *I* often predominates: "I want to sell you a car," "I will not be undersold," "I will match any price in town."

There is no consensus about how effective this type of commercial really is. In all likelihood, the effectiveness of hard-sell spots is related to the educational and economic level of the listener, though more research on the value of such commercials is needed. Whatever their relative worth, hard-sell commercials certainly exist on both radio and television, especially on small- to medium-market radio and independent television stations.

As we did with straight copy, let's look at an example of a hard-sell radio commercial. The spot is for a car dealer and is delivered in a bombastic style.

SOUND	CLOCK TICKING. HOLD BEHIND (USE METRONOME)
ANNOUNCER	Time is running out . . . time is running out! Roger Beasley Mazda's offer of a great little truck for only 5,590 will soon be over! Supplies are running out, and Roger Beasley soon won't have any left to offer! Imagine, the greatest little truck in Austin with steel-belted radials, five-speed transmission, fully carpeted, with tinted glass and many more features. Hurry while supplies and color selection are good.
SOUND	TICKING SOUND UP AND UNDER
ANNOUNCER	Time is running out! Time is running out! Roger Beasley Mazda, 1918 Burnet Road.

Courtesy KASE, Austin, Texas.

Note the sound effect and the short, punchy sentences used in the spot.

◆ Institutional Copy

The chief aim of the *institutional spot* is to keep the client's good name before the public. Some products and services are closely tied to the image of the producer. As a result, what is advertised is the institution rather than the product or service. Power companies, for instance, have no competition. They want their customers to use electricity and thereby increase the company's profit, but because power companies are regulated by state or local agencies, they are more concerned that they project a favorable image to both the public and the regulators. Institutional, rather than product, advertising can be used to maintain that image. Banks use institutional ads to project an image of strength and stability, and petroleum companies use them to tell the public of innovations that promote better living, quite apart from the selling of gas and oil.

Institutional copy can even be thought of as soft-sell advertising. Yes, there is a sales message in an institutional spot—it just doesn't hit listeners over the head. Consider the following commercial, which is one of a series of spots for Franklin Savings featuring Mack and Karen.

MUSIC	UP BRIEFLY AND THEN UNDER
MACK	I remember Grandma's big old Packard . . . driving to the service station . . . wishing I were big enough to run and pump gas . . . polish the windshield . . . know all the customers by name. It's sure different now . . . attendants in glass boxes . . . mechanical voices . . . computer pumps. I just can't imagine my Grandma pumping *her* own gas!
MUSIC	UP SLIGHTLY
MACK	I guess that's why I bank at Franklin Savings . . . They always have time for a smile and a cup of coffee . . . Franklin knows me. They want my business and they show it with every banking service I need . . . plus good, old-fashioned friendship and concern.
KAREN	At Franklin Savings . . . *you* come first. Ten locations and extended business hours make it easy for you . . . for all the service you deserve . . . with a smile.
MUSIC	UP AND OUT
MACK	Franklin Savings. Your Austin savings and loan.

Courtesy Neal Spelce Communications, Austin, Texas.

This Franklin Savings commercial employs several techniques in one piece of copy. It uses a low-key institutional approach. It's a spokesperson spot. It uses two voices and music. And note its use of nostalgia—the reference to the "good old days"—to create listener interest.

◆ Spokesperson Copy

In its simplest form, the *spokesperson spot* features someone speaking in the first person for the client, its product, or its service. It may be the sponsor, a celebrity, an actor portraying a person on the street, or a member of the station's announcing staff who receives a talent fee to speak for the client.

The Sponsor as Spokesperson

Sometimes called the *ego-trip commercial*, this type of spot often takes a hard-sell approach, especially in small- to medium-sized markets. The owner of Joe's Used Cars comes on mike or on camera to tell the audience, "I want to sell you a car. I will not be undersold." On a national scale, it might be the president of an auto manufacturing company telling about the values of his automobiles.

In writing a client-as-spokesperson spot, write a spot that fits the client's delivery. If possible, visit the client and listen to how he or she talks. Does the sponsor have favorite phrases? Does the person use short, choppy sentences? Is his or her normal delivery slow and deliberate, or fast and rapid-fire? As much as possible, you should strive to make the sponsor sound normal. But don't be surprised if he or she rewrites your copy.

Endorsements

A fine line separates endorsement spots from testimonial commercials. *Endorsements* feature a well-known personality, but *testimonials* come from the man or woman on the street. An example of an endorsement is a well-known athlete doing a commercial for a product. A testimonial for a movie, on the other hand, might include recorded comments from actual moviegoers leaving the theater.

The motivational aspect of celebrity endorsement was discussed in Chapter 5. Today, most endorsement commercials appear on television rather than in other media.

Testimonials

Testimonial spots can be a very effective form of advertising because this type of commercial presents the comments of a satisfied consumer. Some effort may be required to gather the testimonial remarks, but the results can be worthwhile. Stations sometimes use the tape-recorded voices of genuine customers to achieve a feeling of credibility. In other instances, the comments are transcribed and recorded by station personnel to provide a more professional sound.

Radio stations often use testimonials in their on-air promotional spots by recording comments from listeners who phone the station. The following spot is typical.

ANNCR	KAAA thanks you for making us your favorite radio station.
TAPE	I love the music. I like hearing the songs that were popular when I was dating, and you play 'em.
TAPE	Ron Hill is great! I listen to him every morning and I love his jokes.
TAPE	KAAA is so good that I listen all day. I have my radio on from morning till night on KAAA.
ANNCR	KAAA-FM, Hits 92. You made us number one and we'll keep playing the hits you want to hear.

You can also obtain comments about a business by taking a tape recorder to the business and talking to customers as they leave. That's what was done in this spot for the Top 40 Guides:

SOUND EFFECTS	STREET NOISES, MALL NOISES, OFFICE NOISES. MUSIC BED
Announcer	We talked with Central Floridians about the Top 40 Guides and here's what they're saying:
1st woman	Oh, I love it! I keep my Top 40 Guide in my phone book. It saves a lot of time. The government numbers in my neighborhood are so easy to find.
1st man	It's about time. I have needed this ever since I moved here.
Announcer	Kind of like a convenience store for your phone book, isn't it?
1st man	Yeah, it is!
2nd man	I only occasionally use the Yellow Pages, but the Top 40 Guide saves me so much time when I do.
2nd woman	It's great! I don't have to use those heavy phone books as much and I don't like flipping through all those pages anyway. I use mine in my White Pages and I haven't broken a nail in six months!

3rd woman	Wow! This is just what I need! Can I have this one?
10-second jingle	"Find it Fast…"
Jingle	
3rd woman:	This is great! It's just great!
Announcer	For a free Top 40 Guide call 648–9694 and we'll send you one for your neighborhood. That's 648–9694.

Courtesy the Yellow Pages Top 40 Guides.

◆ Humorous Copy

Humorous copy should be treated with care and respect—it's serious business. This type of radio copy can be very effective, but it can also backfire. Some sponsors seem to have little or no sense of humor, especially concerning their product or service. Never put humorous copy on the air without first checking with the sponsor. Keep in mind also that humorous copy is difficult to write. You may indeed be the life of the party, but putting your wit on paper in a manner that will effectively sell a product is another thing. Or you may have a gift for writing good, humorous radio copy, but do you have local talent available to perform what you've written? Humorous copy is pointless if it just sits there on your copy paper. And it's even worse if it falls flat because of inept delivery.

If you must write humorous radio copy, be sure to ask yourself the following questions:

- Can the listener identify with the humor? Or is the humor so far outside your audience's experience that no one can relate to it?
- Does the humor sell? Or does the listener remember the comedy and not the product? The copy should not be so hilarious that listeners miss the sales message.
- Will the humor stand up under repeated airing? Listeners tire quickly of the same joke told over and over.

Let's look at two spots that use humor to reach their audience. The first spot is for *Greensheet*, a classified ad newspaper distributed free; the second is for a dental plan for public employees in Texas.

ANNOUNCER	We don't. But then again, we do. The Greensheet delivers interested buyers and sellers right to your doorstep, even though we don't deliver the paper there.
	Finally … and this really gets me … people think the Greensheet is run by elves.
ELF 1	I'll buy that.
ELF 2	You can't, it's free.
ELF 3	Which is why it's read.
ELF 2	But it's still green.
ELF 1	You got a point there.

ANNOUNCER	Find out for yourself how every week the Greensheet delivers classified ads that are read.
ELF 2	And green.
ANNOUNCER	All over.
MUSIC UP AND OUT	

Courtesy Fogarty and Klein, Inc. Houston, Texas.

CHARACTERS:	PATIENT: NEOPHYTE, A REAL "GOLLY-GEE'ER" DOCTOR: SCATTERBRAIN, A W. C. FIELDS TYPE NURSE: SARCASTIC, MAE WEST DELIVERY ANNCR: WARM, BELIEVABLE
MUSIC	ESTABLISH MUZAK TYPE, DENTIST OFFICE SETTING
PATIENT	Gee, my first dental checkup in 26 years.
NURSE	Really? Whew! Mind turning your head, hon?
PATIENT	I almost forgot what a dentist office is like.
NURSE	Honey, you don't need a dentist, you need an exterminator.
PATIENT	Ya see, the Texas Public Employees Association has this great dental plan …
NURSE	Yeah, but did they plan on getting you?
PATIENT	…any state employee can join!
SFX	DOOR OPENS, ENTER DR., ROUTER, DENTAL DRILL
DOCTOR	All right, where's the action, er, patient?
PATIENT	(SHEEPISHLY) Uh, right here.
DOCTOR	Ahem …Okay, we're going in. Open wide!
PATIENT	AaaaaaHhhhhhh!!!
DOCTOR	Mother of Pearl! Bring me my five iron.
SFX	DENTAL DRILL
PATIENT	(MAKES GURGLING SOUND)
DOCTOR	What did he say?
NURSE	He's bringin' the kids in for braces.
DOCTOR	Holy molars!
SFX	DENTAL DRILL UP
PATIENT	(MAKES MUMBLING, GURGLING, CHOKING NOISES)
ANNCR	Join the Texas Public Employees Association and get a dental plan your whole family can sink its teeth into. Plus other great benefits like personal loans, legal service, and auto and home insurance . . . at a price that won't take a bite out of your wallet.
SFX	DENTAL DRILL UP BRIEFLY AND UNDER PATIENT STILL MUMBLING
NURSE	We'll never get this finished.
DOCTOR	Patience, my dear. It's cuspid's last stand.
SFX	DRILL UP BRIEFLY AND OUT
ANNCR	Join TPEA today. Write TPEA, Austin, Texas, 78711.

Courtesy Neal Spelce Communications, Austin, Texas.

Both of these humorous commercials were effective on the air. Why? They were well written, featured professional actors, and were produced under good studio conditions. Both spots contain plays on words: *read for red* in the *Greensheet* copy and *It's cuspid's last stand* in the dental plan copy. Both spots straightforwardly present a selling message. Neither contains a hint of derision about the product or service. Note too that the humor doesn't interfere with the sales message in either of the examples. On the contrary, the humor serves its purpose by holding the listener's attention while the sales message is delivered.

If you're going to write a humorous spot, you have two basic ways of achieving humor:

1. Take a reasonably normal setting and include unusual characters. That's what you find in the spot for the *Greensheet*.

2. Create an outrageous situation peopled with relatively straight characters. The spot for the Texas Public Employees Association uses both an outrageous situation and zany characters.

➤ POINTS TO REMEMBER

- For the copywriter, style can best be defined as the approach being used to sell the client's product or service. You must remember that, regardless of the approach you use, it should fit the product or service.

- The straight announcement—a commercial, station promo, or PSA—is the most commonly used type of radio commercial. It requires only one announcer and presents no production difficulties. When written well and delivered on air in a professional manner, it can be an effective sales message. Hard-sell radio commercials are also fairly common, especially in smaller markets.

- Institutional copy takes the dignified approach of soft sell, keeping the sponsor's good name before the audience.

- Humorous copy can be very effective but must be treated with care. Writing humorous copy is serious business. You should not write this type of copy without first having the client's approval—and also be sure that

your station's announcers can handle the humorous approach in delivery. Agency writers are probably on safer ground with this type of copy than are station writers, because an agency is more likely to be able to cast the right voices for the spot.

- All four approaches—straight, hard sell, institutional, and spokesperson—may be written for a single voice. It's also possible, however, to write for multiple-voice delivery. Hard-sell copy is frequently written for two alternating voices. Humorous copy often lends itself to dialog delivery.

- Spokesperson messages can be delivered in several different ways. A testimonial spot lets the customer speak. Comments by satisfied customers on audiotape or in letters can be effective testimony for the client's business. An endorsement depends on a celebrity delivering a sales message. Or, the client may prefer to present his or her own spot.

EXERCISES

Exercise 1

Write a 60-second two-voice hard-sell radio spot with sound effects for Jenner Ford in Yourtown. Use the following information: This is a "Summer Closeout Sale." The goal is to sell all the leftover models from last year. Prices on last year's models have been greatly reduced.

New models are coming in. Jenner Ford is overstocked. Every Ford model is included: family sedans, sports cars, SUVs, and pickups. The sale is this weekend only. Rebates of up to $2,500 are available. No money down with approved credit. Jenner Ford is at 2290 Airport Blvd. They have a giant U.S. flag flying over their building. Jenner will give the best prices on cars traded in.

Exercise 2

Write a humorous 60-second radio spot for Dynamic Stainstopper Carpet. This carpet is designed to protect against most common food and beverage stains. The manufacturing process ensures that dirt doesn't cling, so the dirt vacuums up easily. Available at Super Carpets of Yourtown. There are four locations. Ask listeners to see the Yellow Pages for specific addresses.

Provide characterizations of the people who will deliver this spot. Use a straight announcer at some point in the script.

Exercise 3

Pick a national or local celebrity to endorse the following product and write a 60-second radio endorsement. The product is Ache Eze, a cream that relieves aches and sore muscles. The product is available at drugstores. The product is not greasy, has no unpleasant odor, leaves no burning sensation, and will not stain. Stress that the product will relieve backache and sore muscles from overwork, exercise, and so on.

Exercise 4

Listen to a humorous radio spot and analyze it. Answer the following:

1. Is a joke told to create humor?

2. Does the humor make fun of the product?

3. Does humor obscure the product?

4. Is humor appropriate to the product?

5. Are you involved in the humor within 10 seconds?

6. Does the humor evoke a smile or a belly laugh? (A smile is best.)

7. Is the humor tightly integrated with the product and its sales message?

8. Does the humor involve zany characters, a zany setting, or both?

You might want to repeat this exercise with TV spots when you get to Chapter 10.

CHAPTER TEN

The Television Commercial: The Mechanics

It's no secret that Americans love TV. People spend many hours a day watching it, and special network programs regularly set viewing records. But television is not the personal and portable companion that radio is. A few people have small, portable TV sets that they can take to sporting events or on picnics. More often, the TV set is the chief element in the living room decor, a large, immovable piece of furniture. Whether a family has one TV set or several, its members usually watch a lot, often more than six hours a day. This makes television an attractive vehicle for advertisers.

Radio relies on sound to reach its audience, but television adds sight, movement, and color. Thus, when you write a commercial for TV, you have a better opportunity to approximate face-to-face communication than in any other means of communication. In fact, local advertisers often want to appear in their own commercials so they can speak directly to potential customers.

◆ Television Today

Television Stations

The two types of television stations are VHF and UHF. VHF stands for *very high frequency* and consists of channels 2 through 13. UHF stands for *ultra high frequency*, and stations in this band broadcast on channels 14 through 69. However, most Americans now receive the UHF and VHF channels via cable, and viewers give little thought to the broadcast channel distinctions.

Individual television stations may affiliate with a network—that is, sign an agreement to carry the programming of that network—or they may be independent and not rely on a network to provide programming. The commercial television broadcast industry now has three full-time networks (ABC, NBC, and CBS) and several part-time networks. Part-time networks provide affiliates with programming for only a limited number of hours each day, often 3 to 4 hours in the evening. Full-time networks make programs available to affiliates through most of the day. Noncommercial broadcasters do not sell advertising but obtain revenue when businesses *underwrite* their programs.

Television advertising is sold primarily in 30-second lengths, although stations sometimes sell 10-, 15-, or 60-second spots. Although not typical, some stations have even sold 1-second spots. Longer advertisements, called infomercials, are also aired on television stations. These are actually advertisements in the form of a program, which typically runs for 30 minutes.

Television spots that run between programs are known as *adjacencies*—in other words, they are *adjacent* to programs. Spots scheduled within program positions are called *participations*. If you watch a typical television program, you will see commercials for several advertisers. These are spots for the *participating* advertisers who share the cost of sponsoring the program.

STRENGTHS OF TELEVISION

- **Television is the most persuasive medium.** No other medium can offer the unique blend of persuasive communication factors—sight, sound, motion, and color. This combination of elements enables television to demonstrate a product, engage viewers' emotions, and show product features.
- **Television is credible.** Consumers believe TV advertising more than ads on any other medium. This may be because people rely most on television for news and

entertainment, and thus on commercials too; or the credibility may come from the persuasive elements mentioned previously.

- **Television is intrusive.** It's about as hard to avoid a television commercial as a radio spot. People watch and talk about the spots that are best written and produced. Advertisers pay premium prices to advertise in the Super Bowl, where the commercials may be as compelling as the game.
- **Television is glamorous.** Television gives advertisers a feeling of importance and an association with the glamour of show business. Local merchants often respond to this glamour by doing their own commercials.

WEAKNESSES OF TELEVISION

- **Television is expensive.** Placing commercials in or adjacent to popular television shows is very costly; only the largest advertisers are able to buy such time. Advertisers can buy time on cable television as an alternative to over-the-air television. This still gives them many advantages of the medium but denies them availabilities next to popular programs.

  Producing television spots is also expensive. Spots shown nationwide can easily cost more than a half-million dollars to produce. Local commercials, which may run in the same cluster of spots as the expensive national spots, require sizable budgets if they are to be competitive.
- **Television is cluttered.** When too many commercials are placed together in a cluster, you have clutter. The more clutter there is, the harder it is for viewers to remember individual commercials.

Radio programming is highly specialized, but just the opposite is true of TV. Television is a mass medium, and generally each network affiliate offers something for everyone—sports, soap operas, and cartoons. This pattern creates an attractive structure for advertisers, who can buy time to reach the specific viewers likely to buy a product.

The material just covered relates primarily to "over-the-air" or broadcast TV, but cable TV is another facet of the industry. The viewer perceives few differences between the two forms of television, but there are major distinctions in the methods of audience distribution.

Cable Television

Cable is distributed through both broadcast and cable-only channels via coaxial cable or optical fiber strung throughout a community on telephone poles or underground. Wireless cable, a variation of traditional cable, uses microwaves to transmit its content to subscribers.

About two-thirds of American households subscribe to cable, and more than 16 million U.S. households own a home satellite dish. Cable systems, depending on channel capacity, typically provide a basic service consisting of the nearby broadcast television stations that cable systems are required by the FCC to carry, one or two superstations (such as WGN or WTBS), and several advertiser-supported cable networks (such as CNN, MTV, ESPN, and TNT).

Pay channels are commercial-free programming services, such as ShowTime, for which subscribers pay extra each month. Pay services are frequently available in packages, called *tiers*. Cable systems charge an extra amount for each tier above the charge for basic service.

Most cable systems have sales staffs that sell advertising time to local advertisers and arrange with national cable reps to sell to national advertisers and agencies.

Systems sell local adjacencies to advertiser-supported cable networks that are generally part of the systems' basic service. The most important advertiser-supported networks are CNN (news), USA (entertainment), Discovery Channel (entertainment), ESPN (sports), and TNT (movies).

STRENGTHS OF CABLE   Cable is television, so it has the persuasive, intrusive, and glamorous qualities of broadcast television. Cable also has the following advantages.

- **Cable can narrowcast.** Cable has a variety of programming formats that appeal to specialized demographic audiences—for instance, all-sports, all-comedy, all-news, and all-music channels. Advertisers can buy commercials in programs focused on narrowly defined audience segments.
- **Cable advertising is inexpensive.** Advertising on cable is much less expensive than advertising on broadcast television. Cable channels do not have the popularity or audience demand of traditional television networks or stations. As a result, advertising slots or *availabilities* are in greater supply.

DISADVANTAGES OF CABLE

- **Cable networks have low ratings.** Cable network ratings are typically much lower than those of the broadcast networks. Advertisers can access availabilities on cable, but the number of viewers may be small. However, if an advertiser carefully narrowcasts and picks the correct cable network, it is possible to reach an audience composed of the most desired viewers, albeit a smaller one than on regular television.

High-Definition Television

High-definition television (HDTV) is a system of program transmission based on digital technology. In the digital system, images and sound are captured by the same digital code used in computers. This replaces the analog or NTSC (National Television Standards Committee) transmission system, which was used for decades.

HDTV enables stations to broadcast programs with much greater resolution than traditional analog television provides. HDTV pictures have more than twice the clarity and resolution of traditional analog television. They are presented in a wide-screen format with a 16-by-9 width-to-height ratio rather than the standard 4-by-3 ratio (see Figure 10.1). The result is that HDTV offers five times more information than the standard analog picture and is accompanied by multichannel, CD-quality sound.

The HDTV picture ratio more closely resembles the screens seen in movie theaters. This wider view is closer to the human field of vision. Enjoyment of the video is enhanced because the viewer is visually drawn more into the action.

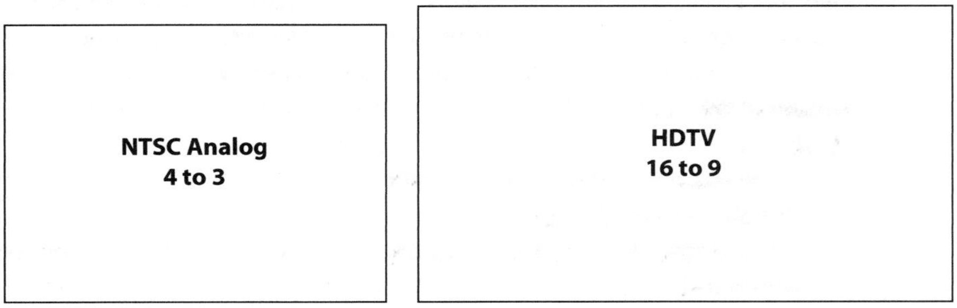

FIGURE 10.1   Television Aspect Ratios

The impact HDTV will have on commercials, PSAs, news stories, and so on is not yet clear. However, producers will certainly use the wide-screen image of HDTV to attract viewers for all levels of programming. Short program elements, such as commercials, will need to stand out so they are not lost in the wide-screen programming presented by HDTV. Practices will be developed once stations begin to switch more local programming to high definition.

Television and the Internet

Increasingly, television stations are using the Internet to expand their services and reach new audiences. The degree to which stations use the Web varies; some have no more than a Web page, while others have extensive sites that mirror their on-air programming. The latter sites often include extensive advertising that includes links to other pages within their Web site as well as links to advertising sponsors' Web sites. Stations that have the resources to use the Web aggressively often find the Internet to be a major new source of revenue.

Content that stations put on the Web falls into four categories. First is promotion and information about the station, its programming, and personalities. News is a staple of these sites, with current events extensively covered. A user gets a brief description of a story with a link to additional details, often including video. Weather is usually presented in detail, with emphasis on the threat of severe local weather, tornadoes, ice storms, and so on. Premium weather coverage, usually requiring payment, is often available for up-to-the-minute alerts and updates. Station anchors and special reports are promoted heavily on these sites. Sports are covered in detail.

A second category of content is informational data of use to consumers. Real estate, job, and automotive listings; traffic reports; airline schedules; community events; school closings; lottery results; and lifestyle stories (beauty, family, and baby) are some of the common data in this category. Some of this material provides direct competition to the classified section of newspapers.

The third category is entertainment. Web sites provide updates on current news about show business events and personalities. The emphasis is on national news, but information about stars and program themes of the affiliated network is also prominent. Listings such as concert dates, movie starting times, and cultural events may also be included.

The final category of content is information about the station. This material explains how to contact the station, jobs that may be available, and more information about the staff and station personalities.

The goal of a station Web site is to provide an instantaneous alternative to consumers who want information in a timelier manner than available on the air. There is no need to wait for a newscast to be broadcast; viewers can select the specific information they want and access it whenever they choose. Web sites do require staffing to update constantly changing data, so a personnel issue is involved. However, if the site gets enough hits and attracts advertisers, the costs can be recouped.

◆ Television Commercial Formats

A television commercial can be presented as a script or a storyboard. One or both may be prepared for a given spot. If the spot is a fairly routine one, production will probably require only a script. If the spot is more complex or if the advertiser needs or wants to visualize the spot, a storyboard may be prepared.

The TV Script

There is a major difference between a TV script and a radio script: The TV script is divided into two columns. The left column is for visual instructions, and the right is for audio (including spoken copy, music, and sound effects). The columns have no prescribed size. In some cases, a standard-sized sheet of paper is divided in two, with half for video and half for audio. In other cases, one-third of the page is for video and two-thirds for audio.

The style rules you should follow in putting the script on paper were introduced in Chapter 2. Let's review them here:

1. Write video in CAPITAL LETTERS.
2. Write all spoken audio in upper- and lowercase.
3. Write audio instructions for sound effects and music ALL IN CAPS, and underline.
4. Write audio talent instructions in parentheses (WHISPER), and underline.
5. Single-space video and double-space audio.
6. Double-space between speaker and shot changes.

You'll notice in the television script examples in this and subsequent chapters that some scripts don't follow our rules. Again, these variations reflect the practices of individual writers, stations, or agencies, some of whom (or which) have no format rules. If you follow the typing format presented here, you'll write a spot that's easy to deliver.

As noted, it is best to capitalize all video instructions. Video instructions tell the director what you want the visual scenes to look like. Abbreviations are used liberally in instructions to conserve space. The following is a completed script on standard two column paper.

VIDEO	TIME	AUDIO
SLO MO VIDEO OF SANTA PUTTING ON HAT	:00–:05	Get ready for the holidays at the Winter Park Mall.
EXTERIOR WS OF STORE CUT OF CROSS PENS WITH PRICE SUPER: $11 AND UP	:06–:15	great gift ideas are yours at Things Remembered where Cross pens are featured AT $11. AND UP with free engraving till Christmas. Engraved gifts are . . . Things Remembered.
WS OF EXTERIOR WITH PUSH TO INSIDE DISSOLVE TO MS OF PICK-UP COUNTER EDIT TO SLIDE SHOWING CU OF FOOD WITH TACO	:16–:25	Spice up your shopping with a break at Taco Viva. Get variety in quality Mexican food at reasonable prices and your choice of 6 savory sauces! When you say Taco . . . say Viva!
VIVA LOGO SUPERED IN UPPER HALF OF SCREEN	:26–:30	A joyous season to all from the Winter Park Mall, your favorite place to shop.

Courtesy SFN Communications of Florida, Inc.

The video instructions in this script use television terminology with which you need to become familiar. The video begins with a slow-motion (slo mo) shot of Santa putting on his hat. In subsequent scenes, wide shots (WS), closeups (CU), and a medium shot (MS) are called for. If you're not familiar with the characteristics and terminology of shot composition, you'll need to pay particular attention to the production section later in this chapter.

LISTEN!

SHOPPING FOR A HOME LOAN
TODAY CAN BE CONFUSING.

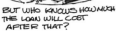
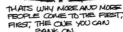

ECU

MANY PLACES TRY TO LURE
YOU IN WITH LOW FIRST-YEAR
MORTGAGE RATES.

MCU

BUT WHO KNOWS HOW MUCH
THE LOAN WILL COST
AFTER THAT?

ECU

THATS WHY MORE AND MORE
PEOPLE COME TO THE FIRST,
FIRST, THE ONE YOU CAN
BANK ON.

HOLD UP
LOGO
'FOLDER'
GOING INTO
OFFICE.

WE DON'T PLAY GAMES, WE
DELIVER WHAT WE PROMISE.
HOME LOANS AS COMFORTABLE
AS YOUR HOME INSELF.

IN
OFFICE

IF YOU'RE IN THE MARKET FOR A
HOME LOAN.

MCU

COME TO THE FIRST, FIRST

FOLDERS

THE ONE YOU CAN BANK ON.

POP ON
THE ONE
YOU CAN
BANK ON

FIGURE 10.2   Typical Storyboard *(Courtesy Fry-Hammond-Barr, Inc.)*

You'll also notice that this script uses a middle column for time. This enables you to specify the amount of time devoted to each scene. In this script, the first scene lasts 5 seconds; the second sequence (two scenes—a wide shot of the store and a closeup of a product) lasts 10 seconds, and so on, up to 30 seconds. This time tally can be useful in helping you allocate the total time into segments for specific scenes.

The TV Storyboard

Because television is visual, it is often desirable for the producer or the client to see a graphic depiction of what each scene (called a *frame* in TV jargon) in a script will look like. This is accomplished in a *storyboard,* which shows, section by section, what the creator of the commercial had in mind, using a series of panels much like a cartoon strip.

Storyboards may be prepared by an individual, but more typically they're prepared by a creative team, often a writer and an artist. A carefully produced storyboard can help a producer or client decide on the suitability of an idea for a commercial. A storyboard is well worth the cost and effort when an advertiser is planning to spend thousands of dollars on a commercial. Figure 10.2 illustrates a professional storyboard. Note that the script is penciled in below the frames and production instructions are placed next to the frames. By contrast, the storyboard in Figure 10.3, although equally rudimentary in

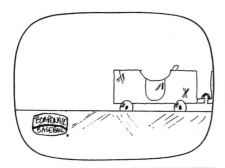

ANNCR: NOW FIND THE BEST PRIZES
INSIDE

SFX: SOUND OF COASTER BRAKES.

VIDEO: MS OF CAR

FREE BOXES OF CRACKER JACK AT
BOARDWALK AND BASEBALL.

SFX: SOUND OF COASTER BRAKES.

VIDEO: CU CRACKER JACK BOX

YOU MAY WIN

SFX: AMBIENT PARK AND CROWD
NOISE.
VIDEO: WS OF THREE PEOPLE

A NEW CAR,

SFX: SOUND OF ENGINE REVING.
VIDEO: CU, WOMAN WITH BOX

A CRUISE,

SFX: SOUND OF SHIP'S HORN.

VIDEO: CU, MAN WITH BOX

FREE PLANE TICKETS,

SFX: SOUND OF PLANE FLYING.

VIDEO: CU, WOMAN WITH BOX

OR ONE OF SEVEN OTHER GREAT
PRIZES!

SFX: PEOPLE SQUEELING HAPPILY
VIDEO: WS OF PEOPLE

CRACKER JACK AND

VIDEO: CU, CRACKER JACK BOX

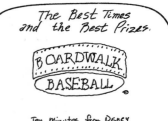

BOARDWALK AND BASEBALL. THE
BEST PRIZES....AND THE BEST
TIMES.

VIDEO: CU, NAME AND LOGO

FIGURE 10.3 Typical Storyboard *(Courtesy WOFL-TV, Orlando, Florida)*

terms of artwork, presents more detailed production instructions. Also, spoken audio copy, sound effects, and video instructions are placed below each frame, and all are typed rather than handwritten.

How many frames should you use in a commercial? A beginning copywriter should plan on using one frame for each four or five seconds of commercial time. Thus, a 10-second spot would have two video changes, a 30-second spot six to eight scene changes, and a 60-second spot twelve to fifteen scene changes. Of course, the actual number of scene changes depends on the pace of the spot. As a general rule, avoid long, static scenes—exposure to one scene for more than 10 seconds will cause the viewer's attention to wander. On the other hand, too many scene changes can confuse the viewer. To achieve the proper pacing, you should read your first draft aloud, acting it out as you go along. It should be apparent if it's too fast or has too many changes, thereby threatening to leave viewers behind.

Building a Storyboard

Which part of a storyboard comes first, the words or the pictures? There is no definitive answer; you should experiment with both ways to find the best pattern for you.

Still, it is always important to think visually in planning a spot. The storyboard focuses more directly on the visual element of the spot and can be planned more efficiently if you follow these steps:

1. Identify the distinctive feature you want to get across in the spot. This feature must stand out clearly, so it's important that you identify it at the outset. Look closely at the spot for the U.S. Navy in Figure 10.4. The distinctive feature is spelled out in the logo "Navy. It's not just a job, it's an adventure." This idea must be presented visually, and not just in the logo but in the rest of the spot as well.

2. Determine what benefit stems from the distinctive feature. In the Navy spot, the benefit is twofold: (a) the adventure and (b) the glamour of a job on the high seas.

3. Decide what setting will help convey the distinctive feature and its benefits. You must visualize a setting that will be appropriate to carry the spot. The Navy spot could do that best by showing activity on an aircraft carrier steaming in Hawaiian waters. Both the glamour and excitement are communicated with this setting.

4. Build on the setting to convey the message. A logical, reasonable progression of visual scenes is necessary. Remember: if the visual could carry the spot alone, you've done a good job. The Navy spot does that. It sets a general scene, follows with a number of shots of specific jobs on the carrier, and concludes with a launching of aircraft. The spot then turns to the distinctive feature at the conclusion. The progression of scenes is logical and easy to follow.

5. Place video instructions and audio lines for each scene under the frame. Use abbreviations, such as ECU (extreme closeup), to describe each scene. The drawing alone may not accurately reflect the desired type of scene.

These five steps can help you prepare a TV spot that accomplishes the job visually and establishes the framework for your script. Use them each time you prepare a storyboard, and you'll be more likely to prepare spots that sell.

Timing Copy

Like a radio spot, a TV spot must be timed carefully. The advertiser is paying for twenty, thirty, or sixty seconds and should get the exact amount, no more, no less. But timing a TV spot is not easy—especially when you're timing the draft of a spot at your keyboard.

U.S. Navy Public Service TV

"FLIGHT OPERATIONS": 30 Seconds (also available in :20 and :10 versions) QUAQ 0837

ANNCR: Flight Operations -
Hawaiian Islands

155 is the

go bird. 10° right rudder.

Bring up 155 on No. 2 elevator.

Cloud tops at 28,000 feet.
Alpha Hotel your wind is down
the deck

at 28 knots.

Launch aircraft.

Stand clear. Stand clear. Most
jobs promise you the world.

The Navy delivers. See your
recruiter.

Navy. It's not just a job, it's an
adventure.

NAVY. IT'S NOT JUST A JOB, IT'S AN ADVENTURE.

FIGURE 10.4 A Logo to Help Identify a Spot's Distinctive Feature *(Courtesy U.S. Navy)*

Your best bet is to do the same thing you would do with a radio spot—read it aloud as it will be presented on the air. This means that you will have to act out those portions of the spot that don't contain audio. If you don't allow sufficient time for the visual portions, the spot almost certainly will run too long when it's produced.

◆ Television Commercial Production Styles

Television commercials are usually classified according to their means of production. Although production styles are not mutually exclusive, the major styles you might encounter in a station with a small- to medium- sized market (not necessarily in this order) are studio, voice-over, and electronic field.

Studio Production

A variety of commercials, often low-budget ones, are produced in the studio using the station's cameras, control room equipment, and talent. Some spots may involve live talent who perform a scripted on-camera presentation. Live talent spots are often supplemented with studio techniques. Camera movements such as pans, tilts, or zooms may be used to create visual interest. Special effects such as dissolves or wipes may also be added to achieve visual variety. Often, the live talent will not appear on the screen for the entire spot but will be interspersed with still photographs or slide pictures. This mixing of production techniques can help achieve visual variety at a low cost.

The following spot shows the script for a typical studio production. An actor was used for most of the scenes, and a videotape segment was inserted to show a man leaving a bus. The announcer was heard but not seen.

VIDEO	AUDIO
OPEN ON SHOT OF A GUY SITTING ON THE FLOOR OF A STUDIO. HE IS DRESSED LIKE A TYPICAL STUDENT AND LIT DRAMATICALLY. BEHIND HIM ON THE WALL IS PROJECTED A TYPICAL COLLEGE CAMPUS SCENE WITH A STUDENT-FILLED COURTYARD. THE YOUNG MAN HOLDS UP THE FOLLOWING SUPER CARD: AN A.A. DEGREE GUARANTEES MY ADMISSION INTO A STATE UNIVERSITY.	Dramatic music up and under.
FLASH/FLARE TRANSITION BRINGS YOU TO A SLOW CU PULL OUT OF A STILL PHOTO STUCK IN BETWEEN GUITAR STRINGS. THE PHOTO IS OF THE YOUNG MAN PERFORMING WITH HIS BAND.	SFX: Transition sound
CUT BACK TO SHOT OF YOUNG MAN ON THE FLOOR, NOW WITH HIS GUITAR. HE HOLDS A NEW SUPER CARD: IN CASE THE BAND DOESN'T GET BACK TOGETHER. HE GIVES THE CAMERA A SLY SMILE.	SFX: Transition sound
FLARE TRANSITION TO REVEAL THE SAME SHOT MINUS THE GUY. VALENCIA LOGO IS PROJECTED ON THE WALL.	SFX: Transition sound
SLIDE PROJECTOR TRANSITION TO PROJECTED TAG. A BETTER PLACE TO START.	SFX: Slide changing music out

Courtesy of Fry-Hammond and Barr, Inc.

Voice-Over

Voice-overs involve both talent and studio production. In a voice-over, the talent (often a staff announcer) is heard but not seen. The entire visual portion of the spot may consist of still pictures or videotape.

Stills are inexpensive, are easy to produce, and can be done in color. This type of spot is common in local production because it does not require use of the studio or studio cameras—only the control room, still-frame storage unit, and announce booth are needed.

A similar approach is to use a voice-over videotape. This involves shooting and editing silent videotape with the announcer's voice then inserted over the tape. Again, the studio and studio cameras are not needed. Unlike still pictures, videotapes have the advantage of showing products in motion.

Electronic Field Production

An electronic field production (EFP) spot is similar to a taped voice-over spot except that all voice and video can be done on location. Small portable cameras (minicams) and portable videotape recorders are used to record the commercial on location and in color. The tape can be replayed immediately to judge the quality of the production. If it is not satisfactory, the spot can be retaped because videotape is reusable.

As a further variation, EFP spots can be enhanced with postproduction special effects in the TV studio. Wipes or dissolves can be added, and items such as phone numbers, prices, or addresses can be inserted over the tape produced in the field. This approach produces a more sophisticated commercial, but it is more complicated and costly than the other techniques discussed.

The Jack Rabbit commercial that follows used a variety of scenes. The first shot was done in the studio, but the rest was shot on location.

VIDEO	AUDIO
SHOT OF CAMERA AND FILM WITH FINGERS WALKING BY AND PICKING UP THE FILM.	So you've taken some pictures and now you have to have them developed.
SUPER DISCOUNT AND DRUG STORE. EXTERIOR SHOT OF JACK RABBIT.	You could take them to a discount store or drugstore, wait a few days, and hope for the best. Or you could take them to Jack Rabbit one-hour photo lab.
VARIOUS SHOTS OF FILM GOING THRU LAB.	Imagine, film developed while you watch, with no extra charge!
PRINTS COMING OFF ROLLER.	At Jack Rabbit, you get high-quality prints on Kodak paper in just one hour!
PAN OF PILE OF FILM.	And for a limited time when you have film developed, we give you a fresh roll of Jack Rabbit film free!
LOGO AND LOCATIONS.	Jack Rabbit, where good things develop fast!

Courtesy WSPA-TV, Spartanburg, South Carolina.

◆ Producing TV Commercials

As in the case of radio, you must know the jargon of the television industry so that your words and sketches can be translated into the desired movement on the screen. In some cases, you'll need to know the specific terminology for desired effects or camera movement. In other cases, you'll use a form of shorthand, especially in designating a desired camera shot. For example, MS is the abbreviation for *medium shot*. This is the jargon by which you, the copywriter, communicate visual instructions to the artists and producers. Your instructions should be specific and sufficiently detailed so that the producer can understand exactly what you intend. If the instructions do not include enough detail, the producer will have to guess at what you want. You may be present at the production session, and you may have the opportunity to offer advice and clarification. But the director usually has the final say about what's done once the copy is written.

Television audio terminology is basically the same as that used for radio, so it will not be covered here. You can refer back to Chapter 8 if you want to review the terms. To help you understand the major terms you need to know, we'll look at four categories of video terminology with which you should be familiar: (1) shot composition, (2) physical camera movement, (3) transitions, and (4) special effects. We also will examine such production considerations as graphics, animation, budgeting, and the question of whether to use film or tape.

Shot Composition

To write a shot-by-shot description of a TV commercial, you must use composition terminology to describe how much of the scene the viewer will see. The actual composition of the shot will be achieved by moving the camera or manipulating lens components (subjects that will be discussed later).

- **Long shot (LS) or wide shot (WS).** This shot provides a full view of a set or background, usually including a full-length view of the talent. Because this shot provides a distant perspective, it should be used sparingly. However, this type of picture does have one advantage: it can show the total visual setting, so it can be used at the beginning of a commercial as a cover or establishing shot that will introduce the entire scene.

- **Medium shot (MS).** This shot is the approximate midpoint between a closeup and a long shot. Medium shots show talent from approximately the waist up. They show more detail of the setting than long shots do because they are not as wide. A medium shot can thus be an effective establishing shot because it will have fewer distracting elements.

- **Closeup (CU).** The closeup is a narrow-angle picture that will present a full-screen image of an object or the talent's face. This shot is also used to focus on individual elements such as the talent's mouth or eyes. It can be used to show an entire object or parts of it. By focusing attention, the closeup gives added emphasis to key elements of the sales message.

The photo board for the U.S. Navy in Figure 10.4 includes examples of each type of shot. The first frame (upper left corner) shows an aircraft carrier in a long shot/ wide shot. The deckhand in frame three (upper right corner) is shown in a medium shot. The shot of the pilot in frame nine (third row, right side) is a closeup. Can you find other examples of these shots in Figure 10.4 or in other photo boards?

There are also variations of the shots just described. For example, a long shot may become a medium-long shot (MLS), a medium shot may become a medium-closeup (MCU), and a closeup may become an extreme- or tight closeup (ECU or TCU).

Finally, more specific shot composition may be called for in some instances. Anatomic and grouping designations offer more precise shot specifications. Terms such as *one-shot, two-shot,* and *three-shot* refer to a scene with one performer, a scene with two performers, and a scene with three performers, respectively. Terms such as *bust shot* and *waist shot* have obvious meanings. An *over-the-shoulder shot* uses the camera to look over a person's shoulder at another person.

Physical Camera Movement

A number of terms refer to instructions that call for movement of the entire camera and its base or movement of the camera alone while the camera base remains stationary. Here are the camera movement terms with which you need to be familiar:

- **Pan (left or right).** To pan is to move the camera either left or right without moving the camera base. A pan might be used to follow a moving object or person or to move the camera's focus from one stationary object to another.

- **Tilt (up or down).** To tilt is to move the camera either up or down without moving the camera base.

- **Dolly (in or out).** To dolly is to move the entire camera base either toward or away from the subject. When a dolly is called for, the subject usually remains stationary. A dolly is best avoided because it is difficult to achieve a smooth shot while pushing or pulling the entire camera. You can achieve a similar effect with better results by using a zoom lens.

- **Zoom.** Movement of a camera lever that adjusts the focal length of a zoom lens to move either toward or away from an object. The effect is similar to that achieved by dollying in or out, but the result is perfectly smooth. A zoom can be used to create all shots, from a long shot to a closeup, without moving the camera.

- **Boom or pedestal (up or down).** This refers to moving the camera up and down using the studio boom or pedestal. This movement can be used to create dramatic perspectives—for example, to move the camera up to look down on a subject.

Transitions

To arrange an orderly change of scenes, you should provide for transitions from one scene to the next. As a copywriter, you'll use transition terms to tell the director whether you want a rapid scene change, a slow scene change, or certain special effects.

- **Dissolve (DS or DISS).** This term refers to the overlapping fade-out of one picture and the fade-in of another. Dissolves are used for slow scene changes, although the speed of the dissolve can be controlled to fit a particular mood. Dissolves may also be used to indicate a change in time or to move from one place to another.

- **Cut or take.** This technique is the simplest transition from one TV commercial scene to another. The final frame of one scene changes instantaneously to that of another.

- **Fade (in or out).** To fade in is to gradually increase the intensity of a video picture from total black to full strength. A fade-out decreases the full brightness of a picture until the screen is dark. Fades can be used to achieve such effects as passage of time. In commercials, fades are used to fade in the opening and fade out the closing.

Special Effects

A number of terms used in television refer to electronic effects produced by the control-room switcher, a device used by the director to see and select the video portion of a production. Most special effects are either a combination of images or a manipulation of them. Because such effects are indeed special, they should be used only as needed to preserve their effectiveness. Here are some terms related to special effects that you'll need to know:

- **Wipe.** A wipe is an optical effect in which a line or object appears to move across the screen, revealing a new picture. A wipe may stop midway and become a split screen. Wipes may be horizontal, vertical, or diagonal; they may come from either side (closing doors) or sweep around like the hands of a clock (iris or circular).
- **Super.** This effect (short for *superimpose*) is a very useful sales tool for showing a picture of one object over another.
- **Split screen.** In this special effect, two or more scenes are visible simultaneously on separate parts of the screen—for example, the screen is split to show two families independently reacting to a given problem.
- **Freeze frame.** A technique for holding a particular scene on the screen for a desired length. It is often used at the close of a commercial to highlight the advertiser's name or slogan.
- **Character generator (CG).** An electronic device using a typewriter-like keyboard to produce printed words optically.
- **Key.** An electronic effect that permits an image (usually lettering) to be cut into a background image. Phone numbers, addresses, and so forth are best produced by keying in the additional material.
- **Matte.** An electronic process similar to keying. Often, the terms *matting* and *keying* are used interchangeably. In commercial production, matting often refers to the electronic laying in of a background scene, such as a client's showroom or storefront, behind a foreground image, such as an announcer.
- **Chromakey.** The electronic combining of two video sources into a composite picture, creating the illusion that the two sources are physically together.
- **Digital video effects (DVE) unit.** A device that permits manipulation of the image by expanding or compressing it, thus modifying its size, shape, and position in a variety of ways. The DVE enables the director to apply a variety of visual effects, such as image rotation, bouncing, or splitting, to achieve a special effect in a spot.

Additional Terminology

The production of television commercials involves so much specialized jargon that much of it is difficult to categorize. The following terms are included to provide a fuller understanding of this specialized language:

- **A-B rolling.** Switching between two or more videotape machines to prepare a composite tape.
- **Aspect ratio.** The ratio between the horizontal (width) and the vertical (height) measurement of the television screen. The ratio in analog television is 4 units wide by 3 units high. In HDTV the ratio is 16 units wide by 9 units high.
- **Crawl.** The gradual horizontal movement of printed words, such as details of a special sale, on the screen. The vertical movement of such words is called a *roll*. Graphics generators have the capability to produce these effects.
- **Depth of field.** The distance within which a subject can move toward or away from a stationary camera without going out of focus.

- **Frame.** The field of view in any particular shot.
- **Montage.** A sequence of short scenes, usually cuts or wipes, that together convey an idea more effectively than any one of them could alone.
- **Postproduction.** Any production work that occurs after taping. Postproduction activity in TV commercials usually involves either editing videotape or adding special effects to tape already shot.
- **Still-frame storage unit.** A digital device used to store individual frames, any of which can be electronically recalled instantly. It is often used in place of slides or camera cards.
- **Studio card/camera card.** A poster board of any size that can be shot by a studio camera. The material may consist of a business logo, a pasteup picture, and so on. Whereas "cam cards" were once shot live in commercials, they are now more frequently used to shoot artwork that will be stored electronically for later use in commercial production.
- **Titles.** Letters or other printed material appearing on the screen, such as a telephone number, store name, or address.
- **Voice-over (VO).** A narrator who is not seen.
- **VTR.** Abbreviation for videotape recorder.

Using Special Effects

The special effects described previously, if used properly, can enhance a spot, but they should not be overused. Here is a spot that makes extensive—and effective—use of special effects. Read the video instructions carefully.

VIDEO	AUDIO
ZOOM IN "PRE-LABOR DAY SELLATHON" GRAPHIC OVER STARFIELD FADE OUT	It's Bellows TV and Appliances Pre-Labor Day Sellathon!
BRING IN "11 HOURS" FROM TOP "FRIDAY, SEPT 1" FROM BOTTOM	For 11 incredible hours this Friday you can save in every department.
CUT TO WS OF APPLIANCE DEPT. SUPER: SAVE UP TO 40%	Save up to 40% on appliances …
CUT TO PAN OF TVS & BIG SCREENS SUPER: SAVE UP TO 50%	Save up to 50% on color TVs and big screen TVs …
CUT TO PULL OUT OF VCRS SUPER: SAVE UP TO 30%	And up to 30% on VCRs!
DISSOLVE TO STARFIELD WITH BELLOWS SELLATHON SUPER	Take a look at Bellows Sellathon prices …
DISSOLVE OUT SUPER AND BRING IN FLOATING PIC OF MAGNAVOX TV WITH PRICE SUPER …TURN FLOATING PICTURE OF TV TO REVEAL ZENITH CAMCORDER WITH PRICE	This Magnavox 19" color TV with remote … only $239. This Zenith VHS-camcorder only 2.3 pounds … just $799.
DISSOLVE CAMCORDER OUT DVE FROM CENTER "FRIDAY ONLY DOORS OPEN AT 10 AM"	Don't miss this Pre-Labor Day Sellathon. One day only! Doors open at 10 a.m. Friday for 11 big hours … at all three Bellows locations.

Courtesy Bellows TV & Appliances.

Consider what this spot did. Words were brought into the picture from the top and bottom of the screen; the product was suspended in air; and a starburst appeared behind one scene. These are some of the effects that can be achieved with a digital video effects unit. A DVE unit can greatly expand the special effects capability of a production department, although not all stations and systems have one.

Using Graphics

Written graphics are generally produced with a special effects device called a character generator (CG). Graphics can be used to show prices, store hours, phone numbers, and so on. Look at the video instructions in the Bellows spot. Can you identify the items that appeared graphically?

Graphics can be used in two ways. First, you can reinforce audio with graphics. For example, if you say, "Up to two-thousand-dollar trade-in on any used car," you can also super, "Up to $2,000 trade-in" over the scene.

Second, you can show graphically information you won't include in the audio. Suppose you want to keep the audio to a minimum in a spot for a furniture sale. You might have the announcer read, "Hundreds of rockers and recliners by famous name manufacturers." Over these lines you could super, "Reductions up to 40 percent." This way you've included key sales data without squandering precious audio time.

Study the scripts in this chapter to see how graphics and other special effects are used. Check with your instructor to see how sophisticated your use of special effects should be.

Film versus Tape

Local television stations seldom shoot their commercials on film, but film is often used by advertising agencies to produce commercials for national and regional distribution. Such commercials are usually shot on 16- or 35-mm film when a larger budget is available for commercials with wider distribution.

Film has several advantages over videotape. It tends to give products, actors, and settings a softer, more cinematic image than videotape. Film editing can also be more precise than videotape editing, and film is preferred if certain optical effects are desired.

Despite these advantages, videotape is the choice of local TV stations especially since the advent of digital technology. The primary reason is speed: tape requires no processing, so directors and advertisers can immediately examine whatever has been shot. If retakes are necessary, they can be done immediately—no need to wait until the tape is developed, printed, and copied. Further, videotape produces a sharp, realistic, though sometimes stark picture that few can distinguish from film.

Animation

In animation, movement is created by drawing a number of still pictures and exposing them one frame at a time on film or videotape. Traditional animation is costly because it requires considerable artwork and production effort. Computerized animation is quicker and costs less. Nevertheless, if live action cannot produce the intended effect, animation may be the best option. For example, cartoon characters such as Tony the Tiger and Smokey the Bear have been used successfully. The same effect could hardly be achieved by having an actor dress in costume and appear in a live commercial. Animated characters can be used to produce a unique spot, either by appearing alone or in combination with actors. Remember, however, that either approach requires a substantial budget, which most local accounts won't be able to afford. The spot in Figure 10.5 illustrates the use of animation.

GENERAL  ELECTRIC

GE WX ELITE PLUS HEAT PUMP

TV Spot for Local Dealer use
:25 with :05 open tag
Produced for Trane CAC, Inc., by Caraway Kemp Communications, Jacksonville, Florida

Hot weather . . .

and rising utility bills are on their way again!

But now you can help beat 'em both with a new,

GE super efficient Elite Plus heat pump system. It cools in summer . . . heats in winter and can save on energy costs all year long.

The GE Elite Plus . . . our most efficient heat pump line . . . and it's a Weathertron® !

Beat the heat this summer . . .

and help save on energy costs all year.

(Dealer name, address & phone)

 5 Animation in a TV Spot *(Courtesy Caraway Kemp Communications, Inc.)*

Television Soundtracks as Radio Spots

In an effort to save money, advertisers often try to make a television commercial do double duty by using the soundtrack of a television spot as a radio campaign. This seldom works unless the television soundtrack uses radio's strength with sound design and music. As we have seen previously, radio commercials are written to appeal to the ear, whereas television spots emphasize a visual appeal. Unless a television message de-emphasizes the visual and emphasizes audio, it probably won't make for an effective message on radio.

Keeping the Spot Producible

The technical sophistication of your station or cable system will determine the nature of the effects you can use. Get to know the directors and learn what is possible at the station for which you work. As a writer, you might not have to do production, but you'll be expected to write spots that can be produced reasonably. Budget, studio time, and the type of special effects the station can accomplish will determine what you can do. Even on a low budget, however, you can create considerable action by moving the camera. You can have the camera pan or tilt, zoom in or out. Virtually any TV station should be able to accomplish such movement. Many stations, however, won't have all the specialized production equipment you might want to use.

A warning: Keep the production simple and to the point. Don't assume a tricky effect will sell the product. Demonstrate the benefits of the product or business and don't let production techniques get in the way.

If the client wants to appear in a commercial with his or her family, proceed very cautiously. Ask the family to say and do very little. Show them in the spot, but don't give them speaking lines unless you're sure they can handle them. People off the street are obviously not professional talent. If you really want to show a typical family on a shopping spree, you'll need a budget to hire professional talent.

Remember also that the spots you write will appear adjacent to higher-budget national or regional spots. Your local, low-budget commercial must look and sound sufficiently professional to hold your viewers' attention.

The Production Budget

Another factor that determines whether your spot can actually be produced is the amount of money the advertiser is willing to spend for production (beyond the station's charge for time). Advertisers want their spots to look professional and to sell their products. But they also want their advertising dollar to buy them the maximum number of appearances on the air. For example, the advertiser who spends $5,000 on your station probably won't want to spend $1,000 of that amount to pay for producing the spot. That wouldn't be cost-effective unless the advertiser planned to use the commercial for a long time or planned to use the spot on a number of stations simultaneously. Even then, production costs would be kept to a minimum.

The account executive will often determine the amount of money the client is willing to spend on producing the spot before a contract is signed. If the account executive is knowledgeable about production, the contract may specify the method—studio production, field production, or other means. In other instances, the account executive may consult with the copywriter before signing the contract to determine what method of production can be used for a given amount of money. In yet other cases, you may be assigned the responsibility of selecting the best method of spending the production budget.

Although it is difficult to generalize, the following methods represent, from least to most expensive, the three basic approaches to spot production:

- **Still photos or videotape with announcer voice-over.** Stills are inexpensive to prepare, and use of the studio is not necessary for production. Videotape without sound is also inexpensive. A staff announcer can deliver the audio portion of the script. Final production of such a spot occurs in the studio.

- **Studio production.** This method requires use of the studio and its cameras and might include still photos or other graphic aids. The complexity of the production and the talent involved—staff announcer or outside talent—will affect the cost of studio production.

- **Electronic field production.** The cost of EFP production is high because the portable videotape equipment must be transported to location. Costs will be even higher if special effects are added from the studio switcher during postproduction. Still, this is one of the most common approaches to the production of spots.

Production costs vary widely according to the size of the market, production methods used, talent involved, and special editing effects added during postproduction.

Advertising agencies also handle production for their clients, but most agencies do not have their own studios and production crews. Depending on market size, agencies negotiate the cost of production with specialized production firms or with local television stations. Representatives of the agency then attend the production session as supervisors.

◆ Guidelines for Writing Television Spots

Most of the rules for writing radio commercials also apply to television audio, but the emphasis on video requires elaboration. The following section provides guidelines for writing television content.

Gaining Attention

Gaining attention early in a television spot is just as important as it is in a radio commercial. If you don't gain viewer attention in the opening seconds, chances are you won't gain it at all. Television is primarily a visual medium, so let's begin with the opening shot of a TV spot. One school of thought maintains that the opening shot should be a long, establishing shot that sets the scene for the viewer. In other words, the video sets the scene, and the audio introduces the sales pitch.

Suppose that you're asked to sell the large selection of used cars at Honest John's Emporium. An establishing shot with John standing in front of a row of cars may be the best way to orient viewers.

Alternatively, you could use a closeup shot in the opening—a shot that will focus on a specific person or item. In this approach, the location may not be important, or you might want to hide it until later in the commercial. If your goal, for instance, is to convince the viewers of Honest John's integrity, it may be preferable to begin the commercial with a closeup shot of John dressed in a business suit. The car lot can be shown later or not shown at all.

Study this spot for *TV Weekly*, in which closeup shots are used until the final scene. The goal of this spot is to focus attention on the magazine, so closeup shots are appropriate.

VIDEO	AUDIO
TABLETOP IN LIVING ROOM SETTING . . . HAND PLACES OLD VERSION OF TV WEEKLY ON TABLE.	ANNCR: The State and Columbia Record's popular television guide, TV Weekly, has been transformed into a thicker, new compact size that you can keep at your fingertips all week long.
HANDS COME FROM THE SIDE AND SQUEEZE THE MAGAZINE VERTICALLY . . . HANDS COME IN FROM TOP AND BOTTOM AND SQUEEZE THE MAGAZINE HORIZONTALLY . . . MAGAZINE DISSOLVES FROM OLD SQUEEZED VERSION TO PRESENT ONE.	
CUT TO CLOSEUP OF TITLE AND ZOOM OUT TO SHOW HAND OPENING COVER, TURNING PAGES . . . DAILY PROGRAM LISTING PAGE SQUEEZES OUT FROM TURNING PAGES ON CURVED TRAJECTORY. PICTORIAL EXAMPLE OF FEATURE . . . EDITORIAL HEADLINE . . . LOGOS FROM HBO, CINEMAX, THE MOVIE CHANNEL, USA, CNN, AND ESPN SLIDE ACROSS THE SCREEN FROM RIGHT TO LEFT IN RAPID SUCCESSION.	This 56-page magazine contains weekly listings for 18 channels on programming from 7:00 A.M. to 2:00 A.M. daily. TV Weekly offers feature articles, editorial reviews, plus extensive movie and sports information. It's the only television guide you'll need.
SQUEEZE SPLIT REVEALS SATURDAY RECORD AND SUNDAY'S STATE . . . HAND DROPS TV WEEKLY ON TOP OF DISPLAY.	Look for it Saturdays in the Columbia Record, and Sundays in the State.
CUT TO SHOT OF PAPERBOY RIDING BICYCLE WHO THROWS NEWSPAPER AT CAMERA LENS . . . SCENE FREEZES, AND TV WEEKLY LOGO WITH SUPER: SUBSCRIBE TODAY 771–8380 SQUEEZES FROM NEWSBOY'S HAND TO 80% FULL FRAME, LEAVING FREEZE SHOT AROUND EDGE.	Call today and have it delivered to your doorstep.

Courtesy WIS-TV, Columbia, South Carolina.

Of course there is no single "correct" shot that will gain attention in a television commercial. Careful analysis of the client and his or her sales goals will help you determine whether a wide shot or a closeup is most appropriate in a given spot.

Finally, don't forget the AIDA formula we discussed in Chapter 6. It applies as much to television as to radio.

Identifying the Client or Product Name

Just as you must interest people in watching the commercial, you must also make certain that you identify the name of the client, product, or service clearly. The message will be ineffective if people can recall some of the action, and perhaps even the general product category, but not the name of the advertiser.

Implant the advertiser's name early and repeat it as often as you can without making the commercial dull or obnoxious. The name of the product or client can be presented both aurally and visually, so you'll have sufficient opportunity to include it. It's also wise to include the name of the client or product in a slogan used in a commercial. For example, the slogan "Visine. Gets the dry out," is short, catchy, and easy to repeat, and it includes the client's name. Above all, don't expect the viewer to remember the client's or product's name if it's presented only once. Include it as often as you reasonably can, and conclude the spot with the name as well. The conclusion is the part of the spot that viewers are most likely to remember, so it's essential that you conclude with strong sponsor identification.

Examine the photo board for the Car Vac commercial in Figure 10.6. Notice that closeup shots of the Car Vac are used to show both the product and product name. The product name is established early in the commercial, and the spot concludes with both the product name and the advertiser's sales theme.

Balancing Audio and Video

The two vehicles of television communication—audio and video—must relate to each other if a commercial is to be cohesive. Nothing is more distracting than to have what is shown conflict with what is said. For example, if the audio for a restaurant spot says, "Choose from the selection of terribly tempting desserts," the video should not show people entering the restaurant, a family eating dinner, or a smiling waitress. Showing the items as they're described lets the viewer comprehend them.

A balanced audio and video presentation can also be used to establish the client's or product's name. When you first mention the name, you should show it. Look at this example:

VIDEO	AUDIO
OPEN ON WS OF COUPLE STUDYING MENU IN RESTAURANT WINDOW. SLOW ZOOM IN AS THEY TURN TO CAMERA AND SHAKE HEADS "NO."	ANNCR (VO): You don't have to be wealthy to dine out.
CUT TO FESTIVAL HOUSE LOGO	At Festival House you can get delicious home-cooked meals at affordable prices . . .

With this approach, you show the client's name as it's spoken. You've also introduced the client's name early. As a result, you are off to a good start in presenting a message that will sell.

You should also balance the audio and video in the closing shot. Either present the client's logo as the final shot and reinforce it with audio, or accompany the final shot with a superimposed title that repeats the audio script word for word. If the announcer's final line is "Festival House . . . . fine food at affordable prices," show that wording on the screen either by itself or supered over a visual. This balances the audio and video and reinforces the key sales idea that you hope to leave in the mind of the viewer.

Examine the script for this commercial for Charles Towne Landing. The spot is built around a slogan, "Families doing things together," which is presented both aurally and visually at the close of the commercial. Notice how each line of audio is balanced by a compatible visual scene.

BBDO
Batten, Barton, Durstine & Osborn, Inc.

Client: **BLACK & DECKER**		Time: **30 SECONDS**
Product: **CAR VAC**	Title: **"GREAT PICK-UP"**	Comml. No.: **BKPT 4013**

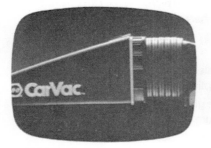

This is Car Vac. . .
from Black & Decker's Car Care Series.

Plug it in,

rev it up,

feel its power. Black & Decker's Car
Vac starts fast,

It's great on the curves,

great on the straightaways.

Its 16 foot cord really goes the distance.

Watch it corner,

maneuver through tight spots.

Car Vac handles like a dream and even
stops on a dime.

Car Vac. It's got great pick-up

because it's the only car vacuum that's
built like a Black & Decker.

FIGURE 10.6 Photo Board with Strong Product Identification *(Courtesy Michael L. Ianzito/Batten, Barton, Durstine & Osborn, Inc.)*

VIDEO	AUDIO
A-&-B-ROLLS FOR *DISSOLVES* BETWEEN SHOTS AS NOTED:	(Music under . . . #105 "Feelin' Free" . . .)
FAMILY WALKS UP TO PAVILION; START SHOT BETWEEN LITTLE BOY'S LEGS & FATHER'S	At Charles Towne Landing, families do things together! They picnic—Dad can grill hot dogs or hamburgers. . . .
DAD AT GRILL W/HOT DOG TO BOY; PULL-OUT TO MOM & KIDS.	
FAMILY BIKES PAST LAGOON.	Or bicycle the many trails as a family. (Music up for split second . . .)
CLOSEUP MAST OF ADVENTURE SHIP & PULLOUT TO FAMILY COMING TO IT.	Imagine ghosts of sailors past on board the Adventure . . .
FAMILY WALKS ACROSS BRIDGE IN GARDENS; USE TODDLER HELD UP.	Reflect on the beauty of the English Park gardens . . .
PUMA CAT & PULLOUT TO FAMILY.	Discover native animals in Charleston's only zoo . . .
FAMILY LEANS OUT FROM LOG FORTRESS.	Roam the 1670 fortifications . . .
FAMILY WATCHING SETTLERS' ACTIVITIES.	Visit dwellings like those of the first settlers!
FAMILY W/FEET IN FOUNTAIN. SCRIPT SUPER:	Charles Towne Landing is . . .
CHARLES TOWNE LANDING . . . FAMILIES DOING THINGS TOGETHER	Families doing things together!

Courtesy WCIV-TV, Charleston, South Carolina.

Emphasizing One Main Idea

As with a radio spot, you should limit a television spot to one main idea. Analyze the information and break it into major and minor selling points. Once you have done this, identify the single strongest sales key and emphasize it in your spot. Don't try to include a number of selling points. Even if you can logically include a number of ideas in the spot, viewers probably won't remember them.

A commercial for a restaurant illustrates what should not be done. The commercial begins by describing the food and service at the restaurant. Midway through the spot a second idea is introduced. The words "Use our executive limousine service" are supered over shots of the food available at the restaurant. It's a second idea, one that has no clear relationship to the first, and one that would better be presented in a separate spot. It draws attention away from the main idea and weakens the sales message.

Avoiding Overwriting

Because television is a visual medium, you should use the video to present more than half the message. As the old cliché says, a picture is worth a thousand words, and it remains true of television commercials.

Of course, you'll want audio copy, but don't use more words than you have to. Circumstances will vary. In some spots, you'll have to rely heavily on audio. This may be true when you have a lot of complicated material to present or when you want a version of the TV spot to be used on radio. In the latter case, the audio must stand alone, reinforced only by exposures to the spot on television, where both audio and video present the message. In other situations, you'll want the video to be the primary message, supplemented with only a minimal amount of audio.

Also keep in mind that television spots as a rule are shorter than radio spots, making it all the more important that each word and scene count. Although 60-second spots are common in radio, 30 seconds is the most common length on television. Television occasionally uses 60-second spots, but many agencies and advertisers believe that shorter spots are more appropriate for cost and viewer attention. Ten-second spots are often used when the message is uncomplicated, and fifteen-second spots, usually run back to back as "split thirties," are gaining popularity with advertisers.

Stressing the Final Shot

The final shot in a spot represents your last opportunity to make an impression on the viewer. As a result, most copywriters conclude TV spots with the name of the sponsor or product, the slogan if there is one, and the address or location. The information may be presented aurally or visually or in some combination of the two methods.

Refer back to the spot for Jack Rabbit Photo on page 146. Note how it concludes with the logo "Jack Rabbit, where good things develop fast," in both audio and video, as well as with the locations of Jack Rabbit Photo. Look also at the Car Vac spot for Black and Decker in Figure 10.6. Here, the final two frames are used to show the product, its name, and the slogan. Finally, examine the script for Charles Towne Landing on pages 158. In this spot, the sponsor's name and slogan are supered over the final scene, and the slogan is presented aurally.

Make it a point to use the conclusion as a final reminder. If the viewer remembers nothing but the name of the sponsor or product, the slogan, and the location, you've done your job. Try watching TV spots closely. You'll see that the conclusion of a spot, often no more than three seconds, is the time to show and tell the key sales information in the spot.

➤ POINTS TO REMEMBER

- The primary advantage of television as an advertising vehicle is that it can use sight, sound, and motion.
- Television scripts are best timed by reading them aloud and acting them out.
- The major styles of television production are: (1) studio production, (2) voice-over, and (3) electronic field production.
- The television script is divided into two columns. The left column is for visual instructions and the right for audio.

- A television storyboard shows what the creator of a spot had in mind frame by frame.
- TV spot production should be kept simple. Trick effects do not necessarily equate with good selling.
- The least costly approach to TV spot production is still photos with voice-over. Studio production is somewhat more costly, and electronic field production is the most expensive.
- Advertising on cable TV is less expensive than advertising on over-the-air TV.

- The opening seconds of a TV spot are crucial because they either gain viewer attention or lose it.
- Television spots run between programs are known as adjacencies.
- The name of the advertiser or product should be presented early in a spot and repeated as often as possible without boring or annoying the audience.
- Audio and video must relate to each other in a television spot.
- A television spot should be limited to one main idea. Secondary ideas should be used only if they have a clear relationship to the main idea.
- Each spot should conclude with the sponsor/product name and slogan.
- Graphics should be used to show key sales data.
- Spots scheduled within television program positions are called participations.
- The video should tell the story. Audio should not be overwritten.
- Television commercials suffer from the clutter of announcements placed in programs.

EXERCISES

Exercise 1*

This is an exercise in the planning of the visual portion only of a TV spot. Do *not* use audio. Include enough visual sales data that the point of the spot will come across without audio. Here are some hints: Use close-up shots of the product showing the product name; use graphics to identify features; use videotape or pictures.

COPY INFORMATION

Product: The Majik Mower by Lawncleaner. Dealer will demonstrate the mower. See the Yellow Pages for dealers.

Features: Variable height settings, self-propelled. Its 4.5-hp engine can cut all types of grass, wet or dry. Majik Mower is a rear-bag model (the bag that picks up clippings is in rear of mower, not on its side). This feature allows for closer mowing near bushes, fences, and buildings.

Special feature: The easy-starting engine.

Exercise 2

Write a 30-second two-column television spot for Yourtown Spas and Fitness Centers. Prepare a spot using electronic field production and graphics.

COPY INFORMATION

Advertiser: Yourtown Spas and Fitness Centers, with four locations in Yourtown.

Facilities: The Centers have swimming pools, hot mineral whirlpools, sunrooms, and scientific exercise equipment. Trained personnel are available.

Emphasis: Stress figure proportioning.

Locations: See the Yellow Pages.

Exercise 3

Prepare a complete storyboard with both audio and video for a thirty-second spot for Quality TV & Stereo, 1620 Grant Street. This spot will be done in your studio, and Harvey Jones, the store owner, will deliver the spot. The event is a video sale. Sample specials include the following: MAG 27" cable-ready color TV with remote, $239.99; regular price is $349. Datawise brand VCR with remote, $225.99; regular price is $269. Brand-name camcorders from $495.99. Use graphics to show sales data. Cameras, VCRs, and so on will be available to show in the spot. Develop a slogan to use in this spot.

---

*At the end of the exercises, storyboards are provided for you to complete each assignment.

Exercise 1

STORYBOARD

Exercise 2

STORYBOARD

Exercise 3

STORYBOARD

Types of Television Commercials

To the typical television viewer, commercials may seem easy to prepare. That's almost never the case, however. A television commercial whose message grabs the viewer's attention and is remembered requires careful planning, writing, and production. Gimmicks alone won't sell. The mind best remembers an idea that is presented in an interesting, cohesive, and relevant manner. That's where careful preparation comes into play.

Your primary task as a television copywriter is to interest the viewer in each spot you write. Your task is somewhat easier than that of the radio copywriter because you can use both sight and sound. But simply pointing a television camera at a person or object usually doesn't produce an effective sales pitch. You must structure the video and audio so that the message involves the viewer and sells the product or service.

If the commercial you've written is weak—if it's uninteresting, confusing, or poorly defined—you'll have lost your sales opportunity. But viewers don't have to leave the room to miss a commercial message. They can simply pay limited attention to a spot that doesn't involve them. You must strive for viewer involvement with each spot you write. In this chapter, we'll examine what you must do to organize and structure a television commercial that will interest and involve the viewer.

◆ The Copy Platform

To write a cohesive television spot, you need to know as much as possible about the client or service. Whom does the firm want to reach? What geographic area does it want to cover? What are the product's main selling points? Who are the principal competitors, and what approaches do they use? Gather as much information as you can. To avoid being overwhelmed, develop a copy platform that helps you identify the most important items for your sales theme.

As you'll recall from our discussion in Chapter 7, the sales theme is the key to a persuasive message. The message can be especially effective if it is developed as a sales slogan, a memorable idea presented in an original phrase. A sales slogan helps viewers recall the advertiser or product name and its selling features. Television can present the sales slogan aurally or visually, or in both ways. A carefully developed sales slogan can be your best aid for recall.

◆ Choosing the Approach

After you've analyzed your material and planned your sales theme, you'll be ready to choose an approach for delivering the information. The approach is the blueprint, the pattern you follow in presenting your sales message. This is the last phase of your planning, and it requires care because choosing the proper style is crucial to creating an effective commercial.

Television spots, like radio spots, may be either hard sell or soft sell. Hard sell, you'll recall, refers to direct selling of the client's product or service, and soft-sell spots use an understated, suggestive approach to create a positive image of the client or the products. Only a few basic styles or approaches are used in television commercials, though there are many variations. We'll stick to six of the most common styles of television spots. They work equally well for local or national copywriters.

Note that the approaches overlap. Almost all spots, for example, include a problem, a solution, and a result. Nevertheless, you should adopt one style as your primary method of presentation. You'll find that choosing an approach will focus your thinking and help you to write a spot that will be noticed. Note also that although we use the terms *style* and *approach,* other professionals use such terms as *technique, format,* or *structure.* The words *style* and *approach* seem most helpful to us in describing ways of organizing commercial data.

The Problem–Solution Approach

One of the most common types of TV commercial is the problem–solution spot. This approach has been used successfully for a variety of products. It works best when the qualities of the product can be demonstrated. A situation might be part of the spot, but it should be subordinate to the problem–solution approach.

Here are some characteristics of an effective problem–solution commercial:

■ The problem identified in the spot must be believable. Whether it is bad breath or water spots on fine crystal, it must be a problem the target audience can relate to. If the problem isn't one the viewer has experienced, heard about, or wants to avoid, the commercial could be offensive.

■ The product must be introduced as a natural, realistic solution to the problem. Too many gimmicks or incredible solutions do little for the credibility of the product. The product's ability to solve the problem and the manner of presentation must seem reasonable to the viewer.

■ The product should be introduced as a solution to the problem, and the solution should show the user experiencing benefits or achieving satisfaction after using the product. That is the high point of this type of commercial. The user may feel better because he or she has solved an annoying problem, saved money, or increased his or her status. Just as the problem must be believable, the demonstration of benefits must also relate to something familiar to the viewer.

■ The name of the product or service must be identified clearly, and it must be associated with the problem the product claims to solve.

The Bank Atlantic commercial in Figure 11.1 illustrates a consumer problem. The problem is evident, and the business is easily identified as the solution to the problem.

The Demonstration Approach

The demonstration spot is one of the mainstays of television because it draws on TV's greatest strength—its ability to show the product being used. It is easiest to demonstrate functioning products like a lawnmower or a reclining rocker. But products whose operation is not observable, like a flashlight battery or an animal flea collar, can also be demonstrated, although it takes more imagination. If a demonstration is properly implemented, it can involve the viewer in the commercial message and provide convincing reasons to buy the product.

Follow these rules in using a demonstration in a commercial:

1. Be certain the significance of the demonstration is clear to the viewer. If you think viewers might not understand, tell them what you plan to do before you do it.

2. Get to the point quickly. Avoid complicated dialog or situations.

3. Write more video than audio into a demonstration spot. The video portion of your spot must be strong because it carries the demonstration. Check your final draft. If the point of the demonstration isn't clear from the video portion alone, rework the spot.

4. Use closeup and extreme closeup shots to enhance the demonstration. Let the viewer see the product as he or she would see it in person. Don't show parts of the product that are too small for the camera to show clearly.

BANKATLANTIC

Television

Announcer: For those of you who are sick and tired . . .

. . . of being ignored, snubbed and kicked around . . .

. . . by big, cold, impersonal banks . . . here's a thought.

Big Man: Ow!!

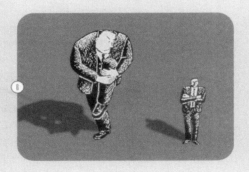

BankAtlantic. The power of positive banking.

FIGURE 11.1 Problem-Solution Commercial *(Courtesy Philip E. Cohen, Harris-Drury-Cohen)*

5. Don't use a lot of technical jargon in the audio portion of the script. Show the viewer how the product works.

6. If possible, show the demonstration from beginning to end. Don't cut away unless necessary. Cuts may create doubts in the viewer's mind and draw attention from the sales message. If you must cut away—for example, to suggest passage of time—tell the viewer what you're doing. Don't make the viewer guess about your use of the cutaway.

7. Keep your message simple and direct. A complicated message and a complicated demonstration won't be remembered.

8. Be certain the product name is displayed prominently. Use the demonstration to show the benefits the viewer might realize from using the product.

9. Prove that the claims for the product are true. Use the demonstration to show the product doing what you've promised.

The Heat 'n Strip spot in Figure 11.2 both shows and tells the audience what the demonstration will do. Note that the visual portion alone is strong enough that it could carry the spot by itself. Extreme closeup shots are used to show the product at work. A concluding shot offers proof that the product works by showing a beautifully restored mantle. The product name is clearly established at the beginning and end of the spot.

The Rubbermaid spot in Figure 11.3 is a somewhat different demonstration. This spot, appropriately titled the "Torture Test," demonstrates the durability of Rubbermaid products. Even with the abuse the product takes, it bounces back into shape. Notice here that the camera shots are wider than in the Heat 'n Strip spot because it was necessary to show a bigger product and more pronounced action.

The Situation Approach

The situation commercial tells a story that establishes a reason for the presence of the product. The story, sometimes called a slice of life, must have a simple plot that can be easily understood. For example, boy meets girl in laundry room. They share a washer and use her detergent because his leaves ring-around-the-collar. The detergent solves that problem. Boy asks girl for date. She declines.

A carefully developed story can gain attention and involve the viewer in the situation. If viewers find the story believable, they will probably feel that the product will work as well for them as it did for the characters in the story. Here are some guidelines for writing situation commercials:

1. Develop a situation that is logical, believable, and easy to follow. Zany, unrealistic situations aren't appropriate. Even though almost anything goes on TV, the situation must be plausible. You'll have less than a minute to develop the situation, so you must keep it simple. The situation is the key to the spot. Present the product subtly.

2. Use the opening of your story to attract attention and involve viewers. The opening sets the stage for the rest of the spot, often by introducing a problem.

3. Use the middle of your story to elaborate on the situation, usually by introducing the product as a solution to the problem.

4. In the final stage, have the product solve the problem. The situation concludes with the characters displaying the satisfaction they've achieved from the product.

5. Be sure to develop the situation logically. Each step must relate to the one that precedes it and the one that follows it.

6. Present the product in a way that promises a beneficial result—the viewer will be healthier, more secure, more confident, and so forth.

7. Identify the product name clearly.

BBDO
Batten, Barton, Durstine & Osborn, Inc.

Client: **BLACK & DECKER**		Time: **30 SECONDS**
Product: **HEAT 'N STRIP**	Title: **"MANTLE"**	Comml. No.: **BKPT 4023**

Somewhere in this room is a beautiful antique,

hidden under layer upon layer of paint.

Now Black & Decker will find it with Heat 'n Strip

the remarkable paint stripper that works with hot air, not caustic chemicals.

Heat 'n Strip bubbles away years of paint

with less work

and a lot less mess.

It makes all other ways of stripping paint antique.

Heat 'n Strip. . .
It's built like a Black & Decker.

FIGURE 11.2 Demonstration Commercial *(Courtesy Michael L. Ianzito/Batten, Barton, Durstine & Osborn, Inc.)*

FIGURE 11.3 Action-Oriented Demonstration Commercial *(Courtesy Rubbermaid Incorporated)*

The Ætna commercial in Figure 11.4 uses a believable setting. The client's name is introduced early and logically. The situation is developed to show a happy event—the wedding—with the father of the bride displaying satisfaction because he's used Ætna's services.

The Spokesperson Approach

In a spokesperson commercial, an individual delivers the sales message on camera. It's a common approach both nationally and locally (where automotive dealers seem to love it). Advertisers often use the spokesperson approach because they feel that consumers will respond to a commercial if they identify with the personality or admire the person delivering the message.

A spokesperson may be a well-known person who endorses the product or service, or a person who claims to have used the product and cites personal experience in the form of a testimonial. Most of the factors in choosing a spokesperson are the same in television as they are in radio. However, there is one difference: the television spokesperson is seen, not just heard. This factor adds a visual concern that can bear on the credibility of the spokesperson.

The spokesperson must be appropriate to the product or service and look and sound sincere. A beautiful actress may be a suitable spokesperson for a line of cosmetics, but the

30-Second Television Commercial Titled: "THE WEDDING"

FATHER OF THE BRIDE
He's not the father of the bride. I am.

He's my Ætna Agent. I met him when my Susie

was her size. And my business wasn't much bigger.

From day one, he's worried as much about my business as I have.

Do I have enough insurance? Or too much insurance? Do I have the right insurance?

Thanks to him, I'm free to worry about other things.

Like how I'm gonna pay for all this.

AVO: Call your Ætna Agent.

THE ÆTNA CASUALTY AND SURETY COMPANY

FATHER: Ætna, I'm glad I met ya!

FIGURE 11.4 Situation Commercial *(Courtesy Ætna Life and Casualty)*

same person would probably be wrong in a spot for vacuum cleaners. You must decide what kind of person is appropriate for the product you're selling, whether it is someone characterized by warmth, humor, glamour, or authority. Here are some guidelines:

1. Describe the person before you write the commercial. What do you want the person to look and sound like?
2. Prepare the copy with your spokesperson in mind. Write for his or her style of delivery. Write copy that seems extemporaneous and can be delivered conversationally.
3. Show and mention the advertiser's name or product throughout the spot. If the name isn't mentioned prominently, the spokesperson may upstage the product.
4. Keep the spot straightforward. Movement and shot changes should be minimal. Focus on the person and his or her presentation of the sales message.

The spokesperson commercial in Figure 11.5 is a buyer's guide that gives consumer information. The presentation uses an anonymous actor who appears knowledgeable and serious. The spot presents information that consumers may not know. The advertiser's name is presented prominently in both the audio and video portions of the commercial.

The Product-as-Star Approach   *cinnabun*

In this format, the product is the star of the commercial. The product is displayed prominently and naturally and is made to appear irresistible.

This approach works well for any product or group of products you wish to put on display. It's a favorite for dairy products, other food items, and soft drinks. If the budget permits, the audio portion will often be a musical background. The commercial may include live-action shots of people enjoying the product. Here's how to make the product the star:

1. Present the sales message with restraint. Hard-sell terms such as *hurry* or *buy now* are best avoided. Use the suggestive approach and build the spot around the sales theme.
2. Use realistic settings and a simple, straightforward message. The advertiser wants the product to be remembered, so the setting should not upstage it. The audio portion shouldn't be complex either, and it should reinforce the video.
3. Use closeup and extreme closeup shots of the product to strengthen the video. Such shots give the viewer the best view of the product and enhance its appearance.
4. Show happy, satisfied people enjoying themselves as they use the product. Make the results of using the product seem rewarding.
5. Explain the characteristics of the product: Communicate its taste, feel, appearance, or other features. Show these characteristics when they appear in the audio.
6. Emphasize the name of the product.

The T.J. Cinnamons commercial in Figure 11.6 features a cinnamon bun up close and in color. A musical jingle that accompanies pictures of the product further focuses attention. Lighting, setting, and the choice of music and announcer are all important in making the cinnamon bun star of the spot.

The Direct-Response Approach

A direct-response spot tries to persuade the viewer to order a product directly from the advertiser, either by mailing in a coupon or calling a telephone number. Direct-response spots are very popular on both television and cable, with the telephone response (usually featuring an advertiser's toll-free number) being the most common.

AMERICA'S FAMILY DRUG STORE

"PRIVATE LABEL GUARANTEE" TV:30

MAC OC: Store brands. There are hundreds of them. And they're not all the same.

In fact there's one that's tested to such high quality national brand standards . . . it comes with a guarantee.

Eckerd Brand. If you're ever dissatisfied with any Eckerd Brand product . . .

we'll replace it with the comparable national brand free.

With a guarantee that strong, we have to make sure Eckerd Brand is as good as you can buy. Period.

If your store brand isn't guaranteed . . . ask yourself . . . why? Eckerd Brand products. You're going to like them. We guarantee it.

W. B. Doner and Company Advertising

FIGURE 11.5 Spokesperson Commercial *(Courtesy Eckerd Drugs)*

T. J. CINNAMONS

Television

Music under

More laughing

Laughing

Music concludes

Music continued

Announcer: T. J. Cinnamons. You're allowed.

FIGURE 11.6 Product-as-Star Commercial *(Courtesy Philip E. Cohen, Harris-Drury-Cohen)*

Direct-response spots are often per-inquiry advertisements. That means the station or cablecaster is paid for each response. These spots hit hard and use every possible inducement to get the viewer to respond. They may advertise an unbelievable kitchen tool, an album of songs by a favorite singer, magazine subscriptions, or jewelry. Direct response spots are often as long as two minutes in length. Here are some guidelines for writing a direct-response spot:

1. **Remember that the video is key.** You must show the product at its best. If you're selling records, the artist should be seen and heard. Show household or shop tools doing as many jobs as you can put into the spot. Jewelry should be made to look attractive and durable. Show the product in as many appealing settings as possible. Make the offer appear desirable.

2. **Don't ridicule the product.** As a writer, you should be aware of the product's limitations. For example, are some of the record cuts made from worn masters? Will the tool work only for one adept at woodwork? If you've accepted the job of writing such spots, you have an ethical responsibility to write a positive message for the client even if you know the shortcomings of the product. Direct-response writing is not for the squeamish or the uninitiated. Some direct-marketing companies sell products of questionable value. Others sell quality items at real savings. A few direct-marketing companies are careless about quality and provide little customer assistance. Others are ethical and make every effort to resolve problems. Writing spots for an unscrupulous direct-marketing firm will certainly test your integrity.

3. **Reach for the impulse buyer.** Direct-response spots seek the person who buys on impulse. It's your job to make such a person grab the phone. Stress that this is a limited offer, that credit cards are welcome, that the item can't be found in stores, and that operators are standing by. Repeat the phone number at least three times. Make the offer appear so good that viewers won't want to pass it up.

The photo board in Figure 11.7 illustrates a direct-response spot. It presents a product that can be effectively advertised on TV.

Variations on Six Themes

As we noted earlier, you can devise other approaches or use variations of the six we've covered here. For example, humor can be injected into many approaches, such as a situation approach, a problem–solution approach, and possibly a spokesperson approach. Animation could be considered a separate approach, but it can be adapted to any of the styles we've discussed. Tony the Tiger, for instance, is a spokesperson for a product.

You might also use an institutional approach. An institutional commercial is designed to enhance the image of the company and to build goodwill toward it. This form of advertising, which is related to the public-service announcement, does not promote specific products or urge the viewer to go to a store or dealer. Instead, it informs viewers about the company's achievements, standards, and activities. Institutional commercials are a favorite of the major oil companies.

The spot in Figure 11.8 is an institutional commercial used by an aerospace company. The commercial does not sell a specific product but generates goodwill for the company by illustrating a service that the company provides.

A final reminder: Before you begin writing a television spot, try to imagine what it will look like. This point cannot be stressed enough. It's your responsibility as a copywriter to visualize what the spot will actually look like when it's on tape or on the air. If you need help, use a storyboard sketch, or have a colleague critique your first draft.

TIMES MIRROR MAGAZINES
OUTDOOR LIFE

TITLE: "MOST DANGEROUS GAME"

COMM'L. NO.: XXGR 0222 (:120)

(MUSIC UNDER)
MAN: You can see it in their eyes. They are some of the most dangerous animals in the world.

The lion -- if it's hungry, it will eat you.

The leopard -- it's a deadly killer because it's small and almost totally silent.

The grizzly -- it stands nine feet tall. Now you can come face to face with them in this special gift from Outdoor Life.

Incredible stories on the animals that strike the deepest terror in man.

It's the <u>Most Dangerous Game</u> -- from the editors of Outdoor Life --

a special <u>free</u> gift for you with a low cost introductory subscription. A full year of Outdoor Life for only $6.97.

Call this number, 1-800-228-2080 and bring home the great outdoors. The action. The information. The pride...

Outdoor Life. I'm talking about hunting and fishing the way you like it --

pages of tips and tactics you can use to enjoy the outdoors even more. Articles on fish and game in your neck of the woods...

on the big ones that didn't get away and the little secrets that make it happen.

Outdoor Life. It's all you need to know -- from what's new in hunting equipment to where the bass are hitting big.

Lures. Boots. Boats. Fathers and sons. Adventure. Close calls and long shots.

That's the Outdoor Life for you. Equipment. Camping. Hunting. Field guides and updates and special reports on everything

from trout to turkey to white tails to mallards.

It's the tradition of caring for the wilderness, of making it on your own, through strength and smarts.

Outdoor Life. It's the man's magazine you can depend on -- every month, every issue. Come with us today and get Outdoor Life's <u>Most Dangerous Game</u> -- free with your paid subscription.

Call now. 1-800-228-2080 and save 53% off the $15.00 cover price. That's 40% off the regular subscription rate of $11.94.

So you get 12 great issues -- for just $6.97.

1-800-228-2080. For the <u>Most Dangerous Game</u>. For the great outdoors. For Outdoor Life. (MUSIC OUT)

FIGURE 11.7 Direct-Response Commercial *(Courtesy Times Mirror Magazines)*

Either way, be certain the visual elements of your spot will be appealing to the viewer. Television is a visual medium, and if the video portion of your commercial is weak, the entire spot is likely to be ineffective.

One way to give a spot visual strength is to write the visual portion before you write the audio portion. If the video portion will carry the message by itself, you'll know that you have a good television spot. Audio can be added as needed.

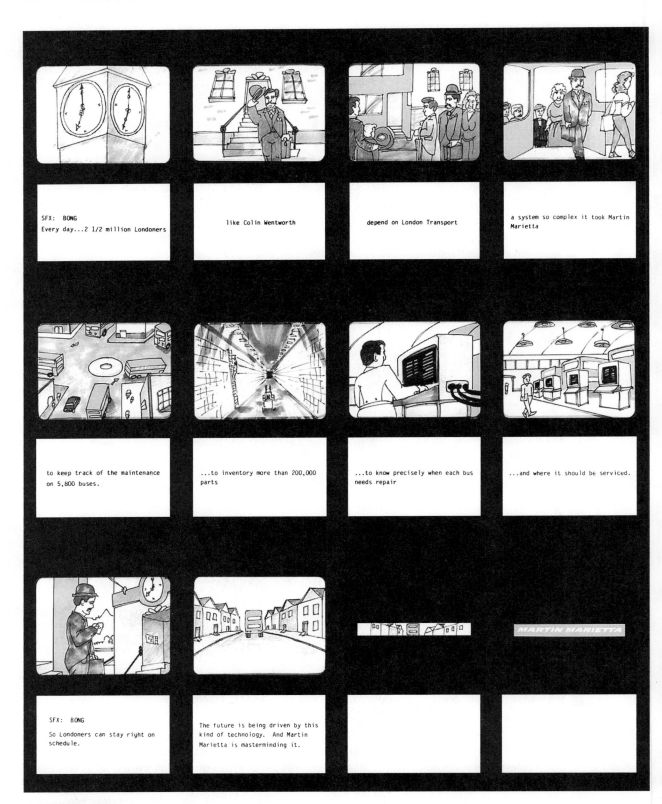

FIGURE 11.8 Institutional Commercial (*Courtesy John H. Boyd, Jr., Martin Marietta Aerospace*)

➤ POINTS TO REMEMBER

- A spot must have a structure that involves the viewer and sells the product or service.

- The problem–solution approach lets you depict a realistic problem and show someone solving it with the product.

- The demonstration approach lets you show the benefits of the product in action.

- A situation commercial tells a story that establishes a reason for the presence of the product.

- The spokesperson approach uses either a well-known person to endorse a product or an unknown person who claims to have used the product and delivers a testimonial for it.

- The product-as-star approach seeks to display the product prominently and make it appear irresistible.

- A direct-response spot persuades the viewer to order something directly from the advertiser. In this type of spot, the visuals must be very strong.

- An institutional approach is designed to enhance the client's image and build goodwill.

EXERCISES

Exercise 1

Write a 30-second problem-solving television spot using the following facts: Yourtown Urgent Care Clinic wants to publicize their services. They provide a walk-in clinic; appointments are not needed. Experienced physicians and nurses are on duty from 8 A.M. to 10 P.M. seven days a week. The address is 2334 North 14th St.

Appeal to working people who need the flexibility and convenience of a walk-in clinic but who still want quality treatment. Illustrate how the target audience might solve a problem by using this clinic. Be sure to show people responding to the benefits of going to the clinic and establish the business name clearly.

Prepare a storyboard that illustrates the spot to accompany your script.

Exercise 2

Grandma's Home-Style Ice Cream has a new flavor, Butter Up. This new flavor combines butterscotch and walnut. Stress that Grandma's ice cream is made with real cream and does not contain artificial ingredients. Grandma's picture is on the label.

Write a 30-second product-as-star television spot for Grandma's Butter Up Ice Cream. The product should be the star of this commercial. Devise a slogan for use in the spot.

Prepare a storyboard that illustrates your spot to accompany your script.

Exercise 3

Write a 60-second television commercial in which you compare two products. Compare a new cold remedy, Kwikure, with an established product, Cold-Eeze. Both products eliminate nasal congestion from common colds. They stop runny nose, sneezing, and watery eyes. However, Kwikure is effective for up to 14 hours. Cold-Eeze works for 4 to 6 hours.

Prepare a straightforward comparison of the features of the two products. Show that Kwikure is clearly superior.

Prepare a storyboard that illustrates your spot to accompany your script.

Exercise 4

Prepare a 30-second situational television spot for the Rapid Fire Microwave Oven. Be certain the spot tells a story with a definite plot. Don't dwell on details. Instead, use the story to introduce the microwave oven in a believable setting. You may wish to base your situation on some of the following features of microwave ovens: They are good for preparing light meals (a portion of lasagna) or quick snacks (a hot dog) or for heating leftovers. They're also good for defrosting frozen foods. Microwaves don't heat up the kitchen, and they usually cook foods faster than a conventional range can. Your goal is to create a situation in which the Rapid Fire Microwave Oven is used for one or more of these reasons.

Prepare a storyboard to accompany your script.

Exercise 5

The Dynamic Corporation has produced a new battery-operated shoe shiner called the Ezeshine. It's about the size of a hair dryer and comes with brushes of different textures. Because of its size and portability, it can be used anywhere. It operates on four "D"-size batteries.

Write a 30-second television commercial that demonstrates the shoe shiner in action. Your goal is to show what the product can do, so don't spend time developing a situation.

Prepare a storyboard to accompany the script.

Exercise 6

Write another 30-second television spot for the Rapid Fire Microwave Oven. Choose an appropriate spokesperson to demonstrate the features of the oven. Develop a sales theme that includes the product name. Use the sales theme prominently in the spot. Use a balance of audio and video to present the sales theme.

Prepare a storyboard to accompany your script.

Exercise 7

Write a 90-second direct-response television spot to sell the following product: a Special Forces men's wristwatch. The features of this watch are as follows:

1. Perpetual calendar displays month and date, along with hour, minute, and second, automatically.

2. Pushbutton illumination lights dial electronically.

3. Stopwatch feature for timing sports, phone calls, and so on.

4. Sturdy construction. Waterproof and shockproof. Can be worn anywhere in all conditions.

5. Rugged flexible band and recessed chronoface reduce chance of scrapes and scratches.

6. The price is $49.95.

7. Watch and band are of stainless steel.

Order the watch by calling toll-free 1-800-123-4321. All credit cards accepted. No postage or handling costs on phone orders. Customers can order by mail. Include additional $6.95 for postage and handling. The address is "Wristwatch," Box 001, Downtown, New York, 10001.

Satisfaction guaranteed. If not satisfied, return within 30 days for full refund.

Special offer: Customers ordering now will get a free surprise gift.

Exercise 1

STORYBOARD

Video:

Audio:

Video:

Audio:

Video:

Audio:

Video:

Audio:

Video:

Audio:

Video:

Audio:

Video:

Audio:

Video:

Audio:

Video:

Audio:

Exercise 2

STORYBOARD

Video:

Audio:

Video:

Audio:

Video:

Audio:

Video:

Audio:

Video:

Audio:

Video:

Audio:

Video:

Audio:

Video:

Audio:

Video:

Audio:

Exercise 3

STORYBOARD

Video:

Audio:

Video:

Audio:

Video:

Audio:

Video:

Audio:

Video:

Audio:

Video:

Audio:

Video:

Audio:

Video:

Audio:

Video:

Audio:

Exercise 4

STORYBOARD

Video:

Audio:

Video:

Audio:

Video:

Audio:

Video:

Audio:

Video:

Audio:

Video:

Audio:

Video:

Audio:

Video:

Audio:

Video:

Audio:

Exercise 5

STORYBOARD

Video:

Audio:

Video:

Audio:

Video:

Audio:

Video:

Audio:

Video:

Audio:

Video:

Audio:

Video:

Audio:

Video:

Audio:

Video:

Audio:

Exercise 6

STORYBOARD

Video:

Audio:

Video:

Audio:

Video:

Audio:

Video:

Audio:

Video:

Audio:

Video:

Audio:

Video:

Audio:

Video:

Audio:

Video:

Audio:

Promotion

As the competition for broadcast and cable audiences increases, stations and cable systems must often seek new listeners or viewers. At the same time, promotional activities are aimed at holding on to those listeners or viewers already in the fold. Promotion has two interrelated goals: (1) to tell the audience about upcoming programs and (2) to keep it interested in regularly scheduled programs.

In larger cities with a number of stations, the competition becomes especially fierce. TV stations battle one another, and radio stations with similar formats fight for listeners. Successful promotion can mean the difference between winning a ratings battle and losing it. In this chapter, we'll cover the elements involved in writing promotional copy for the various media, and we'll examine several common promotional strategies.

◆ Promotion in the Electronic Media

Although the three media of interest here share many of the same promotional concerns and employ many similar strategies, they also have important differences. Let's look briefly at each medium.

Television

Program originators usually supply stations with promotional information. The major television networks prepare promotional packets for every show on their schedules. These packets are sent to the local affiliates before the programs are shown. One major mailing occurs before the fall season, and updates and additions follow as needed. The packet includes publicity releases, star biographies, photos, fact sheets, suggested on-air announcements, and prepared print ads.

The networks also supply the stations with timely news and promotional information—for example, adjustments of the evening schedule because of a presidential news conference or material for special programs. Such information is commonly sent to the local affiliate by fax.

The networks also send their affiliates prepared on-air promotional announcements for both radio and TV. Scripts may be mailed to the station, e-mailed, faxed, or sent as produced promos in a closed-circuit feed from the network to the local station.

Networks may also provide their affiliates with the opportunity to interview a celebrity from a network program. The interview is conducted in the station's studio with a local announcer who talks to the celebrity by satellite. Because the celebrity usually does a number of interviews in one sitting, the local station generally tapes the interview.

Syndicated program producers also send promotional packets to local stations, but they're usually not as extensive as those supplied by the networks. These packets typically include stills, a synopsis of each episode, photos, and prepared print advertisements. Syndicated film companies supply television stations with even less information, usually a synopsis of each movie and photos. Syndicators of special programs—talk shows and news features—supply local stations with on-air promotional material, often fed to the station by satellite along with the programs. Promotional packets are usually also sent to local stations.

The promotional department of a syndicated film or program company often supplies recommended copy for stations to use. Syndicators do this to ensure a consistent level of promotion quality in all markets carrying the program. All that needs to be done is to fill in the blanks with your station's call letters and the time of the program. Similarly, program excerpts are sometimes supplied either by satellite feed or as a part of the promotional packet. If prepared material is not supplied, the promotion writer must write the copy and screen episodes of the program for suitable excerpt material. Screening film or tape is a time-consuming process that the station may choose not to pursue.

Radio

Radio stations rely on the networks for a much smaller percentage of their programming than do television stations. Many radio stations aren't affiliated with a network, and many that are receive only news from it. Others receive network news, talk shows, or both. Stations with a network affiliation generally receive a daily closed-circuit audio feed consisting of scheduling information and, where appropriate, promotion and publicity material.

Some radio stations carry syndicated programs in which well-known disc jockeys present the week's top records. The station usually receives a promo in which the show's host urges people to listen to the program on the local station.

Because there are a large number of radio stations, radio broadcasters must compete for the audience they want or for their share of it. To attract and keep listeners, radio stations rely on giveaways and on-location appearances by station personalities. These activities may be promoted on the air by the station, on TV, and perhaps with direct mail and billboards as well.

Cable

Promotional efforts for cable systems do not differ greatly from those of television broadcasters. Promotion attracts new subscribers; communicates positive images to current and potential subscribers, government officials, and local advertisers; and reduces disconnects. Cable systems can use on-air promotion as well as paid promotion and publicity. Together, these efforts (1) inform viewers about the full array of channels available; (2) convince the public that this complement of channels is the best available, thus reducing disconnects; and (3) create an image of the cable service as the source of desired products—such as MTV.

Cable networks provide local systems with a wide range of consumer marketing and sales materials to aid low-budget local promotions. These materials include on-air spots and IDs, direct mailers, program guides, subscriber information kits, and bill stuffers.

Many national cable networks pay cablecasters for local joint promotion of the system and network. Payment may be made at sign-up time or on an annual basis. Both pay and basic networks use cooperative advertising in which the network and the local system split the cost of radio and print promotion. The major pay-cable networks, such as HBO, also supply local systems with camera-ready materials for use in local print promotion. This service is a great cost saver because many local systems do not have art departments and must hire outside advertising or art firms to prepare print advertising.

Cable systems also want to get maximum use of availabilities in pay-cable networks. Cablecasters usually use any commercial time that has not been sold for self-promotion. These spots may promote some of the system's pay services or some of the system's customer services.

Cable systems can also devote a channel to program listings, public-service announcements, and information about services offered by the system. Program promos focus on locally produced cable programming and may promote offerings on other channels of the system. The information is usually presented by on-air print crawls created by a video character generator. A musical background usually accompanies the visual material, often the signal of a radio station.

◆ Promotion via the Internet

Interactive, online computer services on the World Wide Web have given broadcast stations a new way to promote their products. A Web site enables stations to market to an upscale audience that is technically aware and interested in information. Some call the online services value-added marketing because the World Wide Web provides a source for information that people would normally contact the station to get.

Radio

Radio stations use Web sites to sell merchandise with the station logo or to announce programming lineups and features. For instance, a station's music playlist may be included, as well as information about the station's announcers. Interactive components are also used to let listeners talk with station personalities. This may be to make song requests, listen to music samples, offer comments, or pose questions to talk-show hosts. Sites are also used to promote concerts, shows, and other community events such as station remotes. Weather and news are also often included on the Web, although the amount of such information varies with the format. Figure 12.1 illustrates the initial screen of a radio station Web site for a music station.

Radio station Web sites may be limited to visual components, but some stations stream audio to online listeners. The need to pay performance rights fees has limited the growth of audio streaming.

Television

Television stations use online services for much the same reason as radio stations do: to project and preserve the personality of a station while offering additional programming and services that are impossible to deliver over the air. News and weather is a staple of Web site information for many television stations. They can update and expand news and weather items that appear in newscasts.

In addition, stations and some cablecasters promote special events and program schedules and include some opportunities to talk with station personalities. As with radio, the key is to use Internet services to offer viewers a service the station or system can't readily supply in any other way.

There are two suggestions for stations that use online services. One is that the Web site must be updated daily. People access a Web site to get information or entertainment they don't have. If the browser finds a static page with no changes, he or she is unlikely to check back. The second point is that stations must market their Web sites vigorously, including them in visual promotional material on television and in printed material the stations prepare for their audience.

Welcome to WDIZ Online

Orlando's Radio and Music Information Center

WDIZ lists the ten most played songs for the week in Binburners

Pat Lynch checks out the latest new music and gives you **his** opinion - good or bad - in the WDIZ New Music Review

Meet the WDIZ staff. They each have a web page of their own so be sure and leave them mail while you're there so they don't feel left out

WDIZ Music News contains some of the more interesting and entertaining storys taken right off the wire services

Find out what happened in Rock History this month with WDIZ's Timeline

Check out the new format for the Central Florida Area Concert Schedule

If you read this you might be able to catch WDIZ On The Move. Snag a t-shirt, bolt on a license plate or win some prizes!

Sitting around trying to think up things to do? We already did! Check out these places to go and people to see

Visit Larry The Cable Guy's home on the web. WARNING - Not for the squeemish or easily offended.

FIGURE 12.1 Home Page of a Radio Station's Promotional Web Site *(Courtesy of WDIZ, Rock 100)*

◆ Promotional Strategies

When the goal is to promote a locally originated program or a programming format, you, as copywriter, will work from firsthand knowledge. In this case, you cannot rely on material prepared by network professionals. Instead, you must use your own insight and creativity. A full-time promotion manager or a copywriter handling promotion and publicity can reach the public in a number of ways.

Promos

The on-air promotional announcement, or *promo*, is one of the primary methods of reaching the public. The promo reaches the station's established audience, the people most interested in your message. As with the other types of copy covered in this chapter, you have a different product but the same goal as a radio or TV commercial writer.

On-air promos may be any length—as short as three-second logos or as long as one-minute promos. The commercial load and programming philosophy of the station's management will determine the length. Unsold commercial slots (called *availabilities*) are often filled with promos. There are two types of promos: (1) specific and (2) generic.

SPECIFIC PROMOS   The specific approach asks viewers or listeners to make up their minds, to do something. A specific promo may ask viewers to watch a given episode of a program, to watch a special program, or to watch the station's evening program lineup. A specific promo might also ask viewers to watch a given individual such as the weatherperson or, in the case of radio, to listen to the morning wakeup announcer.

The news promo that follows uses the specific approach. Notice how the spot sells the advantages of listening to this weather forecaster and urges viewers to tune in.

VIDEO	AUDIO
BOYLAN DELIVERS CONCEPT SCRIPT BOYLAN ANIMATION SKYTRACK C.K. SKYTRACK CONSOLE/EXTERIOR WEATHER MAP IN OFFICE WEATHER MAP C.K. BOYLAN ANIMATION	When you need the most accurate weather forecast in town, Ray Boylan delivers! He's the only weatherman in town with Skytrack color weather radar! He tells you what's best to do, come rain or shine. Twenty-five years of weather forecasting experience, working for you on TV-12 Action News. See for yourself, weeknights, at 6 and 11!

Courtesy WTLV, Jacksonville, Florida.

Radio and television promotion is seldom hard-sell, even in a specific promo. The reason is that stations are sensitive to the fact that a hard-sell pitch urging viewers to tune in is likely to backfire and cause them to tune out. Thus, rather than hit too hard in a specific promo, most broadcast promotion managers will use a direct but soft sell. The promo for Ray Boylan weather says, "See for yourself." That's the extent of the pitch to tune in. Hard-sell exhortations are avoided.

Short, ad-lib promos have become increasingly popular on radio stations that feature music formats. Nevertheless, most stations use longer, specific promos to promote special events or special program features. The following promo promotes traffic reports.

SFX	TRAFFIC SOUNDS
ANNCR	If Central Florida traffic congestion makes you ill . . . the 58 WDBO traffic network has just what the doctor ordered.
MUSIC UP AND UNDER	Colonel Richard Bouchard, airborne live, examines the clogged arteries and prescribes bypass alternatives. Dan Schaffer, in the Holler Chevrolet Good Samaritan van, fixes what ails your car, or sends for help via Cellular One telephone. Every nine minutes during rush hours we've got the quick cure for traffic pain. Listen seven days a week for fast relief first . . . from the best . . . your news and weather station . . . 58 WDBO.

Courtesy Bill Patti, WDBO, Orlando, Florida.

GENERIC PROMOS Whereas the specific promo asks directly for a response, the generic promo is understated. It doesn't ask people to watch or listen. Instead, the generic promo helps build and maintain an image. That's what the following news promo does: It communicates the dedication and commitment of a television news department.

VIDEO	AUDIO
00 MS SLIGHTLY HIGH ANGLE BOB OPSAHL AT SWITCHER TURNS TO CAMERA	At Channel 9, there's a spirit, a commitment that makes us Central Florida's leading news station.
06 MS EYE LEVEL, ALYCE AT PAY PHONE. MAN WITH CAMERA ON SHOULDER WALKS BETWEEN HER AND CAMERA. SHE HANGS UP, MOVES FORWARD A STEP. MOVES OUT OF FRAME AT END.	It starts with reporters who know their subjects . . . who dig deeper to develop stories you won't see anywhere else.
10 MLS, DANNY ON WEATHER SET WITH ACCU-WEATHER GRAPHICS TERMINAL.	And that commitment shows, in the way we cover the news . . . from Accu-Weather . . .
12 MS, MARSHA AIRBORNE IN SKYWITNESS OVER EPCOT.	. . . to Skywitness
13 MLS, STEVE TRIGGS IN FRONT OF INSTANT EYE AT CAPE. MAN WITH CAMERA SET UP. TRIGGS TURNS AS THOUGH TO DO LIVE REPORT.	to live satellite and instant eye reports.
16 MLS BOB JORDAN IN COURTROOM. BENCH BG.	Central Florida's largest television news team covers the important stories.
18 MS MIKE STORMS DRIVING RACE CAR PAST DAYTONA SIGN AT SPEEDWAY. SHOT FROM OUTSIDE DRIVER'S WINDOW.	And the interesting ones.
22 TRUCKING SHOT, MLS GEORGE RYAN, CAMERAMAN BG MOVING DOWN BEACH	Wherever the news happens.
26 CU BOB OPSAHL, INSTANT EYE	We work hard to bring you Central Florida's best newscast.
WS, BOB OPSAHL, SKYWITNESS, 2 INSTANT EYES, SATELLITE DISH, AND MEMBERS OF TEAM BG. MUSIC FULL. SUPER	And that's the Eyewitness advantage.

Courtesy SFN Communications of Florida, Inc.

VIDEO	AUDIO
IN OVER-STUFFED SANDWICH EDIT TO SAME SANDWICH LESS MEAT . . . EDIT TO SAME SANDWICH EVEN LESS MEAT EDIT TO SANDWICH, BREAD ONLY. QUANTEL OUT FROM SANDWICH NEWS VIDEO DENNIS REPORTING . . . WEATHER SHOT WITH MENARD SCHWARTZ ON LOCATION AT BUCS PRACTICE LEACH W/CONSUMER REPORT DEESON W/ACTION LINE FONDA INTERVIEW ANTIQUES DETECTIVE/ DR. ___ HEALTH REPORT OVER-STUFFED SANDWICH EDIT TO SAME SANDWICH WITH BITE TAKEN OUT . . . LOGO AND C.G. INFO. OUT	ANNCR: A mid-day newscast should be piled-high with all the news you need. But some stations only offer news by-products, and don't get to the meat of the issues . . . (Pause) At Channel 10's Action News At Noon, we serve you a hearty helping of the most current news . . . up to the minute weather forecasts . . . and a taste of sports you won't get anywhere else . . . _and_, news for the consumer, problem solving with Action Line, personality interviews, and helpful hints to fill your day. Action News At Noon. We make all the news, easy to swallow. Weekdays on Channel 10.

FIGURE 12.2 A Generic Promo (*Courtesy Cyndie Reynolds, WTSP-TV, St. Petersburg, Florida*)

Note that this promo never asks viewers to tune in, and it doesn't indicate the time of the newscast. Rather, the goal is to create an image of a hardworking news team. The generic promo for WTSP Action News at Noon in Figure 12.2 has a similar aim; read it closely and see if you can identify the generic elements.

Cablecasters also promote images they want their operations to convey. The following promo is one of a series designed to show that the cable system has something for everyone.

VIDEO	AUDIO
Fade up to little old lady watching wrestling on USA network.	LITTLE OLD LADY: I just love to watch these beautiful young bodies fly through the air with the greatest of ease.
Little old lady gets on floor and beats up rug.	Then bam! Hit him! Thrash him! Get him!
CV Logo:	CHORUS: See It On CV

Courtesy Katy Gunter, Cablevision of Central Florida

Radio stations can also use the generic approach to create a feeling or image, as the following promo does in promoting WGBH's Summer Radio Festival.

SFX: SOUND OF CRICKETS IN BACKGROUND, NOT CLOSE UP. AUDIBLE THROUGHOUT; UP FULL BEFORE TAG, OUT UNDER. Sorry about the crickets.

After all, they are the longest-running musical tradition of the New England summer. And here we come, right into the heart of cricket country, with our mikes and mobile studios and nervous producers, intent on capturing summer music of another sort. The NEW ENGLAND SUMMER RADIO FESTIVAL series, with host Phyllis Curtin, takes you to the most popular regional music festivals in the Northeast—from the seaside: Newport's Music Festival; inland: to the Connecticut Early Music Festival; then north to Vermont's Mozart Festival . . . and that's just a taste. Because summer in New England is an endless celebration of music . . . and if you sort of "squint" your ears, you'll hear the faint, unmistakable music of crickets. The NEW ENGLAND SUMMER RADIO FESTIVAL . . . Sunday at 6 . . . here on listener-supported WGBH Boston.

Courtesy WGBH, Boston, Massachusetts

This generic promo works hard to create the "theater of the mind" on which radio depends. The spot draws an analogy between two distinct summer sounds, the sounds made by crickets and the sounds made by the New England Summer Radio Festival.

Instead of promoting a specific program or a category of programming, some promos may be used to promote a station's special programming, as this generic promo does.

SFX: JINGLE, CUT #9 TAKE ME OUT TO THE BALLGAME

One of America's favorite pastimes developed from the game of cricket and an old English sport called rounders. In 1839, Abner Doubleday laid out a diamond-shaped field with four bases and named the game baseball. Six years later Alexander Cartwright established standard rules and designed the game almost exactly as it is played today . . . and for over one hundred years Americans have enjoyed the excitement and thrills of major league baseball! Join the fun yourself this season with us, as KFOR brings you Kansas City Royals baseball! VOCAL CLOSE

Courtesy KFOR Radio, Lincoln, Nebraska

Finally, the promo for JOY 108 is a generic spot with a difference. The goal is to "position" JOY 108 relative to its main competitor, STAR 101. This is a battle for the perceptions of the listeners. Read the spot and analyze the logic used in it.

MUSIC: CONTEMPORARY INSTRUMENTAL. UP AND UNDER

ANNCR: There are only sixty minutes in every hour and in that hour every radio station plays about the same amount of music. The difference is that at the new JOY 108 we always play the greatest hits of yesterday and today in four-song music sweeps with absolutely no talk. Four songs in a row with no talk. So when STAR says they play fifty minutes of music each hour that means ten minutes of what—commercials of course. So remember, while STAR guarantees to play ten minutes of commercials an hour, the new JOY 108 guarantees to play only the greatest hits of yesterday and today. Always four in a row with no talk. Now that's a difference worth remembering. The radio station you designed, the new JOY 108.

Courtesy Steve Street, JOY/Orlando—JOY 108.

MORE PROMO BASICS   In a promo, the sponsor is the station, and the station should be clearly identified. Television stations find that viewers identify them most readily by channel number. As a result, you can usually omit the station's call letters.

Radio stations may or may not seek identification by their call letters. Many music stations prefer a verbal logo using a letter from their call letters or a word in combination with their location on the dial. For example, station WHLY might become Y106, or a station may call itself Hits 106. These are promotional logos and should be used in promotional copy. They will also be used on the air by the disc jockey. They cannot be used as the station's legal ID (identification), which by law must include the station's call letters and city of license.

A promotional announcement publicizing a specific program or event or the evening's program schedule should include the name of the station, the title of the program or event, and the day and time of the broadcast.

IDs

The shortest form of on-air promos is IDs, which are usually no more than three to five seconds long. The most obvious use of the ID is to announce the station's legal identification, as required by the FCC. This announcement must be given once each hour, close to the top of the hour. It must include the station's call letters and place of signal origin (city or area of dominant influence). Stations often use the legal ID spot to include brief program promotions as well. A radio station specifies its frequency, whereas a television station identifies its channel number. A promotional theme may also be included. For example, a news/information AM station in Orlando, Florida, uses this legal ID: "This is WDBO, Newstalk 580, Orlando. Central Florida's news, weather, and traffic station. Depend on it!"

Television stations can use audio, video, or both to present their legal IDs. A TV station can thus super its legal ID over program content, insert an audio recording at the proper spot, or broadcast a complete ID with sight and sound. In the latter case, TV stations often use a "shared" ID to link the legal information with a promotional announcement. This can be done by combining a slide with prerecorded audio on cartridge or by combining a short excerpt from a syndicated program with a topical audio announcement. The legal portion of the ID can be supered under a station logo. For example:

Audio: Next on the OPRAH WINFREY SHOW.
Video: Excerpt from OPRAH WINFREY SHOW.

Audio: Watch the OPRAH WINFREY SHOW tomorrow at 4.
Video: Station call letters, name of city, and location.

IDs that are not necessary for legal identification also appear throughout a station's schedule. Radio stations have their DJs read out short, generic IDs to promote the station's format. Television stations may insert IDs in commercial availabilities. They may be the same IDs used for legal identification or modified versions that do not include the legal information (call letters and city).

An ID may also be shared with the network. Networks supply their affiliates with topical ID material. A local voice announcement and a visual logo are all that must be added to complete the ID.

Teasers and Bumpers

Other types of television promotional announcements are the teaser and bumper. These are brief visual announcements, sometimes as short as two seconds, designed to stimulate interest in an upcoming program or event. *Bumpers* are used in network or syndicated programs at the beginning and end of a series of commercials. For example, in the syndicated showing of *Friends*, a station introduces and concludes each commercial cluster with a slide showing the Friends gang, the name "Friends" imposed across the top of the screen, and the station's call letters and location imposed across the bottom.

Teasers are used at the end of a program or a program segment to promote interest in an upcoming program, such as the local newscast. The written copy for a teaser might be very brief, but the wording is crucial. Your task is to write interesting copy that will gain attention without giving away the outcome of the show or news item. For example, a teaser for the late evening sportscast should not say, "The Jackrabbits win by 1 in overtime. Details at 10." With that wording, the suspense is gone, so there's no reason for the audience to stay tuned. A better teaser would say, "The Jackrabbits had a fight on their hands tonight. Details at 10." This teaser doesn't report the outcome and thus maintains suspense. Teasers for syndicated shows or movies call for the same rigorous writing: Tease the viewer with the story line, but don't give it away.

Logos

A *logo* is a brief, identifiable signature representing a station, network, or program syndicator. Visuals are commonly used on television to create effective associations with promotional themes developed by the station. Figures 12.3 and 12.4 show typical station and network logos. Radio stations may also use brief verbal logos to establish their identity, especially when similar formats exist, or to gain listener identification through repetition. One album-oriented rock station may refer to itself as the "real rocker," but another in the same market calls itself the "hot rocker."

Use of a station's logo in its promos is another example of positioning. Just as advertisers seek to position their products in relation to those of their competitors, broadcasters seek to establish a stance for their station in the market. Positioning a station's sound or appearance is especially useful when the market has several stations with similar programming. As a promotions writer, you may be asked to create ID campaigns with logos that will help position your station. In this assignment, you'll have to evaluate your station and its primary competitors to find a characteristic that can differentiate your station in the mind of the listener.

Tie-in packages are available to network-affiliated TV stations. Tie-in packages involve custom animation and music developed by the network and made available to its affiliate stations at modest prices. These materials allow the affiliates to include their own call letters, channel number, and local or syndicated program promotions in on-air promotional packages developed around network themes. Tie-in packages can be used to increase the potential of a promotion budget.

Jingle and Image Packages

Both radio and television stations purchase ID/station image packages from various production companies. Stations use the packages with their own programming and in external advertising.

FIGURE 12.3 A Station Logo (*Courtesy Cyndie Reynolds, WTSP-TV, St. Petersburg, Florida*)

FIGURE 12.4 A Network Logo (*Courtesy American Broadcasting Companies, Inc.*)

Radio stations and cable systems use television rather than print as their primary advertising medium. A radio station wants to promote its format and sound, and television is thought to be a primary source of potential radio listeners. Cablecasters want to attract viewers away from TV stations. Some radio stations produce their own image spots, but others turn to ad agencies. Often, these spots are not of satisfactory quality or are very costly. Preparing an effective image spot to run on television is not easy. The following list identifies some of the pitfalls to avoid in developing a TV campaign for a radio station:

1. Don't overproduce the spot with exotic effects and a dazzling cast. People may remember the spot but not your station.
2. Don't include too many points about the station's format. Stick to one sales point.
3. Don't use a lengthy lead-in that wastes the opening of the spot.
4. Use radio personalities in TV spots with care. They may not transfer well to TV.
5. Keep the call letters prominent. They should be on the screen for most if not all of the spot.
6. Avoid inside information about the station that may not be meaningful to the TV audience.

Rather than risk producing a costly and ineffective TV spot, many radio stations use syndicated packages instead. They are cost-effective because the quality of the spots is usually high and stations using the package in other markets in effect share the cost. Figure 12.5 illustrates the kinds of image packages available to radio stations. Preproduced image packages are also available for TV stations.

Television stations also advertise on radio stations. For the TV station, this may consist of co-op advertising, which splits the cost between the station and the network. Because TV stations often advertise a schedule of evening programming, the network is willing to share the cost of promoting its programs. As a copywriter, you will need to write the copy to fill in a donut, which, you'll recall, is a recorded musical bed with the local station designation sung at the beginning and end. Your staff announcer can usually record the entire spot. Television stations also advertise their evening newscasts on radio, often having one of their news anchors record a summation of the stories to be covered that evening.

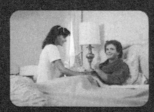

FIGURE 12.5 An Image Package Using Excerpts from Records *(Courtesy Buddy Scott, TM Productions)*

- Television promotion tells a broadcast audience about upcoming programs and keeps them interested in regularly scheduled programs.

- Cable promotion is designed to attract new subscribers and keep current subscribers.

- Radio stations and cable systems use television as their primary advertising medium, and television stations advertise on radio.

- Radio promotion advertises specific personalities or events or the format of the radio station.

- Promos are used to reach a station's established audience, the people most interested in the message.

- Specific promos ask viewers or listeners to make up their minds and then to do something.

- Generic promos are used to promote the image of the station, its programs, or its personalities.

- IDs are brief promos that announce the station's legal identification.

- Teasers and bumpers are designed to stimulate interest in an upcoming program.

- A logo is often used to position a station's sound or appearance.

- The Internet can be used to promote things people would normally contact the station to get.

- Stations that use the Internet for promotion must update the service regularly, preferably on a daily basis.

- If stations are to profit from the Internet, they must market their Web sites vigorously.

EXERCISES

Exercise 1

The radio station you work for, KBBB-FM 104, has been playing contemporary hit music aimed at young adults ages 18 to 25. Ratings have been slipping, so the station manager has decided to change the music format to appeal to an older age group, ages 25 to 35. The new format will include music from the 1960s through 1990s. DJs will now refer to the station as Variety 104. The primary slogan will be "Not too hard, not too light."

- Write a 30-second generic on-air promo for Variety 104. Don't refer to the previous format. Instead, promote the new format as being "all new." Create an image for the station.

- Write a 30-second specific on-air promo for Variety 104. Design this promo to compare Variety 104 with its main competitor, Hot 100, which plays similar music but with a slightly "harder" sound. The slogan of Hot 100 is "The hot hits of the 1960s, 1970s, 1980s, and 1990s." Emphasize the advantage of Variety 104.

Exercise 2

You are the promotional writer for a new TV station in Yourtown, KBBB-TV, Channel 38. This station is an independent and not affiliated with a network. To serve the community, the station presents a live half-hour local newscast at 9 P.M. The other stations in your area present their late news at 10 P.M. The newscast is anchored by Fred Cannon, a veteran newsman in Yourtown. Betty Brown does the weather, and Steve Frasier, former Yourtown College football star, does the sports. The logo for the newscast is Channel 38 Newsline.

- Write a 30-second specific on-air promo urging viewers to watch the news on Channel 38.

- Write a 30-second generic on-air promo that establishes an image for Channel 38's Newsline.

CHAPTER THIRTEEN

Public Service, Issue, and Political Announcements

Broadcast stations and cable systems want to serve their communities. They can be of service to the people in their areas by running public-service announcements of local interest, accepting advertising for or against local issues, and carrying advertisements for political candidates who represent the region.

As a copywriter, you might be asked to write such spots. The rules for writing these announcements are largely the same as for commercial spots. The difference is in the objective—you're not selling a product per se, you're selling ideas and services. Thus, these spots are more like institutional commercials. Nevertheless, the AIDA formula is an appropriate guide in organizing these spots, and the radio and TV formats apply.

This chapter sets forth the guidelines for writing these so-called service spots. Let's begin with public-service announcements.

◆ Public-Service Announcements

Public-service announcements (PSAs) are messages aired free of cost for nonprofit organizations. Broadcast stations and cablecasters air PSAs to respond to community needs and to build their own prestige in their community.

PSAs are aired without charge, so the media have discretion in the number and nature of the PSAs they carry. Stations and systems generally won't devote a lot of costly production to PSAs, and they usually won't schedule many PSAs in prime time.

Choosing the Type of PSA

There are two types of PSA: (1) the informational announcement that tells the audience who, what, when, and where and (2) the announcement that advocates an idea or goal. Local organizations tend to disseminate more informational PSAs, whereas national organizations more commonly seek to sell ideas to the public.

INFORMATIONAL PSAs The PSA that follows is an example of an informational announcement. Although the spot establishes a framework to gain the attention of the audience, its primary goal is to convey information about an event of interest.

VIDEO	AUDIO
GIRL SWIMMING FREESTYLE	Girl voice: She's really stretched her lead. There's no one even close. It's going to be a new world record. :06
LITTLE BOY SHOOTING BASKET, FLASHES GO OFF AS HE SHOOTS.	Boy voice: Jones to Smith. Smith back to Jones. There's the shot, there's the buzzer. It's good! :05
LITTLE GIRL DOING GYMNASTICS.	Female announcer: Here's her dismount. Wow! She really nailed that one! :04.5
KIDS WEARING GEAR FROM THE FAMILY FUN PACK. PEPSI PRODUCTS AND COOLER ARE PROMINENT.	Woman announcer: Join the YMCA now, and receive a free Family Fun Pack. :04

LITTLE BOY AT SHORTSTOP WAITING FOR HIT. BUBBLE BLOWS IN FRONT OF CAMERA	Boy announcer: The crowd is going wild. Today, Day Camp, tomorrow, the World Series. :06
YMCA SUMMER PROGRAMS AND TAG LINE "REAL ACTION, REAL FUN."	Woman announcer: The Y summer programs and Day Camp. Real action. Real fun. :04

Courtesy of the Central Florida YMCA.

IDEA- OR GOAL-ORIENTED PSAs   The announcement in Figure 13.1 illustrates the selling of an idea. The idea is that the warning signs of teenage suicide can be detected, and the goal is to prevent teen suicide. The spot was professionally produced and displays the characteristics of a good television message.

Planning the PSA

A PSA is really no different from a commercial. You're still delivering a sales message, just not for a product. For example, instead of selling a car, you might be selling people on the idea of using their seat belts.

In writing a PSA, you go through the same steps you would in preparing a commercial. Once again, the copy platform can be an effective guide. Here is a summation of the questions, as discussed in Chapter 7, that you need to ask yourself as you plan your spot:

- What objective does this client want to achieve? Is it to raise money, seek volunteers, or create a favorable image?
- What is the target audience for this message? Men, women, families, or teenagers?

The spot in Figure 13.2 targets a group of people, those with respiratory diseases.

- What sales slogan can be developed to promote this client?
- What bonus items, if any, can be introduced?
- What approach (tone, mood, or style) will match this client's message?

Writing a PSA may be more difficult than writing a commercial because you're not selling a product people necessarily need or want. A PSA generally tries to sell an idea that people agree with in theory. But it may be an idea they have trouble putting into practice or one to which they won't give time or money.

Researching the Organization

When you write a PSA, you should analyze the organization's target audience, objectives, methods, and so on. Your first goal is to determine what the organization hopes to accomplish in its PSAs. Does it want to inform the audience about an upcoming event or a new service? Does it want to recruit volunteers? Does it want donations? Does it want people to change their behavior? Like a commercial, a PSA should present only one main idea.

Once you determine the goals of the organization, you must consider the public's image of the charity, which may not always be favorable. People have reasons for disliking charitable organizations, just as they dislike certain businesses. The distrust may be greater when people are being asked to give money or change their behavior out of altruism. You probably can't change a strong negative image, but you must be

A PUBLIC SERVICE MESSAGE — THE EPISCOPAL CHURCH

For Information: Armstrong Information Services, Inc., 141 East 44th St., New York, N.Y. 10017 (212) 986-0910

SILENT NIGHT -- :30 PSA -- #84-152

(SFX) VOICE OVER: Silence... doesn't stop teenage suicide.

Families that deal with the problem succeed in reducing the incidence of suicide.

So, look for the warning signs. Ask the probing questions.

Don't be afraid. You can't give them ideas they haven't already thought of.

You can give them the attention and help

that might save their life.

FIGURE 13.1 Idea- or Goal-Oriented PSA *(Courtesy Armstrong Information Services, Inc.)*

DID THE DOCTOR CHECK YOUR LUNGS?

A public service campaign by:

**NATIONAL JEWISH HOSPITAL/
NATIONAL ASTHMA CENTER
3800 East Colfax Ave.
Denver, Colo. 80206**

30 seconds

OFF-CAMERA VOICE:

GOOD CHECKUP?

A SIMPLE TEST IN YOUR
DOCTOR'S OFFICE WILL
HELP YOU BE SURE.

PRETTY GOOD SHAPE,
HUH?

DID YOU KNOW YOUR LUNGS
WON'T TELL YOU ANY-
THING'S WRONG WITH THEM
UNTIL IT'S TOO LATE...

CHECK EVERYTHING?

BUT THE SPIROMETER
TEST WILL...

HOW ABOUT YOUR LUNGS?

SO ASK YOUR DOCTOR...
NO, TELL HIM...

DID THE DOCTOR CHECK
YOUR LUNGS?

TELL HIM TO CHECK YOUR
LUNGS EVERY TIME YOU
HAVE A CHECKUP...

OH, I KNOW YOU FEEL
OKAY, BUT LOOK...

A Public Service Message
From
**njh
nac**
National Jewish Hospital/
National Asthma Center
Denver, Colorado 80206
and the Parker B. Francis Foundation

IT CAN GIVE YOU THE
BREATHING ROOM YOU
NEED.

FIGURE 13.2 PSA Targeting People with Respiratory Disease *(Courtesy National Jewish Hospital/ National Asthma Center)*

aware of it. Your PSA must present the cause in a positive light and should counter negative images as much as possible.

Identifying Audience Sensibilities

Some PSAs will touch the fears and dislikes of the audience. If those feelings are touched too deeply, people may be turned off by the message. For example, some charities ask for money to fight diseases that can leave people disabled or dead. Most of us don't like to think about death or the possibility of being disabled. Thus, to talk vividly of death or show disabled people may make a point that many listeners and viewers don't want to be exposed to. The same problem may occur when a spot shows people getting shots or giving blood. The cause may be worthy, but many people are afraid of needles or the sight of blood.

You must understand the fears and discomforts of your audience. Don't play on their fears or leave them with a feeling of despair. Impart a feeling of hope no matter how unpleasant the topic may be. But themes that gain attention by startling or disturbing viewers can work—if they're prepared with care. For example, a PSA designed to draw attention to animal cruelty used a startling message. The message focused on the hazards of leaving pets in closed autos during summer days. The car's surface, according to the PSA, becomes hot enough to fry an egg. The heat inside the car could quickly "fry the brains" of a dog. The spot got attention.

Carefully writing and selecting visual material for cable and TV is important if you are to get your message across without frightening your audience away.

Framing the Appeal

A PSA, like a commercial, must appeal to a human need. In fact, the appeal may have to be stronger in a PSA because you'll often be asking people to give for the good of others, not to buy something for themselves.

The human need to which you appeal will relate to the goal of the organization—raising money, recruiting volunteers, disseminating information, and so forth. Supplying information to the public will be the easiest task. Asking people to give time or money will be harder. Asking people to change their behavior—for example, to actually use their automobile seat belts—will be difficult, if not impossible.

The human needs you appeal to will be the same as those discussed in Chapter 5. Human needs to which you might appeal include the need to give and receive love and the need to feel ego satisfaction.

Love and family appeals touch emotions to which we all respond. PSAs have focused on the need to protect infants riding in a car by using a safety seat. Parental love for a child is a strong appeal. Other campaigns urge that individuals eat a sensible diet to avoid high blood pressure or ask them to be aware of the early signs of cancer. These campaigns appeal not only to our instinct for self-preservation but also to the love of family members for one another.

A message can also challenge viewers' self-esteem. The Red Cross did this with the slogan "Together, We Can Save a Life." Finally, a PSA can appeal to self-actualization. The "Living with Asthma" spot in Figure 13.3 emphasizes lifestyles and the fact that asthmatics can live relatively normal and productive lives with proper medication and care.

◆ Radio PSAs

Because radio stations seek specialized audiences, not every station will be appropriate for every cause. Radio stations usually analyze the PSAs they receive and air only those they feel are appropriate for their listeners. For example, a station with adult listeners

LIVING WITH ASTHMA

A public service announcement from

National Jewish Hospital/National Asthma Center
3800 E. Colfax Avenue
Denver, Colorado 80206

30 SECONDS

STARTER: (on bullhorn) RUNNERS ON YOUR MARK...
GET SET....

VOICE OVER: IF YOU HAVE ASTHMA, YOU MIGHT HAVE
FELT LEFT OUT. EXERCISE CAN OFTEN TRIGGER AN
ATTACK.

BUT WITH PROPER DIAGNOSIS AND CARE, YOU CAN
EXERCISE TOO.

MAYBE NOT A MARATHON, BUT ALMOST ANY ACTIVITY
ANYONE ENJOYS. WE KNOW... AND WE CARE...
WE'RE THE NATIONAL JEWISH HOSPITAL/NATIONAL
ASTHMA CENTER.

CALL 800-222-LUNG FOR MORE INFORMATION...
BECAUSE ASTHMA IS SOMETHING YOU CAN LIVE WITH.

FIGURE 13.3 PSA Aimed at Self-Actualization (*Courtesy National Jewish Hospital/National Asthma Center*)

may not be eager to promote a program to teach toddlers to swim if most of its listeners no longer have children at home. If you're writing PSAs, it's best to send stations topics and versions that they're most likely to run. Otherwise, you may waste a good deal of time. Stations prefer PSAs that are easy to produce and run, so a single-voice script is your best bet, and radio PSA scripts are often in single-voice format only. They can be read by the staff announcers and require no production expense. You can add music, sound effects, and multiple voices, but do so only if you know you can get the spot produced.

Radio stations also prefer that PSAs be a standard length. Many stations, for example, run only 10-second PSAs, although others run 20-second, 30-second, and occasionally 60-second announcements. Brevity is especially important in publicizing events of limited appeal—such as class reunions, bake sales, and health-care classes—that don't have to be sold to the general public.

The five W's—who, what, when, where, and why, in that order—should be clear in a standard informational PSA. That basic information alone will suffice for a 10- to 30-second announcement. The following script illustrates how easily a 10-second PSA can be written by using the five W's as a guide.

Who:	Ourtown Little League
What:	is sponsoring a car wash
When:	this Saturday from 10 to 3
Where:	at the Burger Boy on Main Street.
Why:	Proceeds will be used to buy new uniforms.

The addition of a few words, probably in the "why" section, will provide enough material for a 20- or 30-second message.

A wise practice is to prepare three versions of a PSA, as illustrated in the following scripts. Stations can then choose the version that best fits their time requirements. In preparing a PSA with multiple lengths, start with the shortest length. That version must contain the most important information you wish to convey to your audience. Add additional but less crucial details to the longer versions.

10-SECOND PSA

Ourtown Little League is sponsoring a car wash this Saturday from 10 to 3 at the Burger Boy on Main Street. Proceeds will be used to buy new uniforms.

20-SECOND PSA

The kids from Ourtown Little League need your help. They're having a car wash this Saturday from 10 to 3 at the Burger Boy on Main Street. They want to raise money for new uniforms. Drive by the Burger Boy this Saturday and help out our kids as they toil to earn new uniforms.

30-SECOND PSA

The kids from Ourtown Little League need your help in raising money for new uniforms. They're having a car wash this Saturday to demonstrate their initiative. The car wash will be at the Burger Boy on Main Street and will last from 10 to 3. Drive by and get your car washed. It's an inexpensive way to get your car cleaned and the money will help our kids pay for their own uniforms. Remember, the car wash for the Little League, this Saturday, 10 to 3, at the Burger Boy on Main Street.

Stop by.

Not all radio PSAs are single-voice spots. Radio PSAs can, and often should, use multiple voices, as well as more sophisticated production techniques, to gain attention. The following PSA is one that does use more than a straight approach.

SFX:	DRUMS BEATING A FUNERAL TATTOO.
ANNCR:	What do you think kills more Americans every year?
WOMAN:	Cocaine.
MAN:	Heroin . . . Alcohol.
WOMAN:	Suicide.
MAN:	Auto accidents.
WOMAN:	Homicides.
ANNCR:	Sure, those are all deadly. But there is something that kills more Americans every year than all those terrible things combined.
SFX:	DRUM BEATS DISSOLVE TO BREATHING
ANNCR:	Lung diseases. Including lung cancer. Surprised? Then you'll be shocked to know that the mortality rate of lung diseases is increasing faster than that of heart disease and most forms of cancer.
SFX:	BREATHING STOPS.
ANNCR:	Faster than any of the top ten causes of death. Here's another frightening statistic: an estimated one out of ten Americans is stricken with a chronic lung disease. So until we do something about lung diseases, no one can breathe easy. This message is brought to you by the American Lung Association.® Because it's a matter of life and breath.®

Courtesy American Lung Association®

◆ Television PSAs

Television stations appeal to a broader audience than radio stations, so they tend to receive many requests from nonprofit groups for PSAs. Further, most commercial TV stations successfully sell advertising and have only limited availabilities for PSAs—and very few in prime time. Add to this the fact that a TV PSA is more costly to produce than is a radio PSA, and the result is that television stations are highly selective in accepting requests for PSAs. Television stations are more likely to give time to those causes they judge to have the greatest value to their viewers.

The script that follows illustrates the emotional appeal a television writer was able to capture in a PSA for rape prevention. With no budget, the writer used a volunteer for talent.

VIDEO	**AUDIO**
USING DRAMATIC BACK LIGHTING FOR CONTRAST, A WOMAN IN BLACK IS SITTING WITH A WHITE BLINDFOLD. THE FIGURE TURNS TO THE CAMERA AS THE COPY READS " . . . RAPE IS A CRIME OF VIOLENCE,	ANNOUNCER: (SFX HEARTBEAT) It's easy to blind yourself to the facts of rape if it doesn't happen to you. But the fact is rape is a crime of violence, not sex, and it could happen to you or any man, woman, or child.

NOT SEX," AND BEGINS TO LOOSEN THE BLINDFOLD AS PREVENTION TIPS ARE HEARD. THEN JUST BEFORE THE BLINDFOLD IS DROPPED, THE PICTURE IS FREEZE-FRAMED WITH THE FOLLOWING SUPER: GREATER ORLANDO CRIME PREVENTION ASSOCIATION: (305) 422–8718

Help protect yourself from rape . . . be aware and avoid dangerous situations . . . use the buddy system, learn how to survive the rape, and report it. Call the Greater Orlando Crime Prevention Association for important information on rape prevention. Don't blind yourself to the facts.

Courtesy WOFL-TV, Orlando, Florida.

The voice-over is among the most common types of production used for local PSAs. A staff announcer or a spokesperson for the charity may read the script. Slides, videotape, graphic work, or production effects can provide the visual portion of the PSA.

Like radio stations, television stations prefer to keep their PSAs brief to accommodate more organizations. Thirty, 20, and 10 seconds are the most common lengths. Some 60-second announcements are used, mainly late at night or on weekends. Some stations use three- to four-second station ID PSAs.

◆ Opportunities for Writing PSAs

Local organizations often can't afford to hire a writer or an advertising agency to write their PSAs. As a result, many requests from local groups consist of a press release or a letter written by someone from the organization. The organizations hope that the stations will write the PSA for them. Because stations are deluged with PSAs, however, they are not able to honor all of these requests.

This situation has some important implications for the beginning copywriter. Local nonprofit organizations are often looking for someone to write PSAs for them. It's a good opportunity to break into writing for radio and TV. Here are some specific pointers for the volunteer PSA writer:

1. If you're writing radio PSAs for a nonprofit organization, analyze the stations in your area. Determine what audience each station is trying to reach, and send your PSAs to the stations most likely to broadcast them.

2. Include certain noncopy data in your PSA script in the same manner as you would for a commercial. What is the name of the organization? What is its address and telephone number? Who is the contact person? What is the length of the message? Follow the rules outlined in Chapter 2. Include the dates to start and stop airing the PSA. That's crucial information for the station or system, because it's the only information provided that tells when this announcement should be aired. Commercial account executives provide the traffic department, which schedules spots, with a sales order that specifies when the advertising schedule should begin and end. There is no account executive for a PSA, so you have to provide clear start and stop dates on the copy itself.

3. Acquaint yourself with the policies of the TV stations in your area. Most won't want a completed script. They'll prefer a press release and professional-quality visual material that station writers can adapt to the station's specifications. If you're working for the local chapter of a national charity, you may receive videotapes of completed spots. These can be supplied to stations along with sufficient data for a local tag.

4. Submit slides from local organizations to TV stations only if they're 35-mm color slides of professional quality. In addition, pictures in slides must be horizontal images.

5. Include photographs for use in TV spots only if they're 8- by 10-inch matte (dull) finish in horizontal images. If your organization is prominent enough to get on TV regularly, supply each station with a photo or artwork of your logo so that the station has it available.

◆ Issue Announcements

Broadcast stations and cable systems are sometimes asked to run commercials in which the sponsor takes a direct position on an important public issue. For instance, groups might want to buy commercial time to convey their opposition to nuclear power plants, express opinions on environmental concerns, or to take a stand on abortion. If the commercial copy for an issue is highly inflammatory, the station or system likely will either not accept the advertising or ask that the views expressed in the copy be toned down. Some issues, like abortion or AIDS, are explosive and can generate even more controversy if the copy expresses an extreme view.

Issue ads provide a means for citizens groups to spread their message to the public. If you're asked to write an issue ad, it's best to avoid extreme statements and graphic depictions. Use your imagination to convey the point of view, but remember that your boss may ask you to alter the copy if it's offensive.

Stations and cable systems are not required to accept issue advertising, but if they do, they may have to carry announcements from groups wanting to present opposing viewpoints.

Issue ads promote ideas rather than products, so they are similar to PSAs. To be certain the audience won't confuse the two, stations and systems often ask issue advertisers to include a statement in each spot that specifically identifies it as a paid commercial and names the sponsoring organization. Issue ads may advocate a position or rebut a viewpoint. Let's examine the two.

Advocacy Ads

Advocacy ads seek to defend or extend a position or to explain and justify the stance of a group. These spots aim to show that a given position on an issue has benefits for the community. The following spot illustrates the advocacy of a position. The sponsor is a community coalition against illegal pornography.

ANNOUNCER: (MUSIC UNDER) No one is safe from the dangers of illegal hard-core pornography in Central Florida. But there is a way to protect yourself and your family. The Greater Orlando Coalition Against Pornography (GO-CAP) is a nonprofit organization solely funded by individual, private, tax-deductible contributions. We're dedicated to ridding Central Florida of obscene, illegal pornography, because pornography destroys.

Call 855-2811 and find out how you can protect your community. Join in the fight to keep Orlando rated excellent!

(END/FADE MUS.)

Courtesy the Greater Orlando Coalition Against Pornography (GO-CAP).

Ads advocating a point of view may also extend a viewpoint. A group such as GO-CAP, for instance, might use subsequent spots to point out specific instances of the pornography problem or to argue for solutions.

Advocacy ads can also argue that consumers respond in a given way. The two ads that follow urge pregnant women not to smoke.

:60 CRYING IS CUTE

SFX: BABY CRYING AND FUSSING THROUGHOUT.

VO WOMAN	(Talking "baby talk") Aren't you a sick, preemie baby? Did your mommy smoke when she was pregnant? Yes she did.
VO ANNCR	Smoke when you're pregnant, and the price you could pay is having a baby who's sicker than most.
VO WOMAN	Such underdeveloped lungs.
VO ANNCR	And who cries more than a baby born to a mother who <u>didn't</u> smoke.
VO WOMAN	What an unhappy baby …
VO ANNCR	And that means you'll get less sleep, spend more time at the doctor's, have less time and money to do the things you'd rather be doing.
VO WOMAN	I bet you keep your mommy up all night.
VO ANNCR	But you can quit smoking, and we're here to help you do it. Call our toll-free number for your free "I Can Quit" kit at 1-877-951-7797. Call today. 1-877-951-7797.
VO WOMAN	Sick, sick, sick.
VO MAN	Brought to you by Alabama Tobacco Free Families.

Courtesy Myra Crawford, Ph.D., Alabama Tobacco Free Families, University of Alabama at Birmingham.

:60 "DEPARTMENT OF BABIES"

VIDEO	AUDIO
OPEN ON TIGHT SHOT OF SIGN: DEPARTMENT OF BABIES.	SFX: <u>AMBIENT NOISE, HUM AND BUZZ OF FLUORESCENT LIGHTS, ELECTRIC FAN</u>
CUT TO SERVICE DESK WITH MAN BEHIND THE COUNTER. HE IS ALL BUSINESS, VERY MATTER OF FACT. NOT NECESSARILY THE WARMEST, MOST UNDERSTANDING GUY. A WOMAN APPROACHES THE DESK AND HOLDS OUT THE BABY IN HER ARMS. THE MAN NEVER LOOKS UP FROM HIS DESK.	SFX: FUSSY BABY, CRYING/WHINING WOMAN: I'd like to exchange my baby. MAN: What's wrong with that one? WOMAN: I never get any sleep because she cries all the time.
MAN TURNS TO A COMPUTER AND STARTS TYPING.	MAN: (To himself as he types) Wants a baby who doesn't cry as much. (To woman) What else?
CUTS BETWEEN MAN AND WOMAN.	WOMAN: And she's always sick—I'm going to get fired if I take any more time off work. This isn't the baby I was supposed to have … I want a healthy baby. MAN: Smoke when you were pregnant?

CUT TO MAN. HE STOPS WHAT HE'S DOING, BUT STILL NEVER LOOKS UP AT HER. HE POINTS TO SIGN.	WOMAN: Well … yes.
CUT TO PERMANENT SIGN ON WALL: NO HEALTHY BABIES FOR MOTHERS WHO SMOKED WHILE PREGNANT.	MAN: Didn't you see the sign? MAN: Sorry. If you smoked when you were pregnant, you don't get a healthy baby. MAN: Next!
CUT BACK TO MAN. HE'S STILL NOT LOOKING UP TO WOMAN.	WOMAN: But … WOMAN ANNCR: Smoke when you're pregnant and chances are your baby will be sicker and cry more than babies born to mothers who didn't smoke. So if you want a healthy baby, you need to stop smoking now. And if you need help quitting, call this toll-free number for a free "I Can Quit" Kit.
CUT TO TITLE CARD WITH TYPE:	
TOLL FREE 1-877-926-3374 FREE I CAN QUIT KIT LOGO	Because a healthy baby means a better life for you.

Courtesy Myra Crawford, Ph.D., Alabama Tobacco Free Families, University of Alabama at Birmingham.

Rebuttal Ads

Rebuttal ads are used to fight against an established position. Here, a viewpoint has been established, and the goal is to argue against it and seek change. For example, the Florida Association of Broadcasters used the following spot to rebut a state tax on advertising and services. Observe how the spot seeks to bring about change. Note also that this spot identifies the sponsor.

VIDEO	AUDIO
1. SUPER: AN HISTORIC MOMENT (FADE TO BLACK)	1. When Governor Bob Martinez signed his
2. FADE IN ON SHOT OF MAN'S HAND SIGNING PAPER. (FLAG IN BACKGROUND) (FADE TO BLACK)	2. billion-dollar tax increase into law, he broke the record with the single largest tax increase in Florida's entire history.
3. SUPER: AN INSTANT REPLAY	3. But don't worry. He'll let you participate in this
4. FADE IN ON SHOT OF MAN'S HAND SIGNING PAPER.	4. record-breaking achievement by making you pay more for virtually everything you ever buy
5. SUPER: IN SLOW MOTION (FADE TO BLACK)	5. and virtually every service you ever need.

6. FADE IN ON SLOW MOTION SHOT OF MAN'S HAND SIGNING PAPER. (FADE TO BLACK)
7. SUPER: CALL GOVERNOR MARTINEZ (904) 488-4441.
   BROUGHT TO YOU BY THIS STATION AND THE FLORIDA ASSOCIATION OF BROADCASTERS.

6. So let Governor Martinez know what you think of his record-breaking feat.
7. Call him in Tallahassee at 488-4441. We're sure he'd like to know.

Courtesy Les Loggins Advertising/Public Relations.

◆ Political Announcements

It's not hard to tell when an important election is near, because you'll see and hear a lot more political advertisements. Candidates for office have found that radio and television advertising is an efficient way to reach the public. As a result, candidates spend huge amounts of money on political commercials. Many political candidates employ advertising agencies to handle their advertising, but in smaller markets you'll be asked to write political spots as part of your copywriting duties.

Note at the outset that a paid political message is a commercial. But instead of selling a product, store, or service, you're selling the virtues of the person running for office. Naturally, you'll have to rely on what the candidate wants said. That's likely to mean painting a favorable picture of the candidate you're writing for and possibly discrediting the opposing candidate.

Writing a political commercial presents several difficulties. One is comparing candidates. The incumbent will claim to have done a "good" job, one worth rewarding with reelection. Opponents will claim the incumbent has done a "bad" job and point out the reasons why they will do better. Of course, *good* and *bad* are difficult terms to quantify. No one knows whether a particular candidate really can do a better job with the city's garbage removal problem than the incumbent did. And you can only cite what the candidate says he or she *will* do. As a result, it's difficult for the public to make political comparisons.

Another problem is judging what political announcements can actually accomplish. Research has shown that most campaigns don't change people's minds. Most people have already decided which candidate and which political party they'll vote for before they hear the political commercials. Political ads don't change minds, but they do reinforce existing beliefs and voting patterns. Thus, the most realistic goal in many political commercials is to keep the faithful committed and to encourage them to actually vote for the party or person they believe in.

The following are some of the specific goals you might seek to accomplish in political commercials.

Introducing a Candidate

New candidates for office don't have a record to run on and can only introduce themselves to the voters and explain their qualifications. If the candidate has held positions that qualify him or her for the office, that should be pointed out. Significant endorsements should also be noted. Of course, you should also stress party affiliation.

Incumbent candidates sometimes get lost in the shuffle and need to "reintroduce" themselves to the voters. Qualifications, endorsements—and of course, record— should be stressed in familiarizing the voters with an incumbent.

The following commercial for Jim Smith fits into the "introduction" category. The video consists of a finger tracing the number of Smiths in a phone book. The point of the spot is that Jim Smith stands out and should be elected.

ANNOUNCER	(under OKAY, SMITH, SMITH, JIM) . . . It may be a common name, but you couldn't find a more uncommon man to be your secretary of state. For the past twenty years, as chief of staff for two governors, attorney general, and now secretary of state, he's been working to keep Florida great. Keep Jim Smith your secretary of state. (under SMITH, JIM SMITH).

Courtesy Susan Gilbert & Company, Miami, Florida.

Presenting the Candidate's Record

If the candidate is an incumbent or is running for a new political office, stress his or her accomplishments. Candidates like to stand on their records, and well they should. If they have a significant list of achievements, they can point to their accomplishments and promise the voters that they'll do more of the same. This may be one of the easiest political commercials to write, especially if the record is strong.

The TV spot that follows stresses the record of an incumbent candidate. The video shows the candidate at work, while the audio explains his record.

VIDEO	AUDIO
MX: BACKGROUND INSTRUMENTAL/ DRAMATIC UP AND UNDER SUSTAIN.	
SFX: USE B/W PHOTOGRAPHS WITH CAMERA LENS AND PHOTO TAKING SOUND EFFECT WITH TAPE	
CAM CARD: A NEW CONGRESSMAN FOR A NEW DISTRICT	
FROM VIDEOTAPE: INTERIOR OF BATCHELOR IN OFFICE AT DESK. HE ANSWERS PHONE, HAS DISCUSSION.	(up music/sustain) V.O . . . . For the last eight years, Dick Batchelor has helped write a balanced budget for Florida.
ECU: BLACK/WHITE PHOTO OF AUTO ACCIDENT WIPE ON, GO TO BLACK	He chaired the joint legislative auditing committee to rid Florida of waste and fraud in Medicaid, food stamp, and other funding programs.
	SFX: photo lens
FROM VIDEOTAPE: BATCHELOR ON HIGHWAY WITH PATROL OFFICER, FHP CAR, BLUE FLASHING LIGHT.	Drunk drivers on Florida's highways.
SHAKE HANDS.	Dick Batchelor was a prime sponsor of the new, get-tough drunk driver law.
ECU: BLACK/WHITE PHOTO OF LAKE WITH POLLUTION	SFX: PHOTO LENS

| FROM VIDEOTAPE: BATCHELOR ON LAKE-FRONT DECK WITH RETIRED MAN FISHING.

SQUEEZE ZOOM LENS EFFECT
HEAD OF BATCHELOR IN CENTER SCREEN, GREEN BACKGROUND WITH BATCHELOR ... A NEW CONGRESSMAN CAM CARDS PAN LEFT AND RIGHT STOPPING AT TOP AND BOTTOM. | Conservation ... He supported the stopping of the cross Florida barge canal, wrote tough hazardous waste laws, and steered the passage of the law controlling low-level nuclear radioactive waste.
As an eight-year veteran, full-time legislator, the closer you look ...The clearer the choice. (fade) |

Courtesy Susan Gilbert & Company, Miami, Florida.

Arguing the Issues

It's not always easy to tell voters where a candidate stands on the issues because the issues are often complex. Still, candidates may want to use political announcements to tell the public their positions on issues. This may occur when candidates have quite different positions on the issues and may be done in the form of a comparison. As with any commercial, it's best to address a single issue in each spot. The candidate's stand on an issue must be presented clearly and simply. If this is accomplished, the spot can reinforce the idea that the candidate is thoughtful and, in the right situation, show him or her to be in line with majority opinion on the issue.

Building an Image

A frequent criticism of political commercials is that they sell image and not substance. That may well be true, because radio and television aren't as effective at explaining complex issues as they are at dramatizing images. Candidates sometimes try to capitalize on this because it's often easier for them to promote an image. A little show biz can work wonders. For example, the governor of a southern state periodically held "work days" in which he "worked" for a day as a teacher, a farmer, a factory worker, and so forth. The work days made the news and provided material for his campaign commercials, showing him in touch with the people. In another instance, a Florida candidate for the U.S. Senate walked from one town to another, meeting voters as he went. He, too, made news and generated material for his commercials, which depicted him as the hardworking "walking" candidate.

The TV spot that follows builds an image by depicting the candidate as an outdoorsman (the video shows him fishing) who wants to preserve the quality of life.

| JIM SMITH ON CAMERA | Like all of us, I'm concerned about our quality of life. I was born in Florida, went to school here. I raised my children in this great state. I can't imagine a better place to live, and I want to help keep it that way. |
| ANNOUNCER | For the past 20 years, through 3 administrations, Jim Smith has been working to keep Florida great. Keep Jim Smith your Secretary of State. |

Courtesy Kerns & Associates, Inc.

Making Political Comparisons

It's hard for the public to make political comparisons, because they must judge what a candidate says he or she *will* do. Still, candidates might want to compare their records, their backgrounds qualifications, or their stands on the issues in the hope that they'll look stronger than their opponents.

Building Credibility

A political commercial may be used to enhance the credibility of a candidate. In fact, credibility may be a key ingredient in a campaign if there are questions about a candidate's honesty, voting record, or ethics. More than one incumbent has faced legal charges but has managed to get reelected. This type of spot must show the voters all the good things the candidate has done for them and discredit the negative factors.

As noted previously, the candidate will tell you what to say, and his or her concerns may be varied. The candidate may only want to build name recognition or to compare voting records. The possibilities are endless, and they'll usually be tied to the candidate's budget. If that budget is very small, it might only allow messages that say something like, "I'm Joe Jones, Democratic candidate for mayor. Vote for me on election day!"

As you will recall from Chapter 3, a political sponsorship identification announcement is required for all political spots. In the case of the TV scripts reprinted here, the announcement would be presented visually and is not included in the scripts.

➤ POINTS TO REMEMBER

- Public-service announcements are messages broadcast (or cablecast) free of charge for nonprofit organizations.

- If a PSA deals with the fears of the audience, it should impart a feeling of hope.

- PSAs written for radio stations should consider the station's target audience.

- A television PSA should have a strong visual quality even if its production budget is low.

- Radio stations will most readily run PSAs for local nonprofit events if the spot is brief and sets forth the who, what, when, where, and why of the event.

- If stations broadcast issue ads, they may be obligated to sell time to groups holding opposing viewpoints.

- Issue ads seek to advocate or rebut a point of view.

- If the issues in issue ads are too inflammatory, stations probably won't run the advertising.

- Political commercials might not change minds, but they can reinforce existing beliefs and voting patterns.

- It's often easier in a commercial to promote political images than to explain complex issues.

- Political comparisons can be effective if the candidate you're writing for can clearly be shown to be stronger.

- Credibility is a key factor for candidates, and many politicians use broadcast advertising to enhance it.

EXERCISES

Exercise 1

Prepare a 30-second TV PSA in which you urge teenagers not to drink while driving. Appeal to the need for parents to love their children. Emphasize that although drinking might seem like a grownup thing to do, drinking and driving can lead to crippling injuries or death.

Don't use any slogans from previous PSAs on this topic. Be as original as you can.

Exercise 2

This is an exercise in writing radio PSAs of differing lengths.

Visit a service office on your campus (campus police, legal assistance office, placement center, religious organization, and so forth) or the offices of a club. Gather as much information as you can: brochures, handouts, pamphlets. If need be, interview the person in charge.

Prepare three informational PSAs for radio—10-, 20-, and 30-second spots for the same service or organization. Make certain that the PSAs are airworthy.

Exercise 3

Write a 60-second radio commercial for Mary Brown, Independent Party candidate for mayor of Yourtown. Include appropriate sponsor identification. The fact sheet you are given includes the following information:

Resident of Yourtown for 14 years.

Married, three children.

Attended public schools in Yourtown, graduate of Yourtown University.

Lawyer. Partner, law firm of Henson, Earl and Brown.

Member of Yourtown City Council for four years. Worked for improvement of streets and roads, sponsored bill that led to 12 percent pay increase for police and fire department personnel.

Five years on Mayor's Task Force Against Drunk Driving.

The advertisement is paid for by the Citizens' Committee for Mary Brown.

Exercise 4

Write a 60-second issue-oriented radio spot for the Committee to Save Gopher Creek. Use these facts:

Highway 4 follows Gopher Creek near your community. The creek is a beautiful mountain stream, but its beauty is being destroyed. Automobiles and heavy trucks are using the route as a shortcut. The route was once a quiet mountain road, but the heavy traffic is causing air and water pollution. The Committee to Save Gopher Creek wants people to be aware of the problem. They also want trucks and commercial traffic restricted from the route. Use as much visual imagery as you can to illustrate the problem and describe the goals of the committee.

Exercise 5

Write a 30-second PSA for the Summer Youth Employment Program. Emphasize that the city will be hiring high school–age youth to work on city projects—landscaping parks, cleaning roadways, doing maintenance, and so on. The jobs will pay the minimum wage. Also, Yourtown is sponsoring a job placement service with local employers. Its goal is to bring employers and teenagers together to aid in filling summer jobs.

CHAPTER FOURTEEN

The Broadcast Campaign

◆ **Broadcast Campaign Structure**

The Client and Competition Analysis
Analyzing the Client
Identifying Client Strengths and Weaknesses
Analyzing the Competition
Target Audience
Objectives
Sales Slogan
Bonus Items
Positioning
Approach

◆ **Examples of Campaigns**

Middleton Lawn & Pest Control
Florida Libraries
Red Lobster
WHOI-TV
WFTV
Points to Remember
Exercises

S o far in this text we've looked at the basic activity of a broadcast copywriter—writing individual radio and television messages. However, broadcast announcements are not always independently written and scheduled. Announcements of all types— commercial, public service, and promotional—are often written and scheduled as part of a broadcast campaign. A campaign multiplies the effort of an individual order, which includes one or more spots on a single station and may involve writing both radio and television spots. Spots may be placed on selected stations in a given city or region or across the country. A broadcast campaign is complex, so strategic planning is essential if the advertiser's message is to be properly conceived, written, and scheduled.

◆ Broadcast Campaign Structure

A broadcast campaign is a carefully prepared strategy to achieve a specific goal for the advertiser. The goal may be to introduce a new product, store, or service; reinforce brand loyalty; demonstrate a unique feature; or meet any other specific goal.

A broadcast campaign may schedule a commercial or commercials over a period of time—either over a long haul (with spots spread over a period of months) or in a con- centrated blitz (with a heavy concentration of spots in a few days or weeks). Spots in broadcast campaigns are usually related to one another with slogans that, through rep- etition, help build client recognition. The slogans help the consumer to recognize the advertisements easily and eventually to recognize the advertiser. For example, the slogan "Nissan. Driven!" identifies the company and is easy to remember. Unlike inde- pendently run spots, broadcast campaigns provide for planned promotion, which can have a strong cumulative effect. Advertising campaigns can involve other forms of communication in addition to the broadcast media.

Campaigns are used by major clients able to pay for the planning, creative develop- ment, and production of spots. Because the effort is more complex than preparing an independently run spot, campaigns are usually prepared by advertising agencies that have the resources to do the media and creative planning.

The Client and Competition Analysis

A broadcast campaign, perhaps more than independently run announcements, must be planned using the guidelines for creating a copy platform presented in Chapter 7. These now familiar guidelines include the determining objectives, target audience, sales slogan, bonus ideas, and approach. Most of these items require little more mention than we pre- sented in Chapter 7. However, our copy platform for independently run announcements did not include one item that is especially crucial to a broadcast campaign—an analysis of the client for whom you're preparing the campaign and its major competitors. Although you might consider these items in preparing an independently run spot, you probably would not treat them with the depth that is necessary to prepare a campaign.

ANALYZING THE CLIENT   At the outset of a campaign, you must have a good under- standing of both the client and the client's competitors. You must know the client's service, store, or product in depth if you're to promote it successfully. You should know far more about the client than you'll need simply to write the commercials. This insight will enable you to convince the client that you're knowledgeable enough about the product, store, or service to develop an effective campaign.

Clients generally supply a sizable amount of data about their businesses, but just as you can't rely completely on such data for an independently run spot, you should never rely on it for a campaign. You need to meet the client and see the business firsthand.

There are several reasons why you can't completely rely on the data supplied by the client. One is that familiarity with the business could lead the client to overlook items that you can use to advantage in appealing to the public. In one instance, a drugstore chain occasionally mentioned in its advertising that it would meet any other drugstore's prices. All the customer had to do was bring in the competitor's newspaper ad. If the competitor's price for an item was lower, the store would match it. Although this policy wasn't a major part of the chain's promotion, a copywriter from the agency handling the account noticed a customer bring a competitor's newspaper ad into the store she was visiting. She also noticed that the customer got the item at the competitor's price and that the clerk seemed pleased to see that people were aware of the policy. Rather than keeping this policy in the background, the copywriter focused a campaign on it. Because she visited the client for a firsthand look, her commercials emphasized an important selling point.

Another reason a copywriter can't rely only on information supplied by the client is that the client may be reluctant to disclose weaknesses of the product, store, or service. It's understandable that a client might not want to discuss product weaknesses, such as the fact that the chemicals used by a home pest-control service can't completely eliminate crawling insects. It is much easier to pretend that the product does the job, period!

But as a copywriter, you need to know both the good and the bad. If you don't know the shortcomings, both you and the client might be surprised by negative responses to your commercials once customers become aware of them. If sales go down, the client might cancel its contract with your station.

IDENTIFYING CLIENT STRENGTHS AND WEAKNESSES   Whether you visit the client or not, your first step in preparing a campaign is to determine the strengths of the client's business. What makes this product, store, or service superior? Is the store established or new, modern or quaint? Is the service convenient, inexpensive, or reliable? Whatever strengths exist, you need to identify them before you plan your campaign. These are the reasons why a consumer would want to buy a product, patronize a store, or use a service. The strengths are directly tied to the benefits that customers will receive. The advantages may be readily apparent, or you may have to conduct research to discover them.

It's rare to find a product or business that doesn't have some shortcomings, and you must be aware of them *before* you plan the campaign. The store may be inconveniently located, the service may cost more than that of competitors, or the product may not be available in all stores. Whatever weaknesses exist, you must know about them. If possible, try to turn the weakness in your favor. One television dealer does this by acknowledging that his TV sets cost more but emphasizing, in the commercials, that "They're worth it!" If you don't evaluate the shortcomings of the client's business, you may create expectations that the product cannot live up to.

ANALYZING THE COMPETITION   Campaign planning requires more than analyzing your own client. You must also analyze the competition. If your client is a car dealership in a city of half a million people, for instance, it will have competition from a number of other dealers. You don't have to analyze all of them. The ones you must be concerned about are the primary competitors. You'll have to identify them.

You identify the primary competitors by looking at similarities. Which businesses have the same products as your client? Which businesses are seeking the same customers and serving the same geographic area as your client? If your client is a Ford dealer, a Buick dealer across town isn't a primary competitor. However, a Ford dealership across town is a primary competitor because it's selling the same product. A nearby Chevrolet dealership may also be a primary competitor, not because it sells the same product but because it seeks the same customers.

Once you've identified the primary competitors, you should work up a brief analysis of each. The analysis need not be as detailed as the one you do for your own client, but it should be thorough enough to describe each primary competitor's position relative to the strengths and weaknesses of your client. How does your client stack up against competitor A, competitor B, and so on?

If your client does not emerge stronger than its major competitors, you must look for features that distinguish your client from all primary rivals. For example, if your client's service is priced the same as the competition's and is as effective, you can't tout it as being superior. But if your client is an established, family-operated company while the competitors are newcomers to town, you still have an edge to work with. Once you find such a feature or advantage, you can focus on your client as the firm potential customers should use.

An analysis of the competition should also include the type and amount of broadcast advertising that your client's major competitors have been using. This is an important element in assessing a competitor's strengths and weaknesses. If competitors are using radio and television, study their commercials and their schedules. Approximate their budgets and evaluate the approaches they are using in their commercials. Your decision to use radio, television, or both will vary considerably, depending on what the competition is doing. If your competition is spending a significant amount on a highly visible television campaign, you must decide whether you want to use television, and if so, in what way. It would be a reckless waste of your client's money simply to duplicate a competitor's broadcast efforts.

Target Audience

It's important that you target your campaign to a particular group. Go back to your initial analysis of the client. What is the client selling? What are its strengths and weaknesses? What is your objective? Weigh this information carefully. It should guide you in directing the campaign to the appropriate audience.

Remember that you'll typically define your audience on the basis of standard demographics —age, sex, education, income, and so on. You may supplement the demographic data with psychographic research describing the psychological characteristics of the audience.

Objectives

Once you've analyzed your client and its major competitors, you're ready for the key question: What objective do you want this campaign to accomplish? This brings us back to the copy platform and the items we discussed in Chapter 7. For our purposes here, it's sufficient to say that advertising objectives should deal with specific communications activities rather than with marketing goals. State your objectives specifically and thoroughly, as follows:

- Present a price promotion for Subway's Meatball Sub.
- Demonstrate the differences in the newborn, infant, crawler, and walker phases of Pampers Easy Ups training pants.
- Persuade consumers to see a demonstration of SharpVision projection TV in stores.

Similarly, each of the following objectives is for a separate spot in a Honda automobile campaign:

- Promote Honda's resale value as highest in its class.
- Promote Honda's best-selling status as the standard against which other auto makers measure their cars.
- Promote the style of the Honda line.
- Promote the Honda Accord Hybrid.

Note that each of these statements describes a specific goal the advertiser wants to achieve.

Sales Slogan

The sales slogan is the major selling point of your campaign and consists of a major sales point tied to a strong consumer benefit. Preparation of the sales slogan forces you to concentrate on the client's greatest strengths. These strengths are probably the main points you'll want to emphasize anyway, so the time you spend identifying the main strengths gives you more to work with in building a solid picture of your client. If you can build the major selling point into a sales slogan, you'll have developed an even stronger sales vehicle.

As we noted earlier, a slogan has the advantage of building client recognition. Through repetition, the client's sales theme can draw attention to the commercial and thus to the sales pitch. A slogan such as "Before you dress, Caress" is ideal. It's brief, clever, and memorable. The name of the product, a body wash, is included for greater sales power.

Bonus Items

Too many selling points may confuse the audience, so it's best to emphasize one *main* sales idea. You may add an extra copy idea or two, but be certain they relate to the main idea of your sales theme.

The examples of objectives presented earlier in this chapter give several illustrations of bonus items. The Subway sandwich shops promoted a special price for their meatball sub. That was the primary objective of the spot, but the spot also promoted Subway's use of fresh ingredients as a bonus item. Sharp Electronics wanted to convince people to see a projection TV system demonstrated in a store. The bonus item for the spot was to encourage people to enter a sweepstakes giveaway for prizefight tickets.

As you can see in these two examples, the bonus items are really extensions of the main selling points. That's what a bonus item should be, an additional item that can be included but that may not be essential to the spot. Look at the copy information and identify major and optional selling points. Then decide if any of the optional selling points are important enough to be included. If bonus items will dilute a strong, clear sales theme, it's best not to include them.

Positioning

Positioning involves creating a separate identity for your client or product—an identity that helps distinguish your client from competitors.

You may not have the time or resources to position each client purchasing an independently run spot, but you will want to position your client in a broadcast campaign. A planned promotion with a carefully defined objective gives your client the highest possible visibility. Positioning is thus an essential part of a campaign.

One auto dealer could be described as "the volume leader," while another claims to be the dealer that "sells for less." If these claims have real substance—in other words, if one dealer offers good prices because it sells so many cars and the other really does offer lower prices—then both have unique claims. Note that the position must be real. If the product or service doesn't deliver what is promised, the positioning won't work. Refer to the discussion of positioning in Chapter 7 for more details.

Approach

Just as you want to use a suitable tone, mood, or style for an independently run spot, you also need a suitable approach for the commercials you prepare for a broadcast campaign. Will the approach convey elegance, understatement, or an aggressive hard sell?

The approach must match the objective and the target audience, so you should refer to your initial planning. Look at what you want this campaign to accomplish (objectives) and who you want the message to reach (target audience). Those two items will guide you in determining a suitable approach.

Once you've completed your copy platform, you may write some sample scripts for the campaign. The spots may relate to a single objective or to several objectives that the campaign is to achieve.

If the campaign is for television only, your initial efforts will probably be storyboards rather than scripts. Storyboards enable the clients to visualize the spots, whereas scripts do not. If the campaign uses radio, initial scripts may be shown to the client. Neither radio nor television spots will likely be produced until the client approves them— production costs preclude the possibility of producing a spot purely on speculation.

◆ Examples of Campaigns

Up to this point, we have discussed the process of planning a broadcast campaign. To help you appreciate the marketing and creative strategies that make up such a campaign, this section presents examples of actual campaigns. Naturally, we cannot present every step of the planning process, but taken together, the cases illustrate the interaction of marketing dynamics with the creative process.

Middleton Lawn & Pest Control

Bugs present problems both inside and outside many homes. The problem is greater in warm-weather locations where bugs are active much of the year. Businesses compete with each other to offer consumers lawn and pest control service.

Middleton Lawn & Pest Control serves Central Florida, a location with a semitropical climate that is conducive to year-round pest activity. A number of pest control companies, both local and national, serve the area. Middleton launched a campaign of television spots to make people aware of the company name and service. The campaign was a rousing success. Sales to new customers increased by 59 percent in 1999–2000, including growth of 144 percent in May 2000.

Two of the spots from the campaign are "Switch," in Figure 14.1, and "Through the Years," in Figure 14.2.

"Switch"

SFX: DOOR OPENING

MAN: Hi, I'm here to spray for your roaches
WOMAN: I CALLED ABOUT ANTS!

(MAN SWITCHES HANDS)

MAN: Uh, I'm here to spray for your ants??

SFX: DOOR SLAMMING SHUT

WOMAN: URRR!

ANNCR: Time To Call Middleton

FIGURE 14.1 Pest Control Campaign Spot *(Courtesy PUSH Advertising)*

"Through the Years"

SFX: AMBIENT SOUNDS. MUSIC THROUGHOUT.

(MAN AND WOMAN LOOKING AT EACH OTHER LOVINGLY, REMINISCING THROUGH OLD PHOTOGRAPHS)

(MAN POURS LEMONADE)

(WEIGHT OF GLASS CAUSES WOMAN TO FALL THROUGH PORCH)
WOMAN: Aahh!!   SFX: CRASHING

ANNCR: Time to call Middleton.

ANNCR: Now offering Termidor. It's better than baits and kills termites fast.

SFX: AMBIENT SOUNDS.

FIGURE 14.2 Pest Control Campaign Spot *(Courtesy PUSH Advertising)*

Florida Libraries

The library is often taken for granted. The public may be unaware of the extent of its services or volume of business. The campaign for Florida libraries was designed with two goals: to stimulate awareness of public libraries and to indicate the scope of the services provided. The objective of the following script is to inform the public of library services.

VIDEO	AUDIO
CLOSEUP OF A BUSINESSMAN SITTING BEHIND DESK.	Businessman: (TONE OF INCREDULITY) Now, let me get this straight.
SLOW ZOOM OUT THROUGHOUT SPEECH	You have 330 service centers around Florida. You get 15,000 business calls a day and you answer every one. And you have over 11 million resources available to my staff. And most of your services are free. Just who are you, anyway?
EXHIBITS SURPRISE	V.O.: (BOOMING VOICE) We're your public library. We offer all this and more.
SPECIAL EFFECT OF PAGE TURNING TO ART CARD OF LOGO: "WE DO MORE THAN KEEP THE BOOKS AT YOUR LIBRARY"	Narrator: We do more than keep the books at your library.

Courtesy Barratt Wilkins, Florida State Librarian.

Broadcast campaigns may use spots of varying lengths for certain objectives. This 10- second spot is designed to keep consumers aware of the library.

VIDEO	AUDIO
SLOW ZOOM FROM MEDIUM SHOT OF PHONE TO CLOSEUP	Narrator: Who gets 15,000 business calls a day and answers every one?
CLOSE UP ON PHONE AS HAND REACHES INTO FRAME AND PICKS UP RECEIVER.	SFX: Ringing phone
FREEZE FRAME. SPECIAL EFFECT OF PAGE TURNING TO ART CARD OF LOGO "WE DO MORE THAN KEEP THE BOOKS—AT YOUR LIBRARY."	V.O.: Public library Narrator: We do more than keep the books … at your library.

Courtesy Barratt Wilkins, Florida State Librarian.

Red Lobster

Restaurants face the task of keeping customers coming back. To accomplish this, special offers are promoted to attract consumers. These offers may center on certain food items, themes, or prices. The storyboards in Figures 14.3 and 14.4 focus on shrimp. Shrimp lovers are disappointed if a restaurant offers too few shrimp, so Red Lobster appeals with a solution to that concern. The spot in Figure 14.3 focuses on the number of shrimp customers will get and includes a special price. The commercial in Figure 14.4 doesn't mention a price but tries to hook consumers with the notion that they can get a whole

Red Lobster
30 Shrimp:30

Woman 1: "Wow...

Woman 1:...that's a lot of shrimp."

Anncr: "At Red Lobster
for a limited time,

enjoy 30 shrimp for just $9.99."

Waiter: "What sounds good
to you folks tonight?"

Man 1: "30 Shrimp please."
Waiter: "Great choice."

Anncr: "with lemon pepper shrimp,

succulent scampi...

delicious grilled shrimp...

and our famous fried shrimp."

"That's 4 different kinds. 30
shrimp on one plate just $9.99."

Anncr: "At only one place"
Waiter: "Only at Red Lobster."
(Red Lobster music up)

Woman 1:"And kids get shrimp too...

A complete meal just $1.99."
(Red Lobster music out)

FIGURE 14.3   Commercial Storyboard for 30 Shrimp *(Courtesy Wyman Roberts/Red Lobster)*

pound of shrimp at Red Lobster. The two spots complement each other in that both draw attention to the number of shrimp consumers will get, even though the spots make the point somewhat differently. It is hoped that shrimp lovers who see the spots will remember the sales theme: Red Lobster offers a pound of shrimp, 30 of them, for just $9.99.

WHOI-TV

Television station WRAU in Peoria, Illinois, found that it had an image problem. Over a period of time, the station had experienced changes in its on-air staff, and its ratings had slipped. Along with other changes, station management decided it wanted a new slogan that tied in with the viewing area. The station had already changed call letters several times, but a new call letter combination seemed an important part of creating a new image.

The station decided to change its call letters to WHOI, with the letters *HOI* standing for *Heart of Illinois.* This reference was an important part of the new image because it identified the station's primary viewing area. Further, the Peoria area is commonly

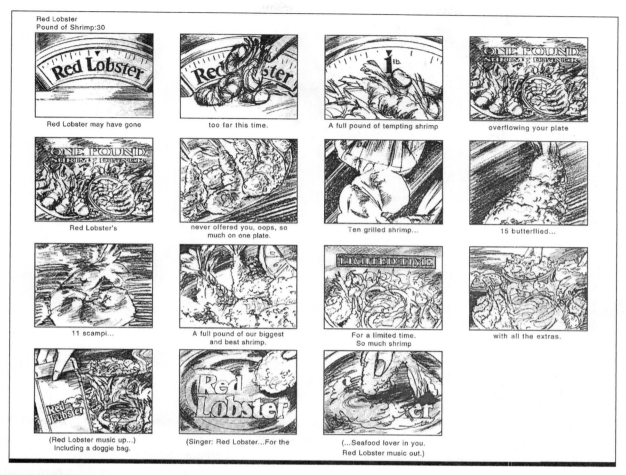

Red Lobster
Pound of Shrimp :30

Red Lobster may have gone	too far this time.	A full pound of tempting shrimp	overflowing your plate
Red Lobster's	never offered you, oops, so much on one plate.	Ten grilled shrimp...	15 butterflied...
11 scampi...	A full pound of our biggest and best shrimp.	For a limited time. So much shrimp	with all the extras.
(Red Lobster music up...) Including a doggie bag.	(Singer: Red Lobster...For the	(...Seafood lover in you. Red Lobster music out.)	

FIGURE 14.4   Commercial Storyboard for Pound of Shrimp *(Courtesy Wyman Roberts/Red Lobster)*

referred to as the Heart of Illinois, so the new call letters established a link between the station and its viewing area. Radio, television, and newspaper advertising were used to promote the new call letters. The newspaper ad is shown in Figure 14.5.

Radio spots that were developed used the audio jingle prepared as a part of the promotional campaign.

JINGLE UP FULL FOR LYRIC . . . "19 WE'RE THE HEART OF IT ALL." (ANNOUNCER)

Now we're the top-rated TV station in the Heart of Illinois. (JINGLE UP FOR FULL LYRIC) "AND YOU'RE A PART OF IT ALL" (ANNOUNCER)

From the time the sun rises . . . until after the day is done . . . throughout the Heart of Illinois— 19 means #1. Every day more men, more women, and more families turn to TV-19 than any other Peoria television station. Viewer surveys by both major rating services agree . . . from sign-on to sign-off, WHOI-TV 19 is far and away Peoria's top-rated TV station. Be part of the action, the adventure, and the excitement. We'll light your life up with the best news and entertainment in the Heart of Illinois.

(JINGLE LYRICS UP FULL) "WE'RE 19—WE'VE GOT IT ALL."

Courtesy Chuck Sherman, WHOI-TV, Creve Coeur, Illinois.

the new heart of Illinois

TV-19 has changed to WHOI. Because we're proud to be part of the Heart of Illinois, we want our name to reflect that pride. So when you tune to 19 for news, entertainment and sports, remember, we're now WHOI. Bringing you the best of the Heart of Illinois.

We've got it all.

FIGURE 14.5 The Newspaper Part of an Advertising Campaign to Change a Station's Image
(Courtesy Chuck Sherman, WHOI-TV, Creve Coeur, Illinois)

WFTV

Whereas WHOI used a campaign to promote new call letters and a new image, WFTV used a campaign to promote a news special. TV stations often run special reports within their newscasts as a means of covering a topic in greater detail. Often, these reports run for several nights. In this case, the objective of the campaign was to get viewers to watch the special report.

The campaign involved advertising in the print media and on radio and running on-air promos on WFTV. A print ad from the campaign is included in Figure 14.6 to give you a stronger feel for the campaign. You'll notice that the radio and TV spots that follow also used a serious, dramatic approach in keeping with the topic.

APPROACH	SERIOUS
MUSIC	SOMBER MUSIC UP AND UNDER THROUGHOUT
ANNCR	Wanted! People to work long hours at night … alone … for little pay. Must be willing to risk injury or death while on the job.
SFX	CASH REGISTER OPENS-SHOT IS HEARD
ANNCR	Last year in the state of Florida more convenience store clerks were killed in the line of duty than police. Watch "Deadly Convenience," a special report on a dangerous occupation, tonight at eleven on the Eyewitness Update on WFTV, Channel 9, Central Florida's news leader.

FIGURE 14.6 The Newspaper Part of an Advertising Campaign to Promote a News Special
(*Courtesy SFN Communications of Florida, Inc.*)

VIDEO	AUDIO
UP ON LS OF NIGHTTIME VIEW OF CONVE-NIENCE STORE	It's one of the most dangerous jobs in America …
MCU OF SIGN FOR POLICE CRIME STAKEOUT	Consumer store clerks take maximum risks for minimum wage
REFLECTION SHOT OF STORE IN SECURITY MIRROR	and more of them are killed each year on duty than are police officers.
MS OF TRIGGS IN FRONT OF CONVENIENCE STORE	I'm Steve Triggs. Join me for "Deadly Convenience," an in-depth look at conven-ience store crime … what law enforcement is doing to stop it
MS OF COP INSIDE CRUISER DRIVING PAST STORE	
CU OF CONVENIENCE STORE SIGN. DISS TO SHOT OF EMPLOYEE	and what convenience store chains can do to better protect their employees.
CG: DEADLY CONVENIENCE, STARTING MONDAY 11 PM, WFTV, CHANNEL 9	It starts Monday on the Eyewitness News Update.

Courtesy SFN Communications of Florida, Inc.

Note that the theme of the campaign is prominent in each advertisement. Use of the same theme not only achieves consistency but also means that each spot can stand alone. In other words, consumers did not have to see or hear all three ads to understand the message. Each spot in a campaign should be able to communicate the message by itself.

➤ POINTS TO REMEMBER

- The schedule of a broadcast campaign may vary, with spots spread over a period of months or a heavy concentration of spots in a few days or weeks.

- An in-depth analysis of the client's business or service is necessary to develop a viable campaign. Identify the client's strengths and weaknesses. Your client's primary competi-tors must be evaluated relative to the strengths and weaknesses of your client.

- Positioning your client in a campaign allows you to create a separate identity for your client, an identity that helps the public distin-guish your client from competitors.

- Spots for a campaign should be able to stand on their own.

- A consistent sales slogan will reinforce the message and will enhance the sales point.

EXERCISES

Exercise 1

Prepare a broadcast campaign for Natural View Skylights. A copy data sheet provides you with the following information: Efficient way to lighten a dark room. Provides natural light for plant growth. Light beautifies a room and makes it seem bigger. Skylight uses natural light, not electricity. Skylight has double-layer construction. Reflects the greatest amount of heat out while allowing sunlight in. Insulation seal prevents outside air from seeping in. Skylight will not shatter. Both skylight and installation are guaranteed. Will not leak. Available in three models to fit all homes. Look for dealer in Yellow Pages.

1. Prepare a complete copy platform.

2. Create a campaign sales slogan to be used in each ad.

3. Write two 60-second radio commercials for the product. Aim one at a Sunbelt audience, the other at a northern audience.

4. Write two 30-second television spots. Use the demonstration approach for the Sunbelt audience and the problem-solution approach for the northern audience.

5. Write a strategy statement analyzing the selling situation. Explain how the advertising will be used to convince the target audience to investigate this product.

Exercise 2

Prepare a broadcast campaign.

1. Obtain brochures or other literature on an existing product or service. Choose from such items as cameras, hair dryers, and health spas. Gather as much information as possible.

2. Prepare a complete copy platform for the product or service.

3. Insofar as possible, analyze the strengths and weaknesses of competitors.

4. Write two 60-second radio commercials using dialog, sound effects, and/or music. Aim one spot at Christmas shoppers, the other at shoppers for Mother's Day gifts.

5. Write two 30-second television commercials. Aim one spot at Christmas shoppers and the other at people shopping for Mother's Day gifts. The TV spots must differ from the radio spots.

6. Write a strategy statement in which you analyze the selling situation. Explain how the advertising will convince the target audience to use the product or service instead of a competing one.

Exercise 3

Contact public service offices on your campus or in your community. Find a nonprofit organization that has a message to communicate to the public but has no budget to prepare it. The health center, for instance, might have an alcohol awareness program, the police department might have a rape prevention program, and the library might have a number of informational programs. When you find a nonprofit organization that wants a public service campaign, gather as much information about the organization and its campaign as you can.

1. Once you've gathered the data, prepare a complete copy platform.

2. Write two radio or television PSAs that are appropriate for this campaign.

3. Write a strategy statement in which you analyze the selling situation. Explain how the announcements will be used to convince the target audience of your major objectives.

Exercise 4

Prepare a radio campaign for Spectrum's Auto City. Spectrum is located at 3738 S. Highway 4. Spectrum is having an all-out sellout. They are clearing out last year's models. Urge listeners to buy now and beat the price increases on the new models. Spectrum offers 2.9 percent APR financing and up to $3,000 in rebates, and they guarantee $2,000 on any trade-in. Spectrum's Auto City is 1/2 mile south of the Interstate on Highway 4.

1. Prepare a complete copy platform.

2. Write one 60-second hard-sell spot aimed at male car buyers. Use two voices, sound effects, and so on.

3. Write one 60-second spokesperson spot aimed at a general audience. Write this spot for Dave Johnson, owner of Spectrum.

4. Write one 60-second conversational spot aimed at female car buyers. Use at least two voices.

5. Write one 60-second two-voice spot aimed at first-time car buyers.

6. Prepare a strategy statement analyzing the selling situation. Explain how the format for each spot relates to the approach used for each target audience.

Exercise 5

Prepare a television campaign for the Blue Lagoon Seafood restaurants. These restaurants feature simple, quality food at reasonable prices. They provide big portions and good service. The menu emphasizes seafood, but steaks, chicken, and so on are also available. The restaurants offer a special menu for children under age 12 with dishes priced at less than $5. There are five locations. See Yellow Pages. Beer and cocktails available.

1. Prepare a complete copy platform.

2. Prepare one 30-second product-as-star commercial in which you emphasize the food.

3. Prepare one 30-second problem-solution spot.

4. Prepare one 30-second situation spot aimed at taking the family out to eat.

5. Prepare one 30-second testimonial spot. Assume that you have comments by satisfied customers of all ages on videotape. Use their remarks to provide positive feedback about Blue Lagoon Seafood restaurants.

6. Prepare a strategy statement analyzing the selling situation. Be sure to explain why you targeted each spot in terms of age and sex demographics.

Writing News Stories

ntil now, the thrust of this book has been to study persuasive messages: commercials, promos, and public service messages. We now go a step further to briefly examine writing news stories. News writing for radio and television is specialized and can cover considerably more detail than will be presented here. Nevertheless, students need a broad background of writing for the electronic media and can benefit from understanding the basics of writing news stories. Therefore, this chapter will cover the basic elements of writing both radio and television news stories.

◆ Newsworthiness

A variety of news events—local, national, and international—occur every day. People in the news business must decide which stories are newsworthy. The criteria for deciding which stories to cover are not scientific but depend heavily on the judgment and experience of news staffers covering events. The following factors can help news people determine which stories deserve coverage.

Prominence

Stories that involve famous people, things, or places make news. People are interested in prominent people. The governor, the president, and even a well-known actress or athlete can capture interest. So can the events such people engage in. When the mayor of your city gets in a public argument with a well-liked city council member, that's news. A popular actor's visit to town to promote his latest movie may also be news. In the latter case, news people must avoid relying on the actor's fame as the only reason in determining if a story is newsworthy.

Conflict

Conflicts between two opposing forces make interesting stories and provide good video. If the president's decision to send troops abroad leads to local protests, the story will probably be covered. If local protests don't develop, it probably won't be. By itself, conflict doesn't make good news. The story must be put in context so that the audience understands why it being covered.

Proximity

Events that happen close to us are important. A tanker truck crash resulting in a chemical spill on the local interstate is newsworthy. However, if the same incident occurred on a rural section of the interstate well away from your city, coverage likely wouldn't be warranted. Generally, local stories are more significant than stories taking place elsewhere. One exception relates to the coverage area of your station. It's not unusual to have one station in a market serve a portion of the geographic area that the other stations don't. If your station provides coverage to the rural area where the accident occurred, the story is important to people who live in that area even though people in your city may be less interested.

Timeliness

Events that are happening now or will happen in the immediate future are newsworthy. That's why public officials often hold press conferences shortly before newscasts and, in some cases, even while newscasts are on the air. But the latter practice is seldom necessary. News operations, including local stations, can often cover stories live. They can also record the live report and keep the reporter on the scene until the next newscast, enabling the reporter to get late developments and deliver a live introduction to the story from the scene. Technology has enhanced timely reporting, but news managers must avoid letting timeliness outweigh other factors in news judgment.

Human Interest Stories

Stories that aren't highly important but are unusual may be newsworthy. People enjoy hearing of intriguing situations that provide a break from hard news. The birthday of an elderly resident or the story of a water-skiing squirrel may amuse people. Human interest stories are sometimes used to conclude newscasts and are called kickers.

Good Video

Television is a visual medium, and the presence of good video contributes to newsworthiness. Few stories are shown if video is not available, and those that are covered are generally kept short. People are accustomed to seeing news events and newsmakers. A newscast with no video would be uninteresting, but a story that's not newsworthy should not be included in a newscast just because video is available.

◆ The Electronic News Lead

The lead sentence in a news story is an attention-getter, a signal for the audience to begin listening. The electronic news lead is not the "Who? What? Why? Where? When? and How?" of the newspaper lead. A radio or television lead may answer one or two of these traditional questions but never all of them. Remember, the electronic news lead is the cue for the audience to begin listening, so important details are not included.

Two of the most frequently answered questions in a broadcast lead are "What?" or "Where?" In other words, the lead focuses on *what happened* (there was a robbery) or *where it happened* (at the Beaver Square Mall).

Telling "What?"

The "What" of a broadcast lead can focus on many things. Frequently, it is a simple statement describing the main point of the story:

The Supreme Court says it will decide whether doctors can prescribe pot.

A lawsuit involving a local election dispute has been moved to the state capitol.

A variation of the "What" lead is used to emphasize the effects of an event on the audience:

> If you've been trying to get a flu shot, you're going to have to wait a little longer.

Telling "Where?"

When a station's signal reaches a wide area, listeners can be better informed if the lead tells them where the event took place. Listeners might presume that a story took place in their community. Whether it did or not, the "Where" should identify the location—usually placing it near the end of the lead:

> A small plane crashed in the woods of northwestern Georgia, killing a local couple.
> A factory worker shot a supervisor to death in Linkville before killing himself.

◆ Lead Structure

The lead has two important responsibilities for a news story. First, it must interest the listener in the story and direct him or her toward the essence of the story. Second, the lead must establish the angle of the story. The remainder of the story must support that angle, but the lead is similar to a purpose statement in an essay.

Hard and soft news leads are both commonly used in electronic news writing, especially in radio news copy. Intermixing them can add variety to a newscast, although a news director's policy may determine the type of lead generally used. Each has advantages and disadvantages.

The Hard News Lead

The hard news lead gives the news immediately; it comes right to the point. This is advantageous in many situations, but the drawback is that the hard lead gives the listener little opportunity to start paying attention. This type of lead works once the newscast has been introduced, because audience attention has been drawn to the news, but without some form of attention-getter, listeners have no opportunity to prepare for what's coming up. Here are two examples of hard leads:

> Florida will gain two seats in Congress following the latest census.
> Americans are turning to the Internet as a main source of political news.

The Soft News Lead

The soft news lead molds the news to catch the ear of the listener whose attention is not entirely focused on the newscast. Soft leads are more creative than hard leads and set the scene for the hard news portion of the story. Unlike the hard news lead, soft news leads are designed to gain attention for the remainder of the news story. Here are two examples of soft news leads:

The black ink keeps flowing.

A federal judge in San Francisco says some seriously ill people are entitled to use marijuana as a medicine.

◆ Story Structure

How do you complete a news story after writing the lead? You need a structure that will fit the broadcast news audience. Newspaper reporters often use an inverted-pyramid structure of story organization, as illustrated in Figure 15.1. This style places as many of the five W's of news reporting (who, what, when, where, and why) in the lead of a newspaper story as possible. The following lead contains the five W's:

State public schools (*who*) may receive additional funding (*what*) next year (*when*) after legislators in the state capitol (*where*) voted to approve $1 billion in growth money to reduce overcrowding (*why*).

Additional facts about the main data are included in the body of a story. Lead sentences written in the inverted-pyramid style may be complex and difficult for broadcast audiences to grasp. For that reason, broadcast news writers generally use a more conversational structure resembling an ordinary pyramid, as shown in Figure 15.2.

This structure begins with a concise lead that emphasizes brevity and some of the five W's. The inverted-pyramid could be simplified as follows:

State public schools will get more money to cope with overcrowding.

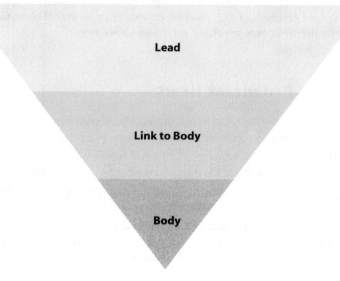

FIGURE 15.1 Inverted-Pyramid News Story Structure

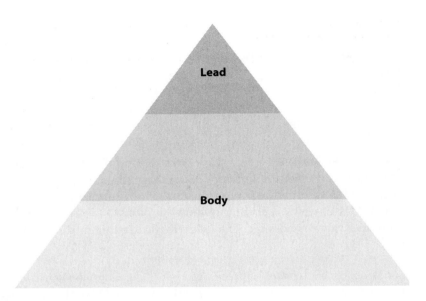

FIGURE 15.2 Pyramid News Story Structure

Three of the five W's are included in this lead. The remaining items could be included in the body of the story.

Here's an example of a broadcast news story illustrating the pyramid structure:

LEAD

There's bad blood between students and homeowners who live near the state university.

BODY

Growing tension between residents in the university area and student apartment dwellers has resulted in the development of a student housing task force. Residents want the university to stop late-night parties and fights in apartments adjacent to residential areas. University officials say they have no control of students off campus, and a spokesperson for the sheriff's office says they are doing all they can.

◆ Writing Rules for Broadcast News

Many of the rules used in writing broadcast news are the same as those employed for other forms of broadcast copy, so you may want to review the style rules discussed in Chapter 2. However, some elements are unique to broadcast news, so we'll cover them here. Always remember that you're writing copy for ease of reading.

- **Abbreviations.** Limit abbreviations to "Dr.," "Mr.," and "Mrs." Commonly used abbreviations such as "St. Louis" are acceptable, but unfamiliar abbreviations such as "Monsig. Foster" should be replaced ("Monsignor Foster").

- **Symbols.** Write out all symbols. Write "5 percent," not "5%." Write "sixty dollars and seventy-five cents," not "$60.75."

- **Numbers.** Simplify numbers. People won't remember if the enrollment increased by 112,538. Instead, write "more than 112 thousand-500 students," or better yet, "more than 100 thousand students." Use digits for sports scores and election returns. Write "the Tigers upset the Hawks 8 to 2," not "8–2."

- **Ages.** Ages are seldom needed in broadcast stories, but if you include them, don't use the newspaper style: "Herbert Jones, 58." Instead, write "58-year-old Herbert Jones," or, for emphasis, "Herbert Jones, who is 58."
- **Dates.** Use dates sparingly. If you must use them, repeat the date at least twice, and if the story is on television, show it graphically. Write out dates using "th," "rd," and "nd" to remind the newscaster to read them as ordinal numbers. For example, write "May 10th," not "May 10."
- **Fractions.** Write out fractions. Write "two-thirds," not "2/3."

Names and Titles

Give the full title of an individual (or an organization) the first time it is used. Subsequent mentions can be shortened for ease of reading.

> State College President Joel Bracket is in Lewisburg. President Bracket will address . . .
> The Center for Disease Control says we can expect a flu outbreak. The center reports . . .

Well-known organizations can be identified by their initials after they have been identified by their full names. Organizations that are not well known should never be identified by their initials.

> The Nebraska Highway Patrol closed Interstate 80 last night. The N-H-P said . . .

Delete middle initials in names unless the public is accustomed to use of the middle initial. Write "Chancellor Jane Johnson," not "Chancellor Jane K. Johnson."

Capitalization and Spacing

Many broadcast newsrooms, especially television newsrooms, type news copy all-caps. However, other stations use upper- and lowercase. Stations may have a preferred policy, or they may leave it up to the individual broadcast journalists. Check with your instructor or news director to verify the desired policy.

Double or even triple space news copy. It's easier for newscasters to read, and it leaves room for handwritten corrections that may have to be inserted later.

◆ News for Radio

Like the radio commercial or promo, news for radio is written to be heard. Writers seek to inform and to create images for the listener. Unlike news for the print media, which is written for the eye, radio news is written so that an announcer can read it with ease and the listener can readily understand it.

Radio news is not the prominent form of program content it once was. One or possibly two radio stations in larger cities may program news and sports or call-in talk shows the entire day. The remaining stations often carry news only during the morning drive time, the prime listening time between 6 A.M. and 10 A.M. when people are beginning their days and driving to work. Listeners are often engaged in other activities when they hear radio news, so radio news stories must catch and hold the attention of potential listeners.

It's easier to gain attention if you write radio news in a conversational style. Use contractions and short declarative sentences. Keep the subject and verb close together and use an informal style.

Types of Radio News Stories

ACTUALITIES　When possible, radio news stories incorporate actualities—the voices or sounds of the newsmakers—as sound bites to provide color. For instance, it's far better to hear a person who witnessed a tornado describe the storm than to paraphrase that person's remarks. Often, radio stations have one of their own staffers read a portion of a news story and use that as a sound bite. This provides vocal variety but lacks the credibility of an actuality.

The following script illustrates an actuality:

> Mowing the lawn may get easier in Adams County. The County Council passed a regulation that requires new homes to limit the amount of yard space that can receive high-volume irrigation. In effect, the plan will limit the size of lawns. County Commissioner Dale Moss explains:
> (sound bite)
> 14 sec.
> Out-cue: ". . . will help save water."

If there is a weakness with the actuality, it is that the story ends with the final words of the sound bite. This may make for an abrupt conclusion. Thus, the sound bite needs to be of sufficient length and clarity that it logically concludes the story. An easy solution to this problem is to use a wraparound format. That's explained next.

WRAPAROUNDS　A story that combines sound and words is known as a wraparound. As the name implies, this approach incorporates the voice of the newscaster at the beginning and conclusion of a news story and the actuality or sound bite in the middle. In other words, the voice of the newscaster is wrapped around the voice or voices of the newsmakers (a wraparound may include more than one actuality or sound bite). Here's an example:

> There's been another tragedy on our roadways. Nine-year-old Chris Gorel of Hempel was killed this morning after he rode his bike in front of a car while on his way to Centerville Middle School. Barry Crow, who was driving his daughter to school, witnessed the accident:
> (sound bite)
> 12 sec.
> Out-cue: ". . . we were devastated."
> The driver of the car, Bob Marks of Forester, was on his way to work when Gorel rode into the front of his vehicle. Police said Marks probably wouldn't be charged. Gorel is the first child in Central County to be killed while walking or riding to school this year.

In writing a wraparound, it's important to avoid having the lead-in say the same thing as the first line of the sound bite. Listen to the sound bite before writing the story and preview the actuality as part of the news story.

Radio News Writing Basics

IMMEDIACY One of the main advantages of radio is its ability to capitalize on immediacy. Thus, if an airplane crashes near your city, the residents of your area will tune to your station for details if it has a reputation for covering local news. To enhance the sense of immediacy, use the present tense whenever possible. For instance: "The president is meeting with Palestinian and Israeli representatives at Camp David," rather than, "The president today held meetings with. . . ." Newspapers use "today" and "yesterday," but radio can use terms with more recency. For instance:

> General Motors says it's never had a better spring. The world's largest auto maker *is reporting* just a 1 percent increase in profits from a year ago . . .
>
> Candidates for governor *are preparing* for their first campaign debate. . . .

LENGTH Broadcast news stories are typically very short. News directors feel that stories get dull after 45 seconds and prefer to cover a larger number of stories in a shorter time. A good rule of thumb is to shoot for a story that's 20 to 25 seconds long, comprising 55 to 70 words and four or five sentences. Some stories will require greater length, but they are exceptions.

◆ News for Television

The primary difference between radio and TV news is that the video tells the story as much as the words do, if not more so. Pictures are essential to a story on television. Words are nevertheless vital, although the number of words varies.

The primary goal for a TV writer is to avoid conflicts with the video. It's not necessary to tell the viewers what they are seeing as long as you have good video. If the pictures tell the story, support the pictures with copy that explains what the video does not present. To put it another way, use words to fill in the blanks, but let the viewer absorb the video.

The most desirable situation is when the video tells a story by itself. If it can't, it's not good video, and you'll need to prop up the video with more written copy. Generally, stories with poor video get pushed aside for those with better pictures. Pictures are that important in television news.

Television News Scripts

THE SPLIT PAGE Like the television commercial format we have seen in previous chapters, TV news scripts use a split page to present both video instructions and the newscasters' words. Scripts are generally created on computers, which send them directly to TelePrompTers. The news reporters use the right side of the split page to read the copy. The left side is set aside for the slug (title of story, date and time of newscast), video and audio instructions, and tape times for the director. As with other

TV scripts, abbreviations are used for the various technical instructions. Here are some common ones:

- **B-roll** is a method used to enhance voice-overs and sound bites by providing video enhancement of what is said. During a B-roll, the anchor or reporter continues to be heard, but the picture changes to scenes corresponding to what is said.
- **CG** refers to a character generator, a device used to insert graphic names and data over videotape or read copy.
- **ENG** (electronic news gathering) indicates that the video is on videotape cassette.
- **ESS** (electronic still storer) systems load, retrieve, and display video from a variety of sources, such as videotape, slides, electronic paint boxes, and satellites. They are used to provide graphs, maps, charts, photos, preprepared graphics, and so on.
- **Natural sound** refers to the actual sound that accompanies the story. Nat sound is used with virtually all on-the-scene news stories to intensify the audio aspect of the story.
- **O/C** (on camera) indicates to the director that the anchor will be on camera at this point of the script.
- **SIL** means "silent" videotape and is used in conjunction with a voice-over (VO).
- **SOT** tells the director that "sound on tape" is a part of the story. The SOT may be a sound bite from a newsmaker or a field report taped earlier.
- **V/O** (voice-over) means the anchor is reading copy while viewers are seeing something else, such as graphics or silent videotape.

Stations use various terms to indicate that names, titles, or other information that will be superimposed over videotape or graphics to identify locations, pictures, or newsmakers. Stations use an abbreviation for the manufacturer of the company name that makes their machine. Many stations use a Chyron and use that term. Others use the term FONT for the manufacturer Videfont. For our purposes, use the term *super*, another term used by stations. Other technical abbreviations are also used to help the director. They will become familiar once you start working with video on a regular basis.

Here is a split-screen television news script for the traffic accident story presented earlier as a radio news story:

SCHOOL FATALITY 9/12 6PM MM JONES

VIDEO	AUDIO
O/C Jones:	A nine-year-old Hempel boy was killed on his way to school this morning. Mary Smith reports.
SOT: 20 SUPER: Mary Smith O/C Jones	Out-cue: ". . . Mary Smith reporting."
	Gorel was the first child to be killed in Central County while walking or biking to school this year. More than a dozen students were injured or killed in similar accidents last year.

Types of Television News Stories

READ STORIES   *Read* (or *tell*) stories are read by an anchor with the only pictures being those that appear in "boxes" next to the anchor's head. Read stories do not make compelling video, but they are an important part of the TV newscast. Read stories may be used because there is no video available, as in the case of a breaking story. They may also be used when video is not necessary or is dull. Yes, it's preferable to use video in television news, but read stories are flexible. The read story may be of enough value to be included for visual variation, or it may be used where adjustments in the length of the newscast may be needed (if the newscast runs long, the story gets dropped; if it runs short, the read story can be used).

VOICE-OVERS (V/Os)   In the *voice-over* story, the anchor reads while video or graphics are shown. The video may have a sound track that is kept low for natural effect (referred to as *natural sound*) or the video might be silent. With voice-over copy, it's crucial to remember that the copy must complement the video. The copy should not state what is obvious to the viewers. For example, if you are showing video of a car accident that occurred at a major intersection, avoid telling your audience, "You are seeing the cars involved in the accident at Highway 50 and Carter Street this morning." Instead, you could say, "A car accident snarled downtown traffic this morning," and let the video show the wreckage.

The following script illustrates a voice-over. Notice that the bulk of the spot involves videotape of the news location.

VIDEO	AUDIO
Anchor: Sara	Cleanup is under way after a tornado struck near Langston.
TAKE VO	(—VO—)
TAPE OF DAMAGE CG: Langston	The tornado hit a residential area near the Crosstown Mall, leaving overturned cars, damaged buildings, and trees blown down. The tornado left a half-mile strip of damage but no one suffered injuries from the storm. Weather Bureau officials say it is unusual to experience a tornado at this time year.

SOUND BITES   The words of the newsmakers are just as important in television news as in radio. The difference is that TV writers can show the newsmakers and present their voices. TV writers frequently weave their stories around sound bites, much as radio writers do with wraparounds. In television, the combination of news copy and sound bites is called a *package,* and it is used extensively.

A news package typically includes sound bites from several people involved in a given event. The script for a package is brief—just long enough for the anchor to introduce the story and the reporter doing the package. The reporter, who is often at the scene of the story, gives more details and introduces the sound bites.

Three sound bites are typical in a news package. For example, a news package about a major traffic tie-up may include a sound bite with a driver involved in the pileup, another with a witness to the event, and a final sound bite with a police officer. Rather than reporting the event in three separate news stories, a news package reports the incident in one comprehensive segment. Since several participants tell the story, packages are longer than voice-over stories, often as long as sixty seconds. Voice-over stories or those using a single sound bite are usually less than thirty seconds in length.

Video instructions are important in a package script, since they tell the director how and when graphics should be used to identify each newsmaker. For instance, the name of the person may be inserted over the sound bite for four seconds to enhance visual comprehension of the story.

Television News Writing Basics

1. **Let the picture tell the story.** Use good pictures and minimize words whenever possible. Some segments of a news story can be left with no news copy, but audiences aren't accustomed to that. Use words to provide additional information not provided in the pictures or to clarify items that might not be obvious in the pictures.

2. **View the video before writing the story.** Whether a station edits the video before the story is written or does the reverse, the writer needs to view the videotape first. Because the picture has primary importance, the words must match the video. The structure of the story, both narrative and video, must progress logically. The writer must clearly understand what the picture looks like for every line of copy.

3. **Identify people shown in stories quickly.** Don't leave viewers guessing about who is seen on the screen. Identify the people seen in the story as quickly as possible. In a related matter, don't provide written material about one person when another individual's picture is on the screen.

4. **Change times and locations in a logical sequence.** Switching back and forth in time or location can be confusing. It might work on radio, but video will look inconsistent if you switch from a daylight shot to a nighttime shot and then back to daylight. Let the video progress logically.

➤ POINTS TO REMEMBER

- In determining whether events are newsworthy, news staffers weigh the following: (a) the prominence of the people or event, (b) the proximity of the situation to the station's main coverage area, (c) conflict between newsmakers, (d) novel people or events, and (e) the availability of good video.

- The lead sentence in a news story signals the audience to begin listening and establishes the angle of the story.

- Hard news leads come directly to the point, whereas soft news leads gain attention for the remainder of the news story.

- Print news stories generally include the five Ws—who, what, when, where, and why—in the lead paragraph. Broadcast leads usually include only two or three of the Ws.

- An actuality in a radio news story is the voice or sound of a newsmaker.

- When the voice of a radio newscaster is wrapped around the voice or voices of newsmakers, the story is called a wraparound.

- Pictures are essential in a television news story, but words are needed to support the video.

- Television news stories use the split page format for video instructions and audio copy.

- The only video in "read" (or "tell") stories appears in boxes near the anchor's head. The anchor reads television news stories with still pictures appearing in boxes next to his or her head.

- In a voice-over television news story, the anchor reads copy while video or graphics are shown.

- Viewers of television news stories that incorporate sound bites can see and hear the newsmaker.

EXERCISES

Exercise 1

Select a news story from a newspaper. Rewrite it for radio or television "tell" style without audio or video.

Exercise 2

Cover a campus meeting. Take full notes. Write a television "tell" story.

Exercise 3

Using the following facts, write a wraparound radio story and a television news package. The wraparound radio story is to be used in a five-minute morning drive-time newscast. Include the actuality statement by Mr. Jennings of the Arkansas Highway Patrol. The story should not exceed 30-seconds. The television news package is to be used in the 6 P.M. newscast on January 20. The television story should not exceed 45 seconds and should include both the voice-over video and the video actuality. You can use portions of each video if time requirements demand.

STORY FACTS

On Monday, January 15, thousands of people continued to be without power while hundreds more were stranded as a result of a major winter storm. The storm hit two portions of the nation's midsection: Texas, Arkansas, Oklahoma, and Louisiana, where ice storms were the problem, and the northern plains, where heavy snow fell in North Dakota, Minnesota, South Dakota, and parts of Iowa and Nebraska.

The southern portion of the storm snapped tree limbs and knocked out power. More than 600,000 homes in Arkansas, Texas, Oklahoma, and Louisiana were without power, some since Friday. At least 41 deaths resulted from the bad weather: 11 in Texas, 22 in Oklahoma, two in Arkansas, and four in Louisiana. A thousand drivers were stranded along Interstate 20 in northern Texas Saturday night. National Guard troops were called out to help move vehicles and rescue trapped motorists. In Arkansas on Sunday, 300,000 homes lost power and most were still without power. A new storm brought freezing rain to Arkansas Sunday night, preventing relief crews from reaching downed power lines.

You have a video statement by Mr. William P. Jennings, Public Relations Director of the Arkansas Highway Patrol. He said: "This is the worst storm in 10 years and winter has just begun. People are without electricity and phone service and there aren't enough relief crews to make a dent in the problem. Arkansas Public Power will be bring in crews from adjoining states to assist their workers. This is going to take awhile."

In the northern plains, snow fell at an inch per hour. Fargo, North Dakota, recorded 8 inches in a few hours. Fort Dodge, Iowa, set a new record for January snowfall, and a 500-mile stretch of the Mississippi River south of St. Paul, Minnesota, was frozen.

The blocked waterway delayed barge shipments of soybeans, corn, and wheat, which are shipped on the Mississippi. In another problem, a Greyhound bus rolled over on an icy stretch of Interstate 80 in Nebraska, injuring 33 passengers.

You have video (no audio) of snowplows clearing an interstate highway. The video is 15 seconds long.

Another storm is developing off North Carolina; it is expected to make its way up the East Coast. This storm could bring a foot or more of snow to such major cities as Philadelphia, New York, and Boston.

Exercise 4

You cover the police beat and read the following investigation report:

DESCRIPTION OF INVESTIGATION

Complainant: <u>Andrew Kelly</u>   Sex: <u>Male</u>   Age: <u>56 DOB 8/4/44</u>
Address: <u>12308 Castelton Lane</u>
Interviewed complainant at Jefferson City Hospital. Victim was hospitalized with severe lacerations and contusions about the head and upper torso. He indicated that an unknown assailant who repeatedly hit him with a firearm beat him. Victim said he did not get a good look at the assailant because the confrontation took place in a darkened hallway between his office and the lounge. He indicated that he was working in his office at the rear of the business (Executive Lounge, 122 Lancaster Street, which he owns) shortly after 2 A.M. He heard a noise in the lounge and left his office to investigate. At that point he was attacked by a man who was described as large and wearing a ski mask. The assailant asked the victim to open the safe; when he refused, the man beat him into unconsciousness. When the victim recovered consciousness, he called 911 and discovered that the safe was open. He estimated that between $12,000 and $15,000 in cash was taken. The amount covered receipts for the lounge. Receipts are deposited in the bank twice a week. Fingerprint crew will go there today to check for prints.

You check police records and find that the lounge has been burglarized twice in the last year and a half. $50,000 was taken in one break-in and $30,000 in another. No one was ever apprehended. Victim had run for county commissioner in 1988 but was defeated.

Write two stories about this incident: (1) a 15-second radio story for a morning drive-time newscast and (2) a 20-second voice-over television story. Assume that you have video of the lounge and a still photo of the owner.

CHAPTER SIXTEEN

Writing for the Internet

◆ **Interactivity**

◆ **Links**

◆ **Planning a Web Site**

Web Target Audience
Goals and Objectives of the Site
Designing the Web Site

◆ **Advertising on the Web**

Measuring Online Advertising
Types of Advertisements
  Banner Ads
  Logos
  Cube Ads
  Pop-Up Ads
  Button Ads
  Interstitial or Intermercial Ads
  Keyword Ads

◆ **News on the Web**

Principles of Web Writing
Television Online
Points to Remember
Exercises

The development of the Internet and the widespread use of computers have brought new dimensions and possibilities to the world of communication. Virtually all the traditional media—radio, television, advertising, newspapers, and so on—make online efforts to communicate with the public. Web-based companies need writers, and many people are adapting to this new medium. The goal of this chapter is to provide a brief understanding of the Internet and the conventions being established to write messages for it. We'll focus on general concepts of writing for the Web and let you apply the concepts as needed.

◆ Interactivity

The concept of *interactivity* is an important feature of Internet use. In many applications of our computers, the goal is to give the user a choice of what to do next. That's where interactivity comes in. The traditional media—TV, movies, and radio—present material in a predetermined fashion, in a straight line, or *linearly*. Thus, we watch a television program through the beginning, middle, and end; there is no opportunity for the audience to control the story. The computer and the Internet provide the opportunity to interact, to control the choice the user or the user's computer makes next. The result is that you must think differently to write for interactivity. You must write in a *nonlinear* fashion, and that is much of our focus here.

◆ Links

The major difference the online writer must emphasize is thinking in terms of links.[1] The Internet is built on links that enable a user to move from one element of information to another. For instance, a television station might present a news story about a scandal involving a public official in city government and refer viewers to the station's Web site to get additional details about the story. The Web page might link to background facts about the public official, to an organizational chart of city government, to budgets allocated to city departments, and so on. When you envision that a user could link from any one box to another, you begin to see the flexibility the user has on the Web.

When content is viewed as a variety of links that individual users may choose to open, the Web writer must anticipate how users will react. You must lead users in a nonlinear fashion: Provide appeals to individual audience members to respond to one of a number of links on an individual basis. Think of giving the user control of the information and anticipate the reactions he or she might have.

However, in many cases you won't want to let the user pick links without guidance. You will want to guide users to choices you believe meet the goals of the Web page. For instance, when advertising is involved, you'll want to guide the user to the objectives the business has in mind, as when a physical fitness business has links to pages about bodybuilding, aerobics, and specially priced programs. Guiding the user requires creativity and an understanding of the computer.

---

[1]A *link*, also known as a *hyperlink*, is anything on a Web page that drives traffic to another Web site.

◆ Planning a Web Site

If you are going to write online materials, you will need to work from a Web page. You might work from a site that has already been developed. If not, you will have to construct a Web site. Our goal is to help you plan a site, not to construct one. Planning is crucial in organizing a Web site. It can make the site's content easy to navigate and can ensure its quality. Use the following considerations as a guide in planning your Web site.

Web Target Audience *who need to stay awake for an extended period of time for the purpose of study*

The initial planning step, as in a commercial or a campaign, is to identify the specific audience that will come to your Web page. To reach this point, ask yourself the following questions: For whom am I developing the Web site? Does education, marital status, financial status, age, or gender affect the audience of my site? The audience directs every facet of your Web design. The visual elements (including color, text, and graphics), the design of information, and selection of graphics relate directly to the target audience.

Goals and Objectives of the Site

Goals establish a broad framework of your site and help you explain its purpose. For instance: the goal of my Web site might be to provide students in my class on writing for the electronic media with quizzes, grade information, and reading assignments.

Objectives are distinct statements about specific content on the Web site. Objectives assist in defining the scope of site information and help organize content. Answer the following question in composing your site objectives: What specific data do I want users of my Web site to know? For example, my home page will provide an overview and links to special services pages. The outside reading page will provide reading assignments to be read by students before certain class dates. The exam page will include online quizzes and instructions for taking them. Additional pages could also be identified and given specific objectives.

Designing the Web Site

You may hire someone to design your Web site or design it yourself. There are two approaches to designing and developing a Web site. One is to use a Web program. These programs do a lot of the work and help you to develop a professional-looking site. The other approach is to build the site yourself, using the interactive and layout elements of the program. This approach is relevant only if you are studying Web site development in detail.

◆ Advertising on the Web

One of the goals of the Web is to generate advertising dollars. Most media Web sites are available to Internet users without charge, so advertising is the main source of revenue. Media Web sites target the areas of their sites that generate revenue—ads on the most popular Web pages.

Broadcast and cable Web sites often include a free online ad when a business buys commercial time on a station or system. Such ads are considered "value added," because they give the traditional broadcast advertiser potential customers who otherwise might not watch or listen to the station. The problem is that there is little evidence of how many Web users actually respond to the Internet ads.

To provide more evidence of users, stations sometimes sell advertising packages that include coupons or other inducements available only on the Internet. For example, a business might include a discount offer with a coupon a viewer can print from the computer screen. By using this form of advertising, the business gets feedback about whether the Web advertising is providing a return.

Some media sites charge separately for online ads and traditional ads. Practices vary, but as time goes by, advertising will play a greater role in financing Web sites and electronic media outlets.

Measuring Online Advertising

Radio stations measure the number of listeners, but broadcast and cable outlets assess viewing. Online media managers also evaluate viewing, but they measure viewing in *eyeballs*, the number of "views" their Web sites get. Eyeballs are measured as *hits* (counting every item on a page when someone accesses it), *click-throughs* (clicking on an advertisement that links to the advertiser's site), and *page impressions* (counting all the elements on a page that is accessed as one "view").

Types of Advertisements

Online ads are quite different from traditional advertisements and have different purposes. The following online advertisements are the most common types.

BANNER ADS   This is the most common type of advertisement. It resembles an online billboard placed across the bottom or top of the Web page. It is housed within a box and links to the advertiser's Web site when the user clicks on it. Banner ads can be static, or they can include some form of movement. The following ad types are examples of banner ads.

LOGOS   With this ad, the advertiser simply places its logo on the Web page with a link to its site. A logo ad works best for well-known brand names. In some situations, the advertiser places the logo on the Web page at no cost. If a user clicks through and makes a purchase, the Web site can receive a percentage of sales or possibly some other form of payment in a barter arrangement.

CUBE ADS   These small-boxed ads can be placed anywhere on the page, typically on the sides or bottom.

POP-UP ADS   This type of ad appears on the screen for about 5 seconds when a user clicks on a page. The ad banner remains on the page after the page loads.

BUTTON ADS   Buttons, like logo ads, feature an advertiser's name. They are often used to enable users to download software such as Netscape's Navigator browsers.

INTERSTITIAL OR INTERMERCIAL ADS Like pop-up ads, these ads are interactive. They appear on the screen for about 5 seconds in a separate window with some type of animation and music while the remainder of the site loads. These ads are patterned after television, but they can attract users to access them with games. Special software is sometimes required to view the animated portion of the ads. Samples of online ads are shown in Figure 16.1.

KEYWORD ADS These ads are featured primarily in search-engine sites such as Yahoo! Type in a search for jogging shoes, and you'll get an ad for jogging shoes. Advertisers can link a keyword ad to a search for a related text word.

Although these are the major types of Internet ads, the online ad picture is changing graphically. Internet ads are delivering more audio, video, and animation in bigger windows that sometimes pop up on Web pages without warning. In addition, technologies exist to determine whether a particular PC user meets the demographic and geographic target for a particular ad.

The television industry is also making changes in the way it relates to the Internet. Stations initially tried to sell and buy advertising on the Internet as if they were dealing with TV spots. Banners, pop-ups, and so on were thought to be similar to spots, but clicking on such an ad didn't produce the same result as that from a TV commercial. Stations are now selling *bundled* advertising packages that use television programming to attract viewers to Web sites where the Internet can give them a chance to find more information. For example, a business might sponsor a section of a site where visitors can ask questions related to the sponsor's specialty (like legal advice or automotive repair).

◆ News on the Web

Many media sites include news coverage, and getting users to read it is as complicated as presenting advertising online. Online journalism leads to a different way of telling a story than happens in a newspaper or television newscast. As with other online elements, the key is allowing users to control information. To help users do this, online journalists have found that they must write in layers. Stories in layers include a headline, an abstract of one or two lines to digest the story, the complete story, and links to related items or other parts of the story. Media sites also offer video and audio components as part of their story. The following example illustrates the use of layering:

Headline Layer:	Trial and error: determining the number one college football team.
Summary Layer:	Meeting reveals new strategies.
Lead Layer:	Can college football gurus really devise a meaningful way to decide the number one team? Coaches and sportswriters' polls don't always agree. Computerized weighting systems aren't consistent. A meeting of college athletic directors Wednesday brought a new approach.

Readers are given directions to the full story if they choose to click on it. Links to other stories and related items are inserted over sections of the full story.

Is layering useful? Media research indicates that people don't read online; they scan. Thus, layering news stories allows users to scan the story and choose as much of it as they want to absorb. Because online users are scanners, layering is a practical way to

Tile / Cube Ads:
These ads are generally 120x90 pixels.

Banner Ads:
These ads are generally 468x60 pixels.

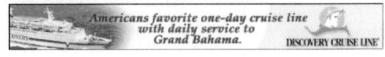

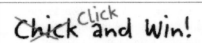

FIGURE 16.1 Illustrations of Online Ads *(Courtesy myCFnow.com/Internet Broadcasting Systems)*

Pop-up Ad:
These ads can be any size and "popup" on top of the screen you're on.

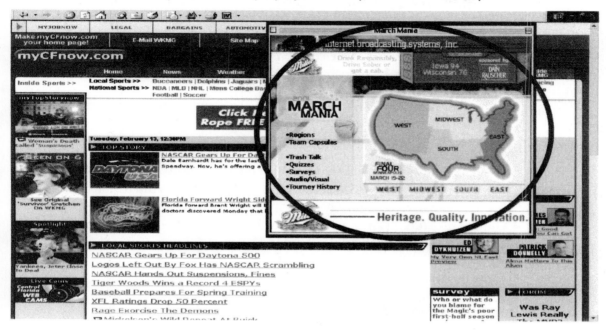

Interstitial Ad:
This is like a pop-up ad with video.

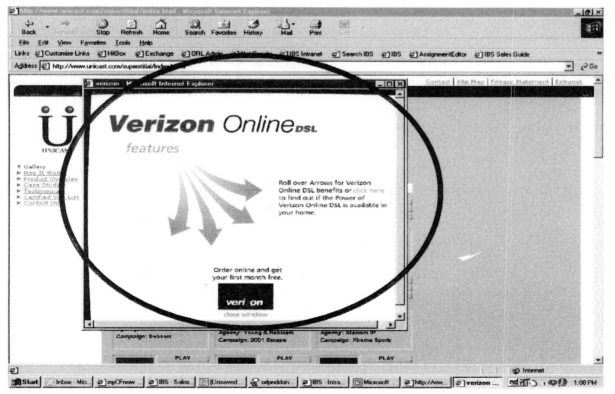

organize a new story. Writing an online story takes care and planning. Rich suggests the following steps[2]:

- **Prescribe the focus.** Identify the main idea or purpose of the story. Write a short sentence to explain the focus of your story.
- **Gather all your material.**
- **Plan visual and multimedia element.** Determine the crucial elements to your story: maps, photos, video? Eliminate graphic items that will add download time but not aid understanding.
- **Write a headline and teaser for your story.** How can you get readers interested enough to click into your story? The headline and teaser must attract their attention.
- **Write a condensed version of your story in 21 lines or less.** This exercise will help you identify the information you must include and will give you an idea of the amount of information that can be written on one page (a desired goal).
- **Plan interactive elements.** Will you use a poll, a game, or a discussion question? Planning these elements will help you plan the content of your story.
- **Outline the story.** What are the main topics, the subheads?
- **Create a storyboard.** Plan pages for each section of the story that will be a separate segment.
- **Write the story.**

Principles of Web Writing

Writing for the Web is different than writing for a print publication. Users read material on a computer screen but are more likely to scan for keywords than start at the top and read each sentence. As a result, you must use eye-catching phrases, short sentences, and short paragraphs. The following rules are important in writing for the Web:

1. Some Web writers suggest that you borrow from the style of brochures or manuals that are written to be scan-read. As in brochures, lists of bulleted items help readers move through online items. Sections with clear titles, subtitles, and key words break up copy for these publications, and Web pages need the same attention getters.

2. Written Web material can't be tedious or stilted. Because of the emphasis on personal style, writing for the Web is more like writing broadcast copy than print copy. Both broadcast and Web copy must be conversational, because you're aiming for a mass audience but thinking of one individual. That's why it's best to "write as you speak," using contractions, short sentences, and flexible grammar. Avoid connecting words such as *therefore*, *however*, and *moreover*. Research of online readers shows that connecting terms and multisyllabic words cause readers to slow their pace.

3. The written word is important, but so is page design and legibility. The default properties for text on Web pages are Times font at standard size (equivalent to 12 points) and black text on a white background. Dark text on a light background is the easiest to read and is popular on most sites.

4. Web headlines must grab attention. They are aimed at readers, not listeners. When you develop headlines, your goal is to draw the reader in to read more. Use clever and playful phrasing. Which is more interesting? *Drink Water Every Day* or *Quake in Your Boots for a Quenching Quaff of Agua*.[3]

---

[2]Carole Rich, *Creating Online Media* (Boston: McGraw-Hill, 1999). pp. 285–286.

[3]Catherine Titta, "Writing Well for the Web," *Jupitermedia Corporation*, January 8, 2001, http://www.webreference.com/content/writing/index.html (accessed November 22, 2006). This Web site includes suggestions for grammatical mistakes, editorial style, and punctuation.

Television Online

Radio writers had to make special adjustments when scripts were needed for television content, and the same type of adaptation is now needed to write for interactive television. Video is streamed (presenting moving visual images) on the Web for both television and film. However, in the cyberspace medium, the streamed visual, whether it is television or film, is presented on a computer screen, and that restricts the writer. There are three major restrictions in writing for video:

1. **The size of the computer screen.** The writer who uses video material does not have the dimensions of a theater or television screen within which to work. This leads to a difference in the viewer's perception of the images. Imposing scenery and large-scale events lose their size on the computer screen. Images become more intimate and less dramatic. In short, the images are compressed. To compensate, you must minimize unneeded detail in pictures and keep backgrounds simple, with even lighting. Avoid dimly lit scenes, because they will not have good picture resolution. The best advice is to concentrate on closeups; they don't lose as much detail. Also, keep scenes and program length short. Remember that the user is in front of a computer screen and will have a shorter attention span than will someone relaxing in an easy chair.

2. **The frame rates of video.** Many computers are too slow to accommodate much movement. To avoid a jumpy, stilted look, limit the movement of characters as well as their number. The lack of speed in the computer also limits how many people can speak at one time. With too much dialog, voice will impinge on voice. Thus, limit the number of people who speak at one time. Concentrate on sharp, crisp dialog and slow the pace of the script. At the same time, be concise. The computer screen is unforgiving, so you must adjust to it.

3. **Bandwidth size.** This problem stems from the level of connectivity offered by Internet providers and by the speed of the user's modem. A slow modem speed can cause a lengthy download. Streaming video plays at a slower speed than does broadcast television. Thus, users with limited bandwidth may lose patience with the time required to download video and may stop loading it after several tries. Not every user will have these problems, but many will, and you must anticipate their concerns.

➤ POINTS TO REMEMBER

- The Web user is also a creator who can search anywhere on the Web for specific or random information.
- Web writers should view themselves as guides who present a goal that the user is guided to follow.
- Web development means thinking of interacting links the user can control.

- Write conversationally for the web.
- Close-up shots provide better resolution than do large-scale scenes for streaming video images.
- Web pages need short sentences and eye-catching phrases to grab attention. Design pages to be scanned, not read line by line.

EXERCISES

Exercise 1

Log onto the Web site for a company such as CBS Entertainment, http://www.cbs.com; NBC Television, http://www.nbc.com; or PBS Online, http://www.pbs.org. Study the Web page. Look for the items that attract your attention. Evaluate the characteristics of these items. What elements caused you to notice them?

Exercise 2

Write news headlines and summary layers on identity theft. Write the item to attract users to the link page that has suggestions on how to minimize the risk of identity theft. The thrust of the item is that identity thieves can take your name, Social Security number, credit card number, or some other piece of your personal information for their own use.

Exercise 3

Evaluate at least 10 online media sites and select your top five choices. Rank your top choices from first to fifth place. Write a brief evaluation of each winner, identifying its strengths and weaknesses. Judge the sites on content, navigation ease, entertainment value, readability, and sponsor identity.

Exercise 4

Reevaluate the 10 media sites you examined for Exercise 3. Which ones present advertising most effectively? Which ones are least effective? Explain your conclusions.

Which static ads are best or worst? Which ads effectively use animation, games, or pop-up appeals?

Exercise 5

Write a news story for the Web, preferably an original news story, including your own reporting. For class purposes, you can rework a story from the campus or local newspaper. If you didn't write it, you must have permission from the source of your story in order to place it on the Web.

CHAPTER SEVENTEEN

Corporate Programs

- **Objectives**
- **Budget**
- **Outline**
- **Research**
- **Production**
- **Evaluation**
- **Script Considerations**

    On-Camera Spokesperson
    Voice-Overs
    Interviews
    Documentaries
    Dramatic Formats

- **Script Formats**

    Two-Column Format
    Screenplay Format

- **Writing Suggestions**

    Points to Remember
    Exercises

Corporate media programming, or as it is frequently called, industrial programming, is big business. Companies use electronic communication in a variety of ways to reach the public and to communicate with their own employees. In addition, educational institutions, government offices, professional and citizen organizations, and associations all use media to reach their audiences.

Writing training scripts and other corporate media jobs might not have the glamour of writing a movie or TV script, but the corporate media offer job opportunities that hold a degree of security not usually found in movie or television work. Corporate media use video, audio, slide-tape, online, multi-image, interactive video, and other combinations of audiovisual to communicate their messages. That is our focus in this chapter—to examine how companies and other organizations use media to inform, persuade, or educate, externally and internally. We'll look specifically at script development for corporate media.

Writers/producers of corporate media programs work with many of the tools used by broadcasters and cablecasters. The differences are the length of programs—corporate media programs are short, usually 10 to 30 minutes, the average being 25 minutes—and the goals of the program. Let's examine the strategy that a corporate writer/producer would follow in preparing a corporate media script.

◆ Objectives

The writer of a corporate media script must start by knowing the objectives of the program. This usually means meeting with managers to learn their goals, target audiences, and motivations. An "in-house" writer may meet with fellow employees, whereas an "out-of-house" writer might look at this task as a client meeting. In either situation, the management meeting should come early in the process.

During the initial meeting to define objectives, as the writer/producer, you must determine what the company wants the media program to accomplish. Is the program to educate and inform? Who is the target audience: the sales force, potential retirees, new employees, or all employees? Education and training are the most common goals of corporate media. If the project involves one of these goals, you must know whom the company wants to reach and what specific objectives are desired.

The second step in defining objectives pertains to the audience. Once you know who the audience is, how do you motivate audience members? Suppose a company wants to implement an employee ethics program so that company employees show respect to the company, other employees, and customers. How do you attract employees' attention and interest? The company regularly communicates with them, and some communication becomes so routine that people pay little attention. As a writer/producer, you must place yourself in the position of the target audience and ask, "What's in it for me?" Is the information being presented as merely another exercise that all employees must satisfy, does it relate to advancements and raises, or does it help employees do their jobs better? Answering such questions will help you consider the appeals and type of media you might use in the program.

◆ Budget

It's essential to know the amount of money available for a corporate media program as soon as possible. You can't write the script and plan the production without knowing how much money you have. Actually, the financing for the project will probably determine the nature of the production you can use, so knowledge of your funding must come first.

◆ Outline

Once the objectives have been defined and the financing is clear, prepare an outline for the program. The outline establishes what will be done, what format the program will take, and what material will be covered. This is essential information for the managers who have requested the program. They may have a general idea of what they want done or they may have very specific goals in mind. Either way, the project proposal requires management approval at an early level. If additional changes are needed, they can be incorporated.

That may be much more difficult if management does not approve the project until a final script is completed.

◆ Research

The goal of a program is to convey specific ideas and information. As the writer, you must have complete, accurate information about the topic. Whether the program concerns the operating details of a piece of equipment or the details of the company's sales success, you must have detailed information in order to write an effective script.

Depending on the topic, you may need to talk with experts about the piece of equipment and its use. You may conduct library or online research to obtain background information. You will also need to consult management about the company's goals and observations.

Finally, you might want firsthand knowledge. If the topic is the operation of a piece of equipment, you might want to go onto the factory floor to have workers demonstrate the equipment and, if possible, let you operate it. In short, you must become an expert on the topic before you can write a script about it.

◆ Production

Whether production of the program is done in-house or at an outside production facility, you, as writer, will be involved through completion. Changes may be requested in the program at any phase. Even though top-level managers may have approved the program in outline form, it's entirely possible that one of them will request changes as the program is finalized.

◆ Evaluation

Once the program has been presented, the final step is to evaluate its effectiveness. This is done through conventional interviewing and testing. The goal of evaluation is to determine if the final product adequately conveyed its message. Was the audience satisfied? Were the goals of management achieved? Remember, as the writer of a corporate media program, you want the production to be informative, entertaining, and interesting. Management may be especially concerned about the degree to which the production met objectives. Both your supervisors and you must know if the program succeeded before the next program or a new project is requested.

◆ Script Considerations

Corporate media productions vary widely in the media used for presentation. Video, film, and slide-tape are the most basic forms of production. Formats vary widely, with writers/producers often borrowing from the commercial media in choosing formats. The following sections identify some formats used by corporate media writers.

On-Camera Spokesperson

In many productions, an on-camera spokesperson serves as a guide who leads the audience through the important elements. The spokesperson must project a personality that is interesting to viewers. It's helpful for the spokesperson to have props or to change locations to add visual variety. The poorest use of a spokesperson is as a talking head.

Corporate media programs often take one of three approaches to using a spokesperson. One approach is to use a company manager as spokesperson. A manager can add strong credibility as an expert on content. Of course, you'll want a manager who has effective camera presence, but if you have such a person, you have an effective tie-in to company employees.

As a variation, you might use a celebrity spokesperson. A celebrity can be appealing to the audience, but you must use someone who complements the video message. A celebrity who is used as host of a series of videos will establish some professional credibility as the series goes on. A celebrity who has no knowledge of the company or product might contradict the goals of the video.

In demonstrating the use of a product or a procedure, a company employee may be an ideal on-camera spokesperson. A knowledgeable employee lends credibility and need not be trained in use of the equipment or procedure. Video is an effective medium because techniques such as close-ups, replays of key steps, and insertion of graphics to reinforce key points can be used.

One demonstration approach is the "wrong way–right way" presentation. This can be effective when a specific sequence of "how to" information is to be conveyed. For example, the police department of a large city needed to train a number of officers in the use of a new pistol being assigned to them. Managers developed a video introducing the pistol, showing the wrong way to grip it and aim it. The second part of the video showed the right way to fire the pistol.

Voice-Overs

Corporate videos frequently use a narrator who talks while visual information is presented. This format is inexpensive, easy to use, and easy to abuse. It requires a strong connection between the voice and the pictures. A video where the pictures seem to have been added to the voice track as an afterthought will not be effective.

Corporate producers often use slides and audio for voice-over projects. A slide program is less expensive than a video, and visual motion is not needed in some training programs.

As with commercials, more than one voice can be used. Further, character voices can be used for special purposes. For instance, a program about a medical procedure can use a patient who experienced the procedure. In general, voice-over programs can be "quick and dirty," with no frills, or they can be done with imagination and variety. The latter will likely produce a more efficient message.

Interviews

Interviews can be an effective way to describe a new procedure because you can talk with a subject expert. The expert might not be capable of narrating a video but can present his or her knowledge as answers to thoughtful questions. You can also use interviews as segments within another format, such as intercutting a narration with an interview of a customer who used both the old product and the new. Interview questions must be carefully prepared both to elicit the maximum information and avoid brief answers that lack information. Some interviews are actually simulated to exercise greater control. One shortcoming of a simulated interview is that the host and guest must make the prepared material seem spontaneous. Where the goal is to convey precise information, a simulated interview can be advantageous.

Documentaries

The advantage of a documentary format is that it can relate what has already happened or what actually exists. For example, a business might want to describe the successful testing of a new tool or describe the impact of a new medicine. Documentaries may conjure up images of dull, news-type presentations, but they can combine other formats to stimulate interest.

As a variation of the traditional documentary, companies often use video magazines as an internal information source to inform employees and build company morale. The advantage of the video magazine is that it can be established as a series, with each episode conveying several topics.

Newscasts are also used to inform and promote. A newscast can be developed with an anchor and an established format. It's tempting to use the talking head in newscasts because it can be expensive to obtain good pictures. On the other hand, employees may not pay attention to a regular newscast that presents little variety.

Dramatic Formats

The term *drama*, as used in corporate video, is given considerable latitude. Large corporations with hundreds of thousands of employees look for effective techniques to reach audiences. Such companies often have substantial budgets for training and to present internal information; they may use corporate media because their communication task is vast.

The dramatic format is widely used in corporate productions for important topics. The imagination and creativity that corporate writers/producers employ in dramatic formats show both an understanding of the popular media and their usefulness in reaching targeted audiences both inside and outside the company.

Consider the approaches that fall within the umbrella of "drama." Suppose that a manufacturer finds a large number of its products to be defective and wants to let dealers know how to explain the signs of trouble to consumers. The writer/producer might develop a dramatic story using a problem-solution format with actors portraying employees, dealers, and consumers.

The downside of using drama in corporate media is that conservative managers may be reluctant to use a dramatic approach that illustrates problems. Managers want themselves and their company to look good even when they are dealing with problems.

Game shows are another form of drama. They might be used in training employees. Actual workers can demonstrate skills and provide information. Employees participating in the program could win points for correct answers.

Courtroom dramas can be used to introduce new procedures. For instance, a human relations manager might be put on trial to defend the need for a new payroll policy. Witnesses could be called to illustrate problem areas or to demonstrate proper procedures. Investigators could present testimony about incidents of ineffective payroll practices.

If the budget is sufficient, the company attitudes tolerant, and your skills sufficient, you might consider adapting successful movies or plays into media programs. For instance, you might use a *Casablanca* theme to explain a new sales approach. Well-known, older titles work best because people remember some of the characters and lines.

You can also develop comedies as long as they focus on the humor of sales points. If your company stresses overnight and on-time delivery, you might parody that with a horse-and-buggy delivery system. If you're training employees to use a new piece of equipment, you might use a James Bond–type character to show how the equipment can do common tasks. Overall, humor should be used with care. As we have seen earlier in this book, humor is difficult to write, and what might seem hilarious to you might not be funny to others. Beyond that, management might disapprove of humor. Finally, humor must be based on the selling or training points. The goal of a corporate media program is to convey information, not to make people laugh. Viewers must understand and remember the information.

Still, within the broad range of "drama," corporate information has been presented in music videos or in parodies of hit TV shows. Given the proper budget and company approval, considerable innovation and imagination can be brought into corporate media programs.

◆ Script Formats

There is no single layout for scripting. Instead, two variations are commonly used: the standard television two-column script and the screenplay format. If you must pick a format for use on the job, pick one that you're comfortable with and use it consistently. If you write a corporate media script in class, follow your instructor's suggestions. Whatever format you use, neatness, consistency of style, and clarity of instructions are important.

Two-Column Format

This script format is best for newscasts and voice-over programs. The two-column format is discussed in Chapters 2, 10, and 15, so you can check those chapters for details.

The following two-column script is an example of one used in company training.

	MUSIC UNDER
FADE UP TO:	
1. MEDIUM SHOT OUT OF FOCUS FOR TITLE—	
TABLE OF FOUR GUESTS, IN GOLF SHIRTS, ENJOYING THEMSELVES; LAUGHING.	

TITLE GRAPHIC: "TAKE TWO"

2. TITLE OUT. INTO FOCUS—
   GUESTS HAVE MENUS BUT
   AREN'T LOOKING AT THEM;
   ANIMATED BEHAVIOR.

SERVER WALKS UP TO TABLE
AND THEY ALL QUIET DOWN.

3. TIGHT SHOT OF GUESTS
   LOOKING CRUSHED.

4. ACTOR PORTRAYING
   DIRECTOR WALKS INTO
   FRAME

5. PROD. ASSISTANT WITH
   CLAPBOARD WALKS IN
   FRONT OF CAMERA

6. CUT TO WIDE SHOT OF
   DIRECTOR (IN PROFILE) IN
   DIRECTOR'S CHAIR WITH
   SCENE IN BACKGROUND.

7. CU TOM

8. MEDIUM SHOT OF GUESTS
   AT 4-TOP TABLE.

9. DIRECTOR WALKS INTO
   FRAME

10. DIRECTOR WALKS AWAY
    FROM TABLE. CAMERA
    FOLLOWS HIM AS HE SITS
    IN DIRECTOR'S CHAIR;
    ADDRESSES CAMERA.

TOM: [pleasantly] Hey, guys! I'm Tom, and I'm going to be your server tonight. Let me tell you about our feature. Tonight we have Chili-Rubbed Grouper. Do you want to start off with an appetizer? How about something to drink?

DIRECTOR: [OFF CAMERA] Cut! Cut!! That's a good start, Tom. [WALKS INTO FRAME] But why don't you take an extra second to personalize your greeting? Notice that the group seems to be celebrating something. Why don't you work that in somehow? Okay, let's give it another try.

CLAPBOARD PERSON: [FLATLY] "Tom greets guests". Take Two!! [Claps Board].

DIRECTOR (OFF CAMERA) . . . . and action!

TOM: Hey, guys! What's the special occasion? You look like you're ready to celebrate something.

BARRY: (HOLDING DRINK SPECIAL MENU) Yeah! We just won first place in the league tournament!

TOM: Great! Sounds like you'll need a round of drinks! I see you're looking at our beer selections. May I suggest a Fosters?

BARRY: Yeah! That sounds great.

RICK: Me too!

ALAN: Fosters for me!!

DOUG: I'll have a lite beer.

TOM: We have Bud Lite, Michelob Lite, and Coors Lite.

DOUG: I'll have the Michelob Lite.

TOM: Okay, beer all around! Take a look at some appetizers. [USING THE APPETIZER MENU] One of my favorites is the fondue, and it's great to share. Think about it. When I come back with the beer, I'll tell you about our feature.

DIRECTOR: . . . and cut! Super! See what a great response you got from your table? Great use of the Tabletop menu. It really showed you knew what was in there! And nice recommendation on that fondue. Okay, everyone; let's go to the next scene!

[WALKING BACK TO HIS CHAIR, NOTICES THE "AUDIENCE"] Ah, hello and welcome. I'm Director Victor Halibut, and, as you know, we have Two Shows Daily. Now, to be an "over the top" crew member here at Red Lobster, you're going to want to show some serious "zip" and really provide Hospitality You Can Taste and Touch! I'm going to show you some ways to add to your repertoire.

I've been directing some of your fellow servers, and I'd like to show you what we've been working on. Come, have a look . . .

. . . and action!

11. CU VICTOR TURNS TOWARD SCENE II

12. MEDIUM SHOT OF JENNIFER AT TABLE WITH THREE SENIOR GUESTS. THEY HAVE JUST FINISHED THEIR SALADS. JENNIFER IS ABSENTMINDEDLY REMOVING SALADS TO TRAY AND POURING ICED TEA.

JENNIFER: Let's see . . . is there anything else I can get you right now?

Courtesy Cindy Layner Darden Restaurants, Inc.

Screenplay Format

This approach works well for dramas or other programs with live action and extensive dialogue. Movies and TV entertainment scripts are commonly written in this format. Action can be broken up into specific scenes, and locations can be easily specified. The following example illustrates the screenplay format (note that the numbers to the left of each segment refer to explanations that follow the example).

1. INT BUSINESS OFFICE—DAY
2. ASHLEY is seated at desk with a stack of cards on it. ALAN, a coworker, passes her desk.
3.   ALAN
4.   I know payday is coming when I see all those time cards.
          ASHLEY
   You're right! I just wish there were an easier way to do it.
5. MOVING
6. Ashley seated at her desk looking at computer screen. MARY stands next to her looking at a brochure. COMPUTER PRINTER starts to function.
          ASHLEY
   Are you serious? I can send in payroll on the computer?

1. Tells whether the setting is INTerior or EXTerior, the location, and the time of day.
2. Describes the action. Names of characters in scene descriptions are only capitalized the first time they are used.
3. Write the character's name in capital letters, centered on the page.
4. Dialogue is indented and single-spaced.
5. Refers to a specific change in visual action. Best used only for major changes of action.
6. SOUND EFFECTS or MUSIC cues are written in capital letters and included within the description of the action.

Script formats can be varied to achieve special needs. The following illustrates the addition of a narrator and a company trainer to a script that opens in dramatic style.

INT OF BUSINESS OFFICE—DAY
Ashley and Mary discuss payroll.

MARY

This new payroll procedure eliminates paper. It's all computerized.

ASHLEY

There's gotta be a catch. How do we learn this?

MARY

Payroll will have training sessions starting Monday.

Fade out Mary and Ashley and cut to:

| Classroom with computers | NARRATOR: The new Painless Payroll system will be explained in classes for three levels of employees: clerks, supervisors, and directors. You'll attend a small class with people who have a job just like yours. |
| Trainer | Experienced trainers will lead you through the Painless Payroll system step by step. You'll be seated at a computer and input data just like you would for payday. |

◆ Writing Suggestions

1. **Think visually.** Corporate scripts are usually visual—video, film, or slides. Think of the pictures and plan for action, shot changes, and so on that enhance the visual.

2. **Use the active voice.** Avoid the passive voice and state facts directly and actively. Read the following example:

   Passive: The new equipment was taken to the work site by the manager.

   Active: The manager took the new equipment to the work site.

3. **Avoid "should" constructions.** This is especially important in writing training programs. "Should" constructions are another form of passive voice. Don't tell people what they "should" do. Just tell them what to do.

   Change: The new software should be used to prepare payroll check requests.

   To: Use the new software to prepare payroll check requests.

4. **Avoid "there" constructions when possible.**

   Change: There are many ways to use the PF 20.

   To: The PF 20 serves many functions.

5. **Maintain an informal style.** The audience has only one opportunity to understand your message in an aural and visual presentation. They can't reread the script. Choose words that are familiar to the audience. Don't include too many ideas, and keep sentences short. Let the visual present much of the message, and write only as much as is needed to clarify what is seen.

6. **Write tight.** Choose words precisely. Leave no doubt about what is being said or shown. Write copy that is easy to say and easy to grasp. Explain and define technical terms. Don't assume that employees will understand them.

7. **Repeat, repeat.** Repetition is important, particularly in training projects. This is where video can be effective. You can repeat important steps, break the project down into small, understandable segments, and use graphics to tell the audience what is crucial.

➤ POINTS TO REMEMBER

- The writer of a corporate media script must first define the objectives of the program.

- An outline of the program is essential early in the project so that those approving it can assess—and modify if need be—the format and material to be covered.

- It's essential to have a budget for the project before you begin writing.

- Presentational formats include using an on-camera spokesperson, voice-overs, interviews, documentaries, and dramatic formats.

- Corporate media scripts often use the two-column TV script for newscasts or voice-overs or a screenplay format for dramas or other live-action approaches.

- Corporate media writers must think visually so that pictures will carry the message.

- The messages in corporate media scripts are often intended to be persuasive. Therefore repetition of key items is essential.

EXERCISES

Exercise 1

Obtain a corporate video from a company or your school's public relations office. Evaluate it. Was the format style (voice-over, interview, etc.) appropriate? Were the main points clear? Was the production appropriate for the message?

Exercise 2

Assume that your company will institute a new computerized message system called *FastMail*. Write a 10-minute script to inform employees that the new system will soon begin (specify a date), highlight new features, and urge employees to attend training sessions to learn the system. Use a voice-over or dramatic format. Prepare an outline and a script for the program.

   FastMail includes the following:

- *Mail.* Send messages to and receive messages from *FastMail* users.
- *Schedule.* Schedule meetings with other users and request resources, such as conference rooms. Users can identify conflicts among individual schedules while scheduling a group meeting. A feature called "Personal Scheduling" allows a user to schedule events such as a dental appointment or a reminder to contact another person on a given date.
- *Task.* Identifies tasks that need to be completed, due dates, and a priority for each task. Jobs may be arranged for yourself or for others. Tasks not completed are carried forward one day.
- *Notes.* Constructs reminders that you list on a specific date on your calendar. Notes can be used to remind you or others of holidays, deadlines, and so forth. "Personal Notes" can be used to provide reminders of paydays, birthdays, and vacation dates.
- *Message Tracker.* Sends information about an office visitor or a phone call to other users. Identification of caller, company, and urgency of the call can be included.

NOTE: Only the Mail feature is on the present system. The Schedule, Task, Notes, and Message Tracker are added features on the *FastMail* system.

Exercise 3

Write a 10-minute script to address the campus parking problem. The goal of the script is to address faculty, staff, and students on the need to pay parking fees to fund campus parking garages. Fees have not been paid in the past but must be paid to generate revenue for the garages. No other revenue source aside from increased tuition is available. Assume that you have video of crowded parking lots, cars with tickets on windows, traffic jams, and similar scenes. The message should be persuasive and in good taste.

CHAPTER EIGHTEEN

Getting the First Job

So far we have looked at the dos and don'ts of writing copy for the broadcast industry, the Internet, and corporate media. Several suggestions for landing a writing job have been offered, but a few more specifics may be helpful. Writing commercials, news stories, promotional announcements, and Web copy can be very satisfying, but finding jobs has become more difficult. Communication businesses have experienced immense cost-cutting in recent years. This has meant job cuts in some cases and in others a requirement that employees be able to do several jobs. An ability to do double-duty will benefit you if you desire to write broadcast copy.

◆ Job Hunting Essentials

Copywriting involves putting your ideas on paper and often having them produced into recorded form in a studio. Material written for the Web remains on the screen until it is changed. As a result, a portfolio of written copy—or better, a tape with recorded samples of your spots—becomes the key to landing a copywriting job.

Radio

There are opportunities for copywriting jobs at radio stations, particularly stations in small markets or smaller stations in large markets. These stations get less advertising copy from ad agencies. Local advertisers frequently don't have advertising agencies to prepare their commercials, so the station must write spots.

Radio stations are very likely to require you to do several jobs. Salespeople often write spots, especially at smaller stations. In addition, a person who can write spots, announce, do production, or even handle traffic can be valuable to a radio station. If radio stations don't employ a promotion director, copywriters may be asked to write promotional material.

Radio executives prefer to hear samples of produced commercials. It's best to develop a tape with recorded samples of the spots you have written. But if you don't have a tape with examples of your spots, sample scripts will do.

Television

Television stations and cable systems offer copywriting opportunities, but not as often as radio stations. There are far fewer television stations, and in larger markets most advertising is prepared by ad agencies. Cable systems in larger cities get most of their advertising copy from advertising agencies, but that is less true in smaller markets. As a result, such stations and systems may not need a copywriter; another staff member, possibly the salesperson, may write spots as needed.

Television stations and corporate programs that do write sizable amounts of local advertising copy often combine the duties of copywriter and producer. This approach works well as long as the producer is well skilled in copywriting or the copywriter is also a skilled producer. Smaller stations and businesses may also ask the copywriter to write promotional copy when it is needed.

While radio stations will want to hear samples of your work, television stations, cable companies, and corporate outlets will want to see examples of produced spots. Seek opportunities to write and record spots in classes, internships, or even volunteer efforts. Be sure taped samples are professional. Amateurish writing and production will quickly be rejected.

Radio and Television News Writing

The people who write news stories at broadcast stations are totally divorced from commercial writing, except in the smaller stations. Their focus is on activities in the newsroom. Copywriters in the sales/production area often write commercials. News writers need to be skilled writers who know writing rules and have the ability to work with material on audio- or videotape. Stations in smaller markets are likely to combine duties such as reporting and writing. They may also ask you to write promotional copy for the news department when necessary.

If the job focus is on writing news stories, sample scripts are desired. Keep copies of your best efforts and retype them so the scripts are clean and error-free. News directors will want to see what applicants can do, so evidence of past work is preferred. Avoid taped samples that include news anchors or reporters delivering a script you have written because the evaluator may focus on the news reader instead of your copy.

Radio stations will likely use sound bites on audiotape, so you should know how to incorporate audio into written stories. This calls for a knowledge of scripting and may require that you edit the sound bite from a recorded interview or on-the-scene event. Thus, basic editing and production skills are important for a radio newsperson.

News departments in television stations tend to break out writing, editing, and reporting duties, especially in larger markets. In other words, a news writer may only write stories, not report or edit them. However, in smaller markets, news staffers often combine several duties. Reporters may cover a story, edit the tape, and write the script. This requires a wider range of knowledge. There's little time to check writing and formatting issues. Reporters usually must produce well-written stories quickly and accurately, using the correct formatting.

You will need clean, error-free sample scripts when you are job hunting, just as you would in seeking a job in radio news. The script reflects your ability and knowledge and should be part of your television news job-hunting package.

The Internet

Most broadcast stations now maintain a Web page with expanded coverage of news stories or program items. The size of the station's staff will usually determine who writes the material for the Web page. Larger stations will likely have specialists who focus on maintaining the Web page and writing its copy. In smaller stations, an employee who has other duties may handle Web duties. An ability to write broadcast news as well as Web copy may makes a prospective employee all the more valuable.

Whom do you contact when you are looking for a job? The news director, production director, sales director, or communications director are the people to contact. Don't contact the manager except at very small outfits. The manager usually hires a production director, news director, and so on, who, in turn, does the hiring for each specialized area.

You need to know the name of the contact person and his or her title. Direct all correspondence to the contact person. Names may be listed on the Web page of the station. If not, call the business and ask for the name and title. Material sent to the wrong person, or one long gone, is likely to be disregarded immediately.

Freelancing

Beginning writers often seek freelance writing opportunities, as do well established professionals. Beginners want to acquire experience, while experienced writers may prefer the flexibility of choosing the clients and firms they work for.

Volunteering to write PSAs for civic or social organizations while you are still in school is a form of freelancing that can help you to build a portfolio to show future employers. Part-time employment with a station, cable system, or a small advertising agency while you are still in school or even after graduation constitutes freelance activity. Volunteer and part-time work both offer the opportunity to gain valuable experience and a chance to work in the "real world" of copywriting. Building a reputation is important in the electronic media, and volunteering can be a good step in getting started.

◆ The Resume

A printed, error-free resume is essential. It should be direct and not be fancy. Proof it carefully. You could be rejected just because of small errors. Use a spell checker, but don't rely on it. Spell-check programs cannot pick up correctly spelled words that are used incorrectly, such as *form* instead of *from*.

There are three types of resumes:

- The *chronological* resume arranges work or study experience with the most current first, working back to your first job or studies last. You may have had few jobs and may have attended only one school, so this may not be the best approach for you.

- The *functional* format organizes your skills, talents, and work experiences by major areas of involvement. For example, this format may apply if you worked on the campus radio station but plan to seek employment in a TV newsroom.

- The *analytical* arrangement may be best for newcomers to the job market. This resume presents your background in terms of skills and accomplishments. The analytical arrangement resume tells what you have done in a straightforward manner. You may feel you don't have much of a background to list. That's true at first, but do list jobs in other fields. They show your initiative. And look for volunteer opportunities in campus media groups and events. They also show your interest and involvement. The following example illustrates an analytical resume for a beginning job-hunter:

Mark E. Johnson
2020 University Avenue
Yourtown, USA Zip code
Phone number and e-mail address

Marital Status:	Single
Career Goal:	Write/produce in medium-market television station.
Education:	List college degrees, date received and any honors received.
Job experience:	1995–1996: Early morning newspaper delivery of *Hometown Herald*.
	1996–1998. Clerk in Video World. Worked up to weekend manager. Offered full-time position of assistant manager.
	2006: Internship with WXXX-TV, ABC affiliate, Yourtown. Production assistant. Assisted floor director on weekdays and served as floor director on weekends.
	2005: Volunteer during Election Night coverage, WAAA, Fox affiliate, Yourtown.
Honors:	List those that are *relevant* to career goals.
References:	On request

Print a hard copy of your resume on plain white paper with no borders, shading, or graphics. Distractions are not needed. You may mail a resume, deliver it, fax it, or send it by e-mail. Avoid paragraph indentations. They may not line up properly if you scan the resume into a computer. Use bullets and dashes to guide the reader and allow for scanning.

- Don't include references, especially if the only ones you have are family and friends. Employers expect them to say good things about you, but relatives and friends may know little about your study habits, work habits, or job skills—the characteristics important to employers. Instead, contact several faculty members who know you and your work and ask them to supply a reference if necessary. Do the same with individuals who may supervise you at an internship or industry volunteer effort. Be sure they know you and have some knowledge of your work.

- List special job skills. Identify special pieces of job equipment you can operate, such as a digital editing system or an audio board. Sell yourself and your abilities!

- If you are replying to an advertisement, use key words from it in your cover letter and resume. Show that you know what is desired and that you can supply it. Don't expect one resume to work for all positions. You must tailor it to respond to the specifics of each job.

- Be sure to spell correctly. In particular, spell people's names and the company name correctly. Use a spell checker, but as mentioned before, you should also thoroughly proofread or have someone else check for words such as homonyms (too/to/two, bare/bear) that can escape spell checking.

Resumes won't get you a job, but they are a necessary part of the process and should be prepared with care.

◆ The Cover Letter

Send a cover letter with your resume. In it explain why you want to work for the station or business and emphasize what you can do for them. For example, if the job involves writing commercials for sales staffers, stress that your work will free sales staffers from writing copy themselves. As a result, they will have more time to make sales calls, thus increasing business. If you have worked with someone at a station who may put in a good word for you, identify the person and your connection to them. In your cover letter, indicate that on a given date, you will call the person to whom you addressed the letter. Make sure to call on that date and, if necessary, be persistent. Leave a message and call back later if you are unable to contact the person the first time you call.

Prepare you cover letter and resume with care. It is estimated that you have no more than three to four seconds to make an impression on a busy reader. Errors and sloppy preparation are likely to get your cover letter and resume rejected. Prepare your paperwork so that potential employers will stop and consider your material.

➤ POINTS TO REMEMBER

- Stations, cable systems, and smaller advertising agencies will likely expect the copywriter to perform other duties in addition to writing spots.

- A resume should be brief, conservative, and error-free.

- A cover letter should explain to an employer how your capabilities will benefit the station or system.

EXERCISES

Exercise 1

Prepare a resume and cover letter for a position you would like to attain when you enter the job market. Be certain both are error-free.

Exercise 2

Invite a copywriter from a broadcast station or cable system to visit class. As him or her to discuss what the job involves and the characteristics needed to get a first job.

Exercise 3

Visit the job placement center on your campus. Look at the resume and cover letter data used by the staff. Ask a staff member to provide job-hunting tips in your field.

Glossary

Account A sponsor on a station or a client of an advertising agency; a buyer of airtime.

Account executive Advertising agency representative in charge of an advertiser's account. May also refer to a station or cable company representative.

Actuality Radio news story that incorporates the voices and sounds of the news event.

Adjacencies The program or time periods immediately preceding or following a program.

Ad-lib Remarks not written into the script.

Advertiser National, regional, or local purchaser of a commercial announcement or program.

Affiliate A local station that is affiliated by contract with a network.

Agency A business firm that gives advertising counsel by planning, preparing, and placing advertising for a client in the various communications media.

AM Abbreviation of *amplitude modulation,* the older of the two technologies of radio broadcasting.

Announcement Advertising message; also called *commercial* or *spot.*

ASCAP American Society of Composers, Authors, and Publishers.

Audio The sound portion of a TV program or announcement.

Availability An unsold segment of broadcast time.

Banner ad Online advertisement stripped across the bottom or top of a Web page like a billboard.

Bed Music that is played behind a commercial.

Billing Charges to advertisers from networks, stations, or cable companies for broadcasting time or services.

BMI Broadcast Music, Inc.

Board The control room audio console.

Board fade A decrease or increase in volume made at the audio control board. Could be either *board fade out* or *board fade in.* See also *mike fade.*

Break (or station break) Time allotted for local sale between or within programs. May also be used for station identification.

Bridge A musical transition linking two segments of commercial copy.

B-Roll Technique in TV news where the anchor or reporter is heard but the picture changes to scenes corresponding to what is said.

BTA (best time available) Spots not scheduled for a specific time period but instead scheduled at the station's discretion.

Bumper A brief promotional scene that precedes and follows a commercial break in a syndicated TV program.

Campaign A planned advertising promotion.

CG Character generator, a device used to insert graphic names and data over commercial or news data.

Chromakey The electronic combining of two video sources into a composite picture to convey the impression that the two sources are physically together.

Client An advertiser.

Cold Describing a program or commercial performed without rehearsal.

Commercial The sponsor's message promoting its products or services as written by the copywriter.

Copy Term used for written scripts of all types such as news copy, commercial copy, and so on.

Copy platform Checklist to aid in preparing a successful sales strategy. Consists of seven items: client and product, service, or store; objective; target audience; sales theme; bonus items; positioning; and approach.

Copywriter The person who writes the script for a commercial, public service announcement, or station promotion announcement. Similar to and often interchangeable with *script writer,* the person who writes the text of a teleplay, commercial, or program. The person who writes Web scripts may be called a *copywriter, script writer, writer,* or *Web writer.* The writer of scripts for radio or television news stories could be described as a scriptwriter but more often may be identified as a *news writer.* A broadcast news writer may have other duties, usually reporting or anchoring, which can lead to other terms, such as *writer/reporter.*

Cross fade To fade from one sound or piece of music to another. Same as *segue.* This is to audio what a *lap dissolve* is to video.

CU Close-up.

Cutaway Any TV shot that briefly switches attention from the main action to some related activity.

Director Individual responsible for the production of radio and TV announcements or programs.

Disc jockey (also DJ, d.j., deejay) The announcer who hosts a program of recorded music.

Dissolve Fade-in of a picture from black or from the picture to black. Used for a transition from one camera to another with slight overlapping of the two pictures.

Donut copy A spot in which the open and close are prerecorded with the middle left open, so a station announcer can read copy identifying local outlets, thus filling "the donut."

Double spotting A station practice of placing two spot announcements back to back.

Echo Reverberation supplementing voice or music, such as the sound of a voice in a cave or extra "life" for music. Echo might be achieved in an echo chamber but more frequently is achieved electronically.

Editing Revision of copy or assembly of film or tape segments.

EFP Electronic field production, or the use of portable cameras and videotape recorders to complete video production on location.

E-mail A system for sending and receiving written messages via computer. Often uses electronic mail services, commercial on-line services, bulletin board system, private networks, or the Internet.

Endorsement Spot in which a well-known person lends his or her fame and credibility to the producer or service.

ENG Electronic news gathering; indicates that the video is on videotape cassette.

ESS Electronic still storer, a system that loads, retrieves, and displays video from a variety of sources, such as videotape, slides, electronic paint boxes, and satellites. They are used to provide graphs, maps,

charts, photos, preprepared graphics, and so forth.

Establish To bring sound effects or music to full volume, permitting the listener to hear enough to understand the sound or music.

Fact sheet A list of facts given to an announcer to use in ad-libbing a commercial.

FM Abbreviation for *frequency modulation*, a radio broadcasting technology that permits a better quality of audio than AM.

Format (1) The organization of each element within a program; a station's established program pattern. (2) The physical arrangement of copy on paper.

Frame A single scene in a video storyboard.

Freelance A nonstaff employee.

Graphics Printed information such as prices, phone numbers, discounts, and so on inserted over TV or cable spots. Also refers to names and dates inserted over news items.

Hard sell Method of commercial presentation characterized by a sense of urgency, short, punchy sentences, repetition, and the use of dramatic music or sound effects.

High-definition television (HDTV) The use of digital code rather than analog technology to transmit television pictures. This produces a wide-screen format based on a 16-by-9 width-to-height ratio rather than the 4-by-3 analog ratio. HDTV pictures have high resolution and clarity, with CD-quality sound.

Hold under After establishing the sound effect or music, fading it to background and "holding" it (as in *bed*) behind the spoken message.

Home page A computer screen, page, or series of such pages that a business, individual, or other organization can use to provide information about services offered from a Web site.

Hook A strategic device used to involve the audience.

Idiot card A cue card.

Independent station A station not affiliated with a network.

Infomercial A commercial, usually 90 or more seconds in length, that supplies information about a product or service—or about a topic relating to the advertiser's product or service—rather than presenting a specific sales message.

Institutional A spot designed to promote image rather than product.

Internet A system of thousands of independently owned computers located all over the world that communicate with one another.

Interstitial ad Online ad where the interstitial pops up in the window of a Web site for a few seconds while the rest of the site is downloading.

Lifestyle A person's pattern of living as expressed in his or her opinions, interests, and activities.

Live Describes a commercial, news story, or program performed as it is being broadcast.

Log The daily schedule of the station's program.

Logo Symbol or slogan used to designate a program or an organization.

LS Long shot. Same as *wide shot*.

Mike fade Result of performers moving away from mike (*mike fade off*), or moving to on-mike position (*mike fade on*) from off-mike position. Mike fade is a decidedly different effect from a *board fade*. In the mike fade, acoustical relationships change because of the performer's movement. In a board fade, only the volume changes.

Mike filter An electronic means for eliminating high and low frequencies. Often used to give the effect of speaking over a telephone line.

Modem An instrument that allows computers to talk over telephone lines.

Motive A need that is sufficiently pressing to direct a person to seek satisfaction.

MS Medium shot.

Music bed Music used as background sound only.

Narrowcast To target programming, usually of a restricted type, to a defined demographic or ethnic group.

Natural sound Actual sound used in a news story, promo, public-service announcement, or commercial.

Network A number of broadcast stations linked together by wire, microwave, or satellite on a regional or national basis.

News reporter A person who specializes in gathering information that can be included in newscasts.

News writer A person who takes information from his or her own research, the station's other reporters, and wire services to produce news copy to be read on the air.

O/C News script symbol for "on camera."

Off(on)-mike Location of talent back from the mike or near to it.

One-shot Close-up of one person in television or cable.

Package A series of ready-for-broadcast programs or announcements bought by an advertiser including components; also a television news story that combines an anchor or reporter reading copy with sound bites.

Pan To move a camera horizontally to right or left to follow action.

Participations Spots scheduled within program positions.

Postproduction The editing in a studio of videotape shot in the field. Special effects and graphics may also be added to the tape.

Prerecorded Describing music, speech, or video recorded prior to its use in a spot.

Production The planning, preparation, and presentation of a commercial or program.

Promo An on-air spot promoting one or more programs carried by the station.

Public service announcement (PSA) A noncommercial announcement carried without charge by a station or cable operation for a nonprofit organization or cause such as the Boy Scouts, a drug abuse program, and so on.

Punch To give special emphasis to a line or spot.

Rates Charges established by a station for air time.

Read (or Tell) news story Story read by an anchor with the only pictures appearing in "boxes" next to the anchor's head.

Reverb Short for *reverberation.* An electronic device sometimes used in lieu of *echo,* though the effects are not the same.

ROS (run of schedule) Spots not ordered for a specific time period but instead scheduled at the station's discretion.

Salesperson The person who calls on the client, makes the sale, and generally collects information about what the client wants stressed in the commercial. The salesperson may sell for a station, cable operation, or agency. Other titles for this function include sales executive, account executive, and time salesperson. The salesperson sometimes writes his or her own copy.

Saturation Intensive use of spot advertising by an advertiser on one or more stations for a specified amount of time.

Schedule The station timetable.

Script A broadcast program or announcement that is completely written.

Segue Same as *cross fade.*

SESAC Society of European Stage Authors and Composers.

SFX An abbreviation for *sound effects.*

Signature Theme.

SIL Abbreviation for "silent" videotape used in a newscast or production.

Sneak To bring music or sound into the background of a spot or program at a low level.

SOT Sound on tape; that is, videotape with a soundtrack.

Sound bite Segment of natural sound of person or event recorded on audio or videotape.

Special effects Electronic effects produced by the control room switcher, such as combining images or manipulating them.

Split screen Electronic effect whereby portions of pictures from two cameras or two similar sources divide the screen.

Spokesperson spot Spot in which someone is paid to speak in the first person for the client, its product, or its service.

Sponsor Advertiser who pays for commercials.

Spot Generally, any commercial announcement; more specifically, commercial time sold independently of a program.

Sting/stab Short, abrupt musical punctuation.

Storyboard A scene-by-scene depiction of the visual portion of a cable or TV spot.

Straight copy Copy written for conversational, informative, one-voice delivery.

Streaming Synchronized video, audio, graphics, and animation sent over the Internet, where personal computers play the media streams directly, without first having to download the entire file.

Sustaining Any program that is not commercially sponsored.

Switcher Electronic device that enables a video director to see and select shots.

Tag Name and address of a local sales outlet "tagged" onto a recorded or filmed announcement furnished by a sponsor.

Talent Actor or announcer who delivers a spot.

Talent fee The production cost of a commercial for music, announcers, actors, and so forth in addition to the time charge.

Talking heads A television shot where the top third of a newscaster's body fills the screen while the newscaster is talking. Talking heads are often used for the opening story of a TV newscast or for shots of the heads of people being interviewed in news stories or documentaries. The term "talking head" has negative connotations because it indicates unimaginative use of the medium.

Teaser (1) A spot that seeks to build interest while hiding the name of the product or service until near the conclusion. (2) A short promo used at the end of a program or program segment to promote interest in an upcoming program.

Teleplay A script written for production on television.

TelePrompTer Device mounted above the lens of a camera permitting the performer to follow the script.

Testimonial A spot in which a consumer speaks on behalf of the product or service.

Tilt To move a camera vertically up or down.

Traffic The office that handles all programming and scheduling in a broadcast station.

Truck To move a camera parallel to the set background, or to move with a person crossing the set.

Under Music or sound as background for voice. "Up and under" means to start music or sound at full volume and then to fade under voice.

Video The visual portion of a TV commercial or program.

V/O (voice over) Refers to a TV or cable spot in which the announcer is heard but not seen.

Web sites Independently owned computers that are hooked into the Internet.

World Wide Web (WWW or Web) A system that helps users navigate the Internet. The system enables a user to link Internet files so that the user can access related files by selecting a key word.

Wraparound A radio news story that uses the voice of the newscaster at the beginning and conclusion of the story with an actuality in the middle.

WS Wide shot. Same as *long shot*.

Zoom Electronic change of camera shot from long shot to closeup without losing focus.

Bibliography

Part 1: The Broadcast Copywriter

Chapter 1: The Broadcast Copywriter

Broadcasting Publications. *Broadcasting/Cablecasting Yearbook.* Washington, DC: Cahner's Business Information, 2006. Lists all U.S. broadcast stations and cable systems.

Broadcasting Publications. *Broadcasting & Cable Magazine.* Washington, DC: Cahners Business Information, 2006.

Part 2: Copywriting Elements

Chapter 2: Copywriting Style—Basic Mechanics

Burton, Phillip Ward. *Advertising Copywriting.* Lincolnwood, IL: NTC/Contemporary Publishing Group, 1999.

Kessler, Lauren, and Duncan McDonald. *When Words Collide,* 6th ed. Belmont, CA: Wadsworth, 2004.

Chapter 3: The Legal and Ethical Implications of Writing Copy

Contest Lotteries and Casino Gambling, 2nd ed. Washington, DC: National Association of Broadcasters, 2003.

Political Broadcast Catechism, 16th ed. Washington, DC: National Association of Broadcasters, 2004.

Part 3: Advertising Basics

Chapter 4: Consumer Behavior

Menon, Satya. *Managing Consumer Motivation and Learning: Harnessing the Power of Curiosity for Effective Advertising Strategies.* Cambridge, MA: MSI, 1999.

Ries, Al, and Jack Trout. *Positioning: The Battle for Your Mind.* New York: McGraw-Hill, 2001.

Shiffman, Leon G., and Leslie Lazar Kanuk. *Consumer Behavior,* 9th ed. Upper Saddle River, NJ: Prentice Hall, 2006.

Chapter 5: Motivation

Gobe, Mark. *Emotional Branding: The New Paradigm for Connecting Brands to People.* New York: Allworth Press, 2001.

Mullen, Brian, and Craig Johnson. *The Psychology of Consumer Behavior.* Hillsdale, NJ: Lawrence Erlbaum, 1990.

Chapter 6: Organizing the Broadcast Commercial

Jeweler, A. Jerome, and Bonnie L. Drewniany. *Creative Strategy in Advertising,* 8th ed. Belmont, CA: Wadsworth, 2005.

Chapter 7: Broadcast Copy Preparation

Hilliard, Robert L. *Writing for Television, Radio, and New Media,* 9th ed. Boston, MA: Thomson Learning, 2008.

Part 4: Radio Copywriting

Chapter 8: The Radio Commercial: The Mechanics

Hausman, Carl, Philip Benoit, Frank Messere, and Lewis O'Donnell. *Modern Radio Production: Production, Programming and Performance,* 6th ed. Belmont, CA: Wadsworth, 2007.

Keith, Michael C. *The Radio Station,* 7th ed. Boston: Focal Press, 2007.

Chapter 9: Types of Radio Copy

West, Hall, and Jim Conlan. *Radio Advertising 101.5.* West Palm Beach, FL: Streamline Press, 1998.

Part 5: Television Copywriting

Chapter 10: The Television Commercial: The Mechanics

Kanner, Bernice. *The 100 Best TV Commercials.* New York: Times Books, 1999.

Zettl, Herbert. *Television Production Handbook,* 9th ed. Belmont, CA: Wadsworth, 2006.

Chapter 11: Types of Television Commercials

Book, Albert C., Norman D. Cary, and Stanley I. Tannenbaum. *The Radio and Television Commercial,* 3rd ed. Chicago: National Textbook Company, 1996.

Richter, Thomas. *The 30-Second Storyteller: The Art and Business of Directing Commercials.* Boston: Thompson Course Technology, 2007.

Part 6: The Electronic Media: Other Writing Needs

Chapter 12: Promotion

Eastman, Susan T., Douglas A. Ferguson, and Robert A. Klein. *Media Promotion and Marketing for Broadcasting, Cable, and the Internet,* 5th ed. Boston: Focal Press, 2006.

Chapter 13: Public Service, Issue, and Political Announcements

Political Broadcast Catechism, 16th ed. Washington, DC: National Association of Broadcasters, 2004.

Chapter 14: The Broadcast Campaign

Crostjens, Judy. *Strategic Advertising.* New York: Nichols Publishers, 1990.

Schultz, Don E., and Beth E. Barnes. *Strategic Advertising Campaigns.* Lincolnwood, IL: NTC Business Books, 1995.

Chapter 15: Writing News Stories

Block, Mervin and Joe Dirso, Jr. *Writing News for TV and Radio (with Interactive CD).* Chicago: Bonus Books, 1998.

Tuggle, C. A., Forrest Carr, and Suzanne Huffman. *Broadcast News Handbook,* 2nd ed. Belmont, CA: Wadsworth, 2004.

White, Ted. *Broadcast News Writing, Reporting, and Production,* 4th ed. Boston: Focal Press, 2005.

Chapter 16: Writing for the Internet

Kaye, Barbara K., and Norman J. Medoff, *Just a Click Away—Advertising on the Internet.* Needham Heights, MA: Allyn & Bacon, 2001.

Maciuba-Koppel, Darle. *The Web Writer's Guide.* Boston: Focal Press, 2002.

Rich, Carole. *Creating Online Media.* Boston: McGraw-Hill, 1999.

Sammons, Martha C. *The Internet Writer's Handbook.* 2nd ed. Needham Heights, MA: Longman, 2004.

Chapter 17: Corporate Programs

DiZazzo, Ray. *Corporate Media Production,* 2nd ed. Boston: Focal Press, 2003.

Van Nostran, William J. *The Media Writer's Guide.* Boston: Focal Press, 2003.

Chapter 18: Getting the First Job

Bennett, Scott. *The Elements of Resume Style.* New York: AMACOM, 2005.

Newlen, Robert R. *Writing Resumes That Work.* New York: Neal-Schuman, 1998.

Index

psychographic targeting, audience and, 97–98
public service announcements (PSAs), 216–223, 231, 233
  audience sensibilities and, 220
  choosing type of, 216–217
  copywriter's opportunities in, 224–225
  costs of, 223
  definition of, 4, 216
  framing appeal for, 220
  idea/goal oriented type of, 217, 218
  informational type of, 216–217, 223–224
  issue announcements and, 225–228, 231, 234
  planning of, 217
  for radio, 220–223, 231, 233
  researching organizations for, 217, 220
  self-actualization appeal used in, 221
  targeting audience in, 219
  for television, 223–224, 231, 233
  writing opportunities for, 224–225
puffery, 41, 51
punctuation, 23–25, 31
  comma, 24
  dash, 24
  ellipsis, 25
  exclamation point, 24
  hyphen, 25
  importance of, 23, 31
  period, 23
  question mark, 23

quality, as motivation for buying, 78
question lead-ins, 22–23, 255–256

race, of target audience, 97
radio
  basics/terminology of, 114–115
  copy/commercial formats for, 17, 113, 115–121, 122, 126–133
  copy types for, 115–120
  copywriting for, 114, 122, 259–261
  delivery of, 112–113
  gaining listener's attention in, 114
  Internet and, 121, 202
  job hunting essentials for, 292
  mass communication and, 112
  news stories for, 259–261
  as other medias' advertising medium, 210
  playlists for, 112
  promotion in, 201, 212, 213
  PSAs for, 220–223, 231, 233
  satellites and, 113
  single-voice copy for, 115–116, 132
  sound effects in, 114, 115, 118–120
  station types and, 5, 112
  strengths of, 113, 122
  target audience and, 113
  timing copy for, 114, 122
  TV scripts v. scripts for, 17, 140
  two-voice copy for, 116–117, 123
  weaknesses of, 113–114, 122

radio commercial(s). *See also* advertisement example(s); commercial(s); sample script(s)
  elements of, 112, 122
  formats for, 17, 113, 115–121, 122, 126–133
  hard-sell copy example of, 127
  institutional copy example of, 128
  straight-copy example of, 126
radio news stories
  types of, 259–261
  writing basics for, 261
radio spots, 113
  music in, 114, 115, 118–120
  television soundtracks for, 153
Rainwater, Lee P., 55
rational appeals, 76–78, 81
read (or tell) style, in television news, 262–263, 264, 265
rebuttal ads, 227–228
receivers, 3, 9
reference groups, consumer behavior and, 56, 58, 59, 63, 66
reflexive pronouns, 26–27
regulations
  federal, 38–42, 50
  state, 43–47
reinforcement, 71
religious subcultures, 54–55
research
  for advertisement data, 42
  for corporate media programs, 281
  of organizations for PSAs, 217, 220
response, 3, 8
resume, 294–295, 297
  with cover letter, 295, 297
  do's and don'ts for, 295
  sample copy for, 294
  types of, 294
reverb, in radio, 115
Rich, Carole, 274, 274n2
rigged demonstrations, 40–41
rules for writing, 30–31, 258–259

safety needs, consumer behavior and, 69
sales goal(s), 87, 89
salesperson, 4
  as copy source, 106
sales slogan(s). *See also* slogans
  in broadcast campaigns, 236, 239, 248
  copy platform and, 100–102, 170
sales theme, copy platform and, 100–102, 105, 170
sample script(s)
  for advocacy ads, 225–227
  AIDA formula used in, 88–89
  for attention getting, 155
  for balancing audio/video, 156, 158
  for Coors beer campaign, 106
  for corporate media campaigns, 284–287
  in dialog copy format, 117
  for EFP spots, 146
  five Ws in, 222, 257–258

of Florida libraries' campaign, 243
for generic promos, 205–207
with hard leads, 256
of hard-sell radio copy, 127
for humorous commercial, 78–79, 130–132
for IDs promo, 208
for illegal teaser, 38–39
for image building, 245, 246, 248
for informational PSA, 216–217, 223–224
for institutional spots, 45, 128
for issue ads, 225–228
for layering stories, 271
with music copy format, 119–120
with names and titles, 259
of news stories, 257–258
of news story actuality, 260
for political ads, 229, 230
political sponsorship identification, 40
for professional services ads, 44–45
for quality appeal, 78
for radio, 16, 207
with radio format conventions, 16–17
with radio news immediacy, 261
for rebuttal ads, 227–228
for screenplay format, 286–287
in single-voice copy format, 116
for soft leads, 257
for soft-sell approach, 126, 128
with sound effects, 118, 119
special effects and, 150–151
for special promos, 246–248
for specific promo, 204–205
for split-screen television news, 262
with storyboards, 141–142, 157, 244–245
for straight copy, 126
of straight radio copy, 126
with strong product identification, 157
for studio productions, 121, 145
for television, 17, 205–206, 262, 263
with television format conventions, 17–18, 140
for testimonials, 129–130
for timing promos, 140
for traffic report promo, 205
for two-column copy format, 284–286
for two-voice copy format, 116–117
with voice-over, 263
for WHOI-TV campaign, 245
with wraparounds, 260
screenplay formats, 286–287
script(s). *See also* format(s); sample script(s)
  corporate media types of, 282–283
  for radio v. TV, 17, 140
  for television, 17–18, 140–141, 159, 261–262
  two-column format for, 284–286
segue, in radio, 115
self-actualization needs, consumer behavior and, 69
self-discipline, 6
self-expression, 70–71
self-regulation, 47–50

Straight copy – 1 voice
　　　conversational
hard sell
institutional – no comp
Sponsor　spokesperson
endorsement – well known
testimonials – from common people　259　　261-4
Humor　　　　　　　　　　　　　　　　　284-8

　　　　　　　　　　　　16-18
　　　173　　115　122　126-33

　　　　　18　20　45
　　　　　17　　　　　140 145-6
　　　　　　　　159　　261-2

　　　　　　　　270-1

Single voice announcements
two voice spots
dialog spots
fact sheets

live
live ad-lib
　donut
　prerecorded

　　　　　radio
　　　　30 sec theek
　　　　　　words
　　　　　　SE
　　　　　　music

　　　phy. form of copy

　One voice
　2 voice
　Dialog copy

SFX – gun fire　　　keep the ball rolling
　　bacon sizzling　sizzling
baby crying
glass breaking
　　rake & leaf blower
cheerleading jingles crowd roaring
spark & announcer

TV　　　Still pres or videotape w announcer
　　　　　　voice over
WS　　　voice over
Close V　Electronic fred production
med shot　　　　　on location

banner ads top body
logo w link – evaluation
cube ad – boxes
pop up
buttons – ad many